Studies in Upplandic Runography

Studies in Upplandic Runography

Claiborne W. Thompson

UNIVERSITY OF TEXAS PRESS, AUSTIN AND LONDON

The publication of this book was assisted by a grant
from the Andrew W. Mellon Foundation and by partial
support from the Horace H. Rackham Publication Grant
Program at the University of Michigan

Library of Congress Cataloging in Publication Data

Thompson, Claiborne W   1940–
    Studies in Upplandic runography.

    Bibliography: p.
    Includes index.
    1. Inscriptions, Runic—Uppland, Sweden. I. Title.
PD2007.U7T5   439′.6′17   74-22284
ISBN 0-292-77511-3

To My Parents

CONTENTS

MAPS

FIGURES

PLATES

(following page 84)

The seventy-five photographs reproduced here do not represent every runic inscription mentioned in the text, but almost all of the stones relating to Asmund (chap. 8) are included. They are ordered according to number: first Uppland, then the three stones from Gästrikland.

All of the photographs are from the Antikvarisk-topografiska Arkivet, Stockholm. Photographers include Iwar Anderson (U617, U629, U645, U859, U860, U866, U871, U875, U884*B*, U885, U899, U932, U945, U956, U969, U987, U998, U1009, U1012, U1035, U1043), Harald Faith-Ell (U29, U80, U240, U344), G. af Gejerstam (U692), and Nils Lagergren (U824). The woodcuts of U343 and U346 are by Peringskiöld; the drawing of U301 is by Rhezelius; U986 is an unsigned woodcut (Bautil 384).

ACKNOWLEDGMENTS

Most of the groundwork for this book was done in Sweden during the academic year 1967–1968, with the financial help of a fellowship from Harvard University and a Swedish Government Grant. I am also grateful for the generous advice of Professor Einar Haugen of Harvard University and for the assistance provided by the Swedish office of Runverket in the Riksantikvarieämbetet.

A generous subvention from the Horace H. Rackham Publication Grant Program, University of Michigan, helped to defray part of the manufacturing costs of this book.

For permission to reproduce the photographs in this book I am indebted to the Antikvarisk-Topografiskt Arkiv (copyright) and the Kungl. Vitterhets Historie och Antikvitetsakademien, Stockholm. I would also like to extend thanks to Mr. H. A. Shelley for drawing the maps and rune forms and to the press and printer for their patient work on what must have been a difficult task.

My greatest debt is to Börje Westlund, Stockholm, who introduced me to the Swedish runes, guided me through much of the early field work, and spent long hours discussing problems of Upplandic runography with me.

Studies in Upplandic Runography

1. Introduction

This book is concerned with runic writing in part of Scandinavia and represents a chapter of the more general topic of runology.[1] As is well known, the runic alphabet, or *futhark*, was not confined to Scandinavia, but was the writing system of various ancient Germanic peoples, including the English, and diverse tribes of continental *Germania*. We know of over 5000 inscriptions preserved in runes, widely distributed in space and time. Of these, however, almost 3000 are found (and continue to be found) within the borders of Sweden.[2] The vast majority date from the late Viking Age (10th–11th centuries) and are written in what is called the younger futhark.

In particular, the custom of erecting commemorative monuments (rune stones), relatively rare during the period of the older futhark, spread rapidly into Sweden and seems to have flourished most intensively in the province of Uppland during the eleventh century. Upplandic stones account for more than one-third of Sweden's runic monuments and exhibit a homogeneity that renders them especially suitable

---

[1]There are a number of recent surveys of runology, though little has appeared in English. Perhaps the best treatment is Lucien Musset's *Introduction à la runologie*. Two useful German handbooks are Wolfgang Krause's *Runen* and Klaus Düwel's *Runenkunde*. Reference might also be made to R. W. V. Elliott's *Runes: An Introduction* and Sven B. F. Jansson's *The Runes of Sweden*.

[2]Inscriptions from the provinces of Skåne, Halland, and Blekinge are not considered Swedish, since these areas were part of Denmark in former times.

to runological investigation. It is these stones which form the subject of the present work.

Ancient Uppland (which included part of present-day Västmanland) formed the political, religious, and cultural center of Svealand, the kingdom of the *Svear,* or Swedes.[3] Uppland was an area of wooded and fertile plains, most readily traveled by its abundant waterways, though such land routes as the famous "Eriksgata" also played an important role.[4] Administratively, it was made up of the divisions called Fjädrundaland, Attundaland, and Tiundaland, together with the coastal area known as *Upplands rod,* or *Roden.* The first three names are based upon the ancient "hundred" (four, eight, and ten of these, respectively), a district supplying 100 or 120 men for military purposes. The *rod* were divided into *skeppslag,* or ship districts. (See map 1.)

For Uppland the eleventh century was a time of change. The year 1050, which for our purposes represents a midpoint, is at the same time a traditional date for the close of the Viking Age, a period of immense vitality that saw the rise and fall of such Swedish trading centers as Helgö and Birka, the founding of such towns as Sigtuna and Uppsala, and extensive Swedish forays and settlements abroad. Swedish merchants plied the Baltic, founded Staraja Ladoga (a precursor of Novgorod), settled parts of Russia, and explored the Russian rivers to the Black Sea and indeed as far as the Baghdad Caliphate. Swedish Vikings in the east served in the Byzantine imperial guard; to the west they were among the troops of Canute during his conquest of England. Of these activities the rune stones give eloquent (if sparse) testimony.[5]

The story of the Vikings at home has, perhaps understandably, attracted less attention than tales of their exploits abroad, but it is nevertheless of considerable interest.[6] It is clear, for example, that the eleventh century was a time of great economic prosperity in Sweden, especially in Uppland. The economy was predominately a rural one, agriculture (grain) and cattle-raising playing the major roles, supplemented by ex-

---

[3]Svealand included the provinces of Gästrikland, Uppland, Västmanland, Södermanland, and eastern parts of Dalarna, Värmland, and Närke. To the south lay Götaland, the kingdom of the Götar, or Geats. The north was largely uninhabited.

[4]The waterways were much more extensive in those times, since the water level was higher than it is today ("postglacial uplift").

[5]See for example Jansson, *The Runes of Sweden,* pp. 17–70.

[6]Peter Foote and David Wilson have tried to correct the balance by stressing the Vikings at home in their book *The Viking Achievement.*

tensive hunting and fishing. The contemporary historian Adam of Bremen wrote around 1070 that "the Swedish country is extremely fertile; the land is rich in fruits and honey besides excelling all others in cattle-

MAP 1

raising, exceedingly happy in streams and woods, the whole region everywhere full of merchandise from foreign parts."[7] Though Adam's observations are not always reliable, they are supported in this case by the wealth of grave goods uncovered by the archaeologist's spade and by the evidence of the rune stones themselves, raised by prosperous landowners in honor of deceased members of the family.

It is possible to distinguish anywhere from three to six social classes in ancient Sweden, but the group we know most about was the middle class of free peasants, or yeomen. The prosperous yeoman farmer *(bóndi)* was the backbone of society, and the family farm—in some cases of considerable size—was the basic unit of economic life in eleventh-century Uppland. The importance of the family in this social system can scarcely be overemphasized. Embracing a much wider field of application than our modern term suggests, the family included kinsmen by marriage, as well as distant blood-relations, and formed the core element of society. Pride of kinship and loyalty to the family were highly esteemed, as the rune stones make clear. "Memorial stones seldom stand by the road, unless raised by one kinsman for another," says the gnomic *Hávamál*, a repository of proverbial Norse wisdom, and the rune stones of eleventh-century Uppland bear this out. Indeed, these monuments sometimes permit us to trace a family (e. g., Jarlabanki's of Täby) through four or five generations.

The eleventh century was also an age of transition in religion, for it was the period of Sweden's Christianization. Although the first Christian mission to Sweden had been established as early as the 830s, no real success was achieved in Christianizing the people until the early years of the eleventh century, under the rule of Olof Skötkonung, a firm supporter of the Christian faith. Missionary work continued under the kings who followed: Anund Jakob (Olof's son), Emund the Old, and Stenkil, all of whom were Christian. Nevertheless, pagan sentiment was widespread. The first bishop of Sigtuna (established under Stenkil) was driven out about 1066, and toward the end of the century heathen reaction installed the pagan Blot-Sven (Sacrifice-Sven) as king for a time. Not until the early twelfth century can one safely speak of a Christianized Sweden.

Presumably, the adherents to the new religion came largely from the upper social classes and especially from the wealthy yeomen who

[7]Adam of Bremen, *History of the Archbishops of Hamburg-Bremen*, pp. 202–203.

raised our rune stones. At any rate, most of the stones are demonstrably "Christian," and, though it can be argued that the new faith challenged the supremacy of the family to a certain extent, it may also be true that the Christian church was itself a contributing factor in the proliferation of runic monuments commemorating deceased kinsmen. Thus, Otto von Friesen argued that, since the Christian practice of interment in consecrated ground conflicted with the ancient custom of burial among one's ancestors on the family estate, a kind of compromise was reached by which the person was buried in a churchyard but at the same time commemorated by a rune stone on his ancestral property.[8]

The publication of the Swedish runic inscriptions began in 1900 with the first volume of *Sveriges runinskrifter,* a monumental enterprise (hereafter often referred to as *Runverket*) sponsored by the Royal Academy of Letters, History, and Antiquities. It is customary to cite the inscriptions by number according to the system employed in these volumes. Thus, for example, Sö101 is the runic inscription at Ramsundsberg in Södermanland, numbered 101 in *Södermanlands runinskrifter,* the multi-volume edition of the runic inscriptions of the province of Södermanland (forming volume 3 of *Sveriges runinskrifter*) published by Erik Brate and Elias Wessén between 1924 and 1936. Swedish inscriptions not yet published in *Runverket* are numbered according to the old edition of Johan Gustaf Liljegren, *Run-urkunder* (= L). The monuments are also frequently identified by a place name within a parish, and in such localizations I have retained the Swedish abbreviation *sn.* (for *socken* 'parish') and the word *kyrka* 'church'.

Most of the Upplandic monuments are published under 1181 entries in *Upplands runinskrifter* (= U), edited by Elias Wessén and Sven B. F. Jansson, which forms volumes six through nine of the great Swedish *Runverket.*[9] Not all of these 1181 items represent actual rune stones, however; in at least one case, a single stone is mistakenly treated as two separate ones (U199 and U235), and in other cases fragments listed under different numbers may be combined into larger units.[10] One small fragment, found just before publication, entered the work without a

---

[8]Otto von Friesen, ed., *Runorna,* pp. 166–171.

[9]An otherwise unmarked reference to either Wessén or Jansson indicates the discussion of the inscription in question in the appropriate volume of this work.

[10]See Börje Westlund, "Om runstensfragmenten vid Hagby i Täby socken," *Fornvännen* 59 (1964): 152–156, for an example of this.

number (vol. 4, p. 467). Even if the figure of 1181 is accepted for conven-
ience, it should be recognized that about 21 percent of these represent
small fragments and that about 22 percent of the 1181 items are no longer
extant, but are known only through older sources. Of the approximately
750 extant and (more or less) whole stones that then remain, some 34
contain no inscription, while another 26 have garbled inscriptions best
understood as attempts by illiterate carvers to imitate "real" runic inscriptions.[11]

In addition, new rune stones (most of them fragments) continue to be
found, and old ones (known earlier but subsequently lost) are re-
found in Upplandic soil or embedded in church walls. Those discovered
since the publication of *Upplands runinskrifter* can be studied in the
yearly reports published in the journal *Fornvännen*.

The Upplandic inscriptions are not distributed evenly throughout the
province but are concentrated in clusters no doubt related to population
and wealth in Viking times. The stones exhibit a striking density in the
parishes around Lake Vallentuna (Täby, Vallentuna, Skånela, Hammarby, Fresta) and in the area immediately northwest of Uppsala (e.g., Bälinge parish has 36 monuments). There is evidence that fashion played a
large role in the proliferation of the monuments, so that to a certain extent one may say that "one rune stone breeds another." Thus, one often
finds two inscriptions that have been executed only a few yards apart,
one of them clearly an imitation of, or at least inspired by, the other.[12]

All but two[13] of the Upplandic rune stones are carved in the younger
runes, the vast majority in the variant called the "Danish," or "normal,"
futhark. In the present study the runes are often named after their Latin
letter equivalent, for instance, "the m-rune," "the f-rune," and so forth.
It should also be noted that the old a-rune, which after the period of the
older futhark developed the new sound values of /aⁿ/ and /o/, is referred
to here (following Swedish practice) as the "o-rune" and transliterated
accordingly. All transliterations of runic inscriptions are reproduced in
bold-faced type. What the Swedes call a *skiljtecken* I translate as "word

[11]See C. W. Thompson, "Nonsense Inscriptions in Swedish Uppland," in *Studies
for Einar Haugen*, ed. E. S. Firchow et al., pp. 522–534.

[12]Thus, judging from the first volume of *Upplands runinskrifter* alone, U59 seems
inspired by U58, U81 might be an unsuccessful (and abandoned) attempt to copy U80,
and U146 is perhaps an imitation of U145.

[13]U877 (Möjbro, Hagby sn.) and U1125 (Krogsta, Tuna sn.), which are excluded from
this study.

divider," even though it might not serve this function alone. In describing the physical shape of a rune I call a *huvudstav* a "mainstaff" and a *bistav* a "branch" or "bar."

Since the runic inscriptions are practically our only source of the Swedish language until the thirteenth century, the language in which they are composed is generally called "Rune-Swedish" *(runsvenska)*. Over the years, and especially in the volumes of *Runverket*, scholars have evolved a uniform spelling system for this language, which differs somewhat from the later Swedish of the manuscripts (Old Swedish) and from the Old Icelandic or Old Norse of the handbooks. Such normalized Rune-Swedish is found italicized in this study.

Most of the rune stones with which the present work is concerned are memorials honoring dead kin, and such messages, above all, are what the inscriptions wish to communicate.[14] One finds a basic commemorative formula again and again: "X had this stone raised in memory of Y, his father (or son, etc.)." Not infrequently the inscription is extended beyond this stereotyped formula, perhaps informing us that a bridge or a causeway, a road or a mound has been constructed in honor of the deceased, describing briefly the circumstances of his death, or enjoining the Christian deity to aid his soul.

Besides the messages concerned with the commemoration of the dead, we possess, on slightly less than two hundred rune stones, information concerning the artists who executed the inscriptions. This information is usually found in the form of a brief statement, such as "Fot carved the runes" or "Gunnar hewed the stone," appended to the main inscription, and these "signatures" (as they are called) permit us to identify more than half a hundred Upplandic rune-carvers by name. The runic monuments in Uppland are often works of great beauty, and these carvers are Sweden's first known artists. By investigating the stones signed by a particular carver, it is possible to isolate features that distinguish this carver from all others. When these features are found in an inscription bearing no signature at all, one can tentatively attribute the unsigned inscription to the known carver. Finally, after the questions of attribution are settled, one can investigate the relationships among the Upplandic carvers in an attempt to discover chronological, art-historical, and runological trends.

---

[14]Some 26 inscriptions constitute exceptions, being executed for self-glorification, e.g., *at kvikvan sik* "to himself while still alive."

For the runologist who works mainly with Scandinavian runic material, the lack of a standard English terminological tradition can be a source of some embarrassment. Though it is possible (for once) to sympathize with George Stephens, who believed that "we have watered our mother-tung long enough with bastard Latin" and was not afraid to create words like "rune-rister," "stone-smiths," and "rune-ristings," I have frequently chosen to describe the practice and methods of rune-carving by the term "runography," an anglicization of Latin *runographia,* employed by many seventeenth- and eighteenth-century antiquaries. Similarly, the term "runographer" *(runographus)* is used along with its more familiar equivalent "rune-carver." The adjective "runographic," then, is not limited to matters of orthography (as Stephens used it), but refers to the whole complex of features that distinguish one rune-carver from another.

These features are usually grouped into five categories. Design, or ornamentation (Sw. *ornamentik*), indicates the artistic patterns, usually zoomorphic, which decorate the surface of the stone. By technique, or technical considerations *(huggningsteknik),* is meant the manner in which the carver chooses, shapes, and executes the stone with the tools of his profession. Variation in the shapes of the runes (allographic variation) falls under the criterion of rune forms *(runformer),* while orthography *(skrivning)* refers simply to the manner in which a carver renders Rune-Swedish sounds with runic symbols. Under formulation *(formulering)* are grouped the various ways in which the basic memorial formula, the prayer, and additional information are expressed in the inscriptions.

In the following pages each of the five criteria will be discussed and evaluated as the problem of attribution is treated first in a general way (using the entire Upplandic corpus) and then with specific reference to the runographic tradition of the carver Asmund Karasun.

2. Formulation

Most of the runic monuments of Uppland bear commemorative inscriptions of a rather uniform type. Typically the inscriptions convey information about (1) the person who authorized the monument, (2) the person who is honored by the monument, and (3) the relationship of "1" and "2."

There are several groups of exceptions to this rule. First of all, the two Upplandic stones inscribed in the older futhark (U877 and U1125) belong to an earlier tradition and can be excluded from my discussion. From early medieval tradition come five stones (U15, U184, U541, U559, U799) that employ a *hic iacet* formula and two inscriptions in the dotted alphabet (U219 and U220) identifying stonemasons who worked on Vallentuna Church. In addition, there are inscriptions that contain only names (e.g., U989), prayers (U528, U804), part of the runic alphabet (U754), ownership identification (U316), or the signature of a rune-carver (U257, U268, U544). Finally, there is the remarkable Hillersjö inscription (U29), a legal document concerned with rights of inheritance.[1]

---

[1]There are other monuments (e.g., U73, U188, U344, U348) that appear to contain a different type of inscription, but they are actually continuations of inscriptions from other stones and can be included in what I call "additions" (see p. 17). Mention should also be made of the interesting, but not yet fully interpreted, U359, clearly a non-commemorative inscription.

Aside from these few exceptions,[2] the runic inscriptions of Uppland are formulated in accordance with a number of specific, stereotyped patterns, which nevertheless permit considerable variation. It can be shown, moreover, that in many cases these variations are characteristic of specific periods of time, certain geographical areas, or the styles of particular runographers.[3]

In analyzing commemorative inscriptions it is convenient to distinguish four parts of the formulation: the memorial formula, the prayer, the addition, and the signature. These divisions may be illustrated in the following way, using U356 (Ängby, Lunda sn.) as an example:

1. Memorial formula: *Ragnfriðr let ræisa stæin þenna æftiR Biorn, sun þæiRa KætilmundaR.*
2. Prayer: *Guð hialpi hans and ok Guðs moðiR.*
3. Addition: *Hann fell a Virlandi.*
4. Signature: *En Asmundr markaði.*

It is clear that every commemorative inscription should contain the memorial formula in some form; the remaining parts of the formulation are optional.

THE MEMORIAL FORMULA

In order to demonstrate the range of variation in the first part of the formulation, we may cite U142 (Fällbro, Täby sn.): *Ingifastr let ræisa stæin ok bro gæra æftiR Jarlabanka, faður sinn ok sun JorunaR, ok Kætiløy let at bonda sinn.* This memorial formula (I have omitted the signature at the end of the inscription) is composed of a number of elements that can be described as follows:

1. The name of the person who sponsors the memorial *(Ingifastr).*
2. The act of commemoration *(let ræisa stæin ok bro gæra).*
3. The expression denoting "in memory of" *(æftiR).*
4. The name of the commemorated and his relation to others *(Jarlabanka, faður sinn ok sun JorunaR).*

[2]And eliminating, of course, more than 300 monuments that are (1) fragmentary or otherwise unclear in formulation, (2) not inscribed with runes at all, or (3) nonsense inscriptions (non-linguistic creations of illiterate carvers).

[3]In addition to variation in the basic patterns, there are two general ways in which the formulation may vary. Inscriptions differ in length (according to the number of patterns strung together). Thus, the early, unornamented stones are often quite lengthy (cf. U323, U617). Second, some inscriptions (about 25) are distinguished by containing poetry. The runographer Balli was particularly fond of formulating his inscriptions in verse (cf. U703, U707, U729, U735, U739, U808, U838).

5. Additional commemoration (*ok Kætiløy let at bonda sinn*).

With the exception of personal names, the carver may vary his memorial formula by choosing from a number of possible words or expressions to fit a pattern.

Not infrequently there are several sponsors of the memorial and thus several names for the *Ingifastr* of U142. In this case it is most common to link all names with *ok* 'and', as in U539 (Husby-Lyhundra kyrka): *DiarfR ok Orøkia ok Vigi ok JogæiRR ok GæiRhialmR, þæiR brøðr alliR*... A few inscriptions, however, omit the conjunction, as U510 (Mälsta, Kårsta sn.): *Frøystæinn, Þorbiorn, Fasti, Viniutr, UlfR, GunndiarfR, þæiR brøðr*... As can be seen from these two inscriptions, it is not uncommon to summarize all the names with the pronoun *þæiR* (*þaR, þau*), as more than a hundred inscriptions testify. This summarizing is especially characteristic of "unornamented" stones.

A greater and more interesting variation is possible with the next element in the memorial formula, the verb phrase that describes the method of commemoration (*let ræisa stæin ok bro gæra* in U142). First of all, the auxiliary verb *lata* may be omitted, as in U504 (Ubby, Närtuna sn.): *Kætilfastr ræisti stæin þenna æftiR Asgaut, faður sinn*... The omission of *let* or *letu* is especially characteristic of the runographer Æirik, while the carver Viseti is distinguished by his use of the present tense (*þæiR lata*, for example) instead of the past. In one inscription (U4), the word *let* is replaced by *bað* 'commanded, ordered'. In the overwhelming majority of cases, however (about 84%), the Upplandic inscriptions describe the commemoration with some form of *lata*.[4]

The most common expression for the execution of the memorial is *ræisa stæin*. This expression may be omitted, reduced, augmented, or replaced. Omission is rare; inscriptions like U742 (Myrby, Boglösa sn.)— *Ari let æftiR*...—can best be understood as abbreviations of the normal, complete formulations.[5] Reduction of the phrase results in truncated formulas, such as *let ræisa, let stæin, ræisti*, and *gærði* (see table

---

[4] It is uncertain to what extent this phrasing reflects a real situation; that is, does the expression *let ræisa* mean that the sponsor actually commissioned others to raise the stone (and conversely the expression *ræisti stæin* indicate that the sponsor played an active role in the raising himself)? It is probable that in eleventh-century Uppland the wording had become strictly formulaic and no longer corresponded to reality. In contrast, the Danish inscriptions, which are as a rule earlier, seem to be an accurate reflection of the event, in that the auxiliary verb is characteristically used in connection with royalty (cf. DR42, DR55).

[5] U40, U52, U93, U311b, U742, U917, U1017b.

2.1). The rarity of these variants often points to a connection between inscriptions and may give strength to an attribution. Most of the cases of *let haggva*, for example, are from an area just northwest of Uppsala and seem to be from the latter part of the eleventh century; at least three of them (U1048, U1050, U1060) are no doubt the work of a single carver.

TABLE 2.1

Expression	With *let*	Without *let*	Total
ræisa stæin	354	88	442 (59%)
retta stæin	102	9	111 (15%)
haggva stæin	57	2	59 (8%)
gæra mærki	28	2	30 (4%)
rista runaR	16	3	19 (2.5%)
gæra bro	15	1	16 (2%)
haggva hælli	6	1	7
ræiŝa mærki	6	0	6
rista stæin	4	0	4
sætia stæin	1	2	3
rista hælli	2	0	2
rista mærki	1	1	2
haggva mærki	1	1	2
ræisa kumbl	1	1	2
gæra kumbl	2 (1 = *baŏ*)	0	2
marka stæin	1	0	1
retta mærki	1	0	1
haggva runaR	1	0	1
ræisa runaR[6]	0	1	1
gæra þingstaŏ	0	1	1
braut ryŏia	1	0	1
ræisa stæinhæll	1	0	1
gæra stæinmærki	1	0	1
retta kumbl	1	0	1
Reduced formulas			
haggva	12	2	14
ræisa	3	6	9
stæin	3	0	3
retta	2	0	2
gæra	0	1	1
mærki	1	0	1
Seven inscriptions with only *let*.			

[6]An excellent proof of the formulaic nature of the inscriptions, U897 combines *ræisa stæin* and *rista runaR* with the result that the nonsense formula "raised the runes" is created.

An example of an augmented variant is found on U142, quoted above: *let ræisa stæin ok bro gæra*. Bridge-building, in fact, constitutes the most common subject of augmentation (more than fifty examples), although roads (U149), mounds (U135, U269), assembly places (U212), fords (U996), and the like are also mentioned.

The replacement of *ræisa stæin* may be partial (e.g., *haggva stæin*) or complete (e.g., *rista runaR*). A favorite expression of the rune-carver Asmund is *retta stæin*, while Öpir often uses the formula *gæra mærki*. The various expressions for the act of commemoration can be summarized in table 2.1.

Not infrequently the nouns of these expressions (*stæin, hælli,* etc.) are modified by a demonstrative pronoun, so that the inscription reads "raised *this* stone" and the like. In such cases (about 250) the carver may choose among several forms. In the masculine accusative singular (constructions with *stæin* account for most occurrences), there are three possibilities: *þenna* (most common, with 71%), *þennsa* (25%), and *þennsi* (4%).

The third element in the memorial formula is a preposition that renders the notion "in memory of." The normal word for this in the Upplandic inscriptions is *æftiR*, which occurs in almost 70 percent of the cases. Most of the remaining 30 percent use the preposition *at;* a handful of inscriptions, usually older ones, have *aft* or *æft*.[7] The object of this preposition is usually a personal name, followed by an expression that clarifies the relationship of this name to the other names in the inscription.[8] Thus, a typical inscription is U1122 (Stavby kyrka), commissioned by the brothers Svæin, Sibbi, and Gunnar *at Hæmkil, faður sinn*.

This normal formulation can be varied in several ways. The omission of either the name or the noun of relationship is rare and perhaps inadvertent (U4, U116, U373, U795). Reversal of word order from *N. N. faður sinn* to *faður sinn N. N.* is less rare and is associated particularly with the carver Viseti, although it is by no means limited to him (cf. U573, U629 [Þorfast], U663, U1007 [Manni], U1010 [Manni?], U1018, U1019, U1023, U1039, U1094, U1119, U1127, U1132).

---

[7] The forms *fyr, fyriR* also occur, but usually with expressions like "his soul," and meaning something like "for the benefit of."

[8] In the inscriptions that honor the sponsor himself, the expressions *sik kvikvan* or *sik sialfan* are used.

Finally, the expression may be supplemented with more information. A common modification consists simply of further identification of family relationships, as in the aforementioned U142: *æftiR Jarlabanka, faður sinn ok sun JorunaR.* Equally frequent is the identification by means of a place name, such as in U371 (Lövhamra, Skepptuna sn.), in memory of *Ulf i Laughambri,* and U338 (Granby, Orkesta sn.), *æftiR Biorn i Granby.* Finally, and perhaps most common, is the addition of a simply laudatory word or expression, as the following examples testify:

U56 (Glia, Bromma församling, Stockholm): *faður sinn, mann nytan.*
U186 (Gillberga, Össeby-Garns sn.): *faður sinn goðan.*
U289 (Vik, Hammarby sn.): *faður sinn, dræng hæfan.*

Occasionally a runographer will combine two of these modifications in a single inscription, as in U18 (Stavsund, Ekerö sn.), commemorating *mag sinn goðan i Viki.* This practice is especially characteristic of Balli, who seems to have learned it from his master, Lifstæin.

The fifth and final portion of the memorial formula consists of an optional extension that usually includes a second sponsor whose relationship to the deceased differs from that of the main sponsor(s). Thus, it seems to have been the practice for sons to sponsor the memorial for their father, the commemoration by the wife being added after that by the sons. This type of memorial formula appears quite frequently, especially in stones that have been linked to Fot or his school, for example U463 (Ala, Vassunda sn.): *Veðraldi ok Vigi letu ræisa stæin æftiR Holmstæin, faður sinn, ok Holmfrið at bonda sinn.*

Many of the variations that are possible in the main memorial formula can be found as well in the additional commemoration. In this connection it is interesting to note that the preposition *at* 'in memory of' occurs with greater frequency in the extension than in the main formula.

Although the additional commemoration usually involves persons in the same family as those in the main part of the memorial formula (being simply a way of including wives, sons, and other sponsors who bear different relationships to the deceased), there are cases in which the two commemorations are wholly unrelated (cf. U842, U1065, and perhaps U952).

THE PRAYER

The invocation of divine aid for the soul of the departed is a familiar feature of Upplandic commemorative inscriptions, and it is therefore surprising to learn that prayers occur on only about 26 percent of the stones.[9] None of these involves the invocation of a pagan deity.

By far the most common formulation (41%) of the prayer in Upplandic inscriptions is *Guð hialpi and hans* (alternatively *hans and, and N. N.'s,* etc.). Other prayers can be interpreted as variants of this norm, in that the elements *Guð, hialpi,* and *and* are replaced by other members of the same form class. A common substitution for *and,* for example, is *sal* (or *sial*). Occasionally both *and* and *sal* are used, a tautology frequent in early stones (cf. U201, U358, U490, U518, U617). *Guð* may be replaced by *Kristr* (in one case by *Michael*) or supplemented with *ok Guðs moðiR. Hialpi* is replaced only rarely (U440 *bergi,* U867 *letti,* for example). Occasionally the prayer is lengthened with an additional formula, for instance, *bætr þan hann gærði til* 'better than he deserved'. A survey of the various prayers is found in table 2.2.

TABLE 2.2

Prayer	Number	Percentage
Guð hialpi and hans (*hans and,* etc.)	82	41
Guð hialpi sal hans	31	16
Guð hialpi hans sal ok Guðs moðiR	15	8
Guð hialpi hans and ok Guðs moðiR	13	7
Guð hialpi hans and ok salu	6	3
Miscellaneous		
Misc. with *bætr þan hann gærði til*	8	
Misc. with *Kristr hialpi*	8	
Guð + other verb (*bergi,* etc.)	6	
Guð hialpi + misc. expressions	8	
Without *Guð* or *Kristr*	2	
Prayer unclear	19	

THE ADDITION

While most Upplandic runic inscriptions convey information that is largely predictable (the memorial formula, the prayer), over 150 of them bear additional information of particular interest to the modern historian or linguist. From what is known of the chronology of the Upplandic monuments it appears that inscriptions from the early eleventh century (unornamented, Gunnar, Asmund) are especially distinguished in this

[9]Out of 754 inscriptions that can be put to the test, I count only 198 with prayer.

respect. Later, as the custom of raising rune stones spread and the formulation of the inscriptions became more rigid, the amount of additional information seems to have decreased.

Most frequently this information concerns the honored dead: his exploits, the manner of his death, his relationships to others. The Assur for whom U617 (Bro kyrka) was erected, we are told, *vaR vikinga vorðr með Gæiti*. On U778 (Svinnegarns kyrka) it is revealed that the deceased, a certain Banki or Baggi (the orthography is ambiguous), *atti æinn seR skip ok austr styrði i Ingvars lið*. A particularly succinct and extremely suggestive formulation is the simple addition concerning the Asgaut of U504 (Ubby, Närtuna sn.): *SaR vas vestr ok austr*.

It is but a short step from references to the exploits of the dead to the mention of the circumstances surrounding his death. Thus, U661 (Råby, Håtuna sn.), a stone that, like U778 above, refers to the famous voyage of Yngvar (or Ingvar) the Far-traveled, honors Anund, *es vas austr dauðr með Ingvari*. Among other stones that append information concerning the death of the commemorated the following may be mentioned:

U130 (Nora, Danderyds sn.): *hann varð svikvinn a Finnhæiði.*
U140 (Broby, Täby sn.): *hann ændaðis i Grikkium.*
U180 (Össeby-Garns kyrka): *hann do i Viborgum.*
U201 (Angarns kyrka): *hann fors uti Grikkium.*
U533 (Roslags-Bro kyrka): *hann vas drepinn a Virlandi.*
U539 (Husby-Lyhundra kyrka): *saR varð dauðr a Jotlandi.*
U611 (Tibble, Granhammar, V. Ryds sn.): *hann uti fioll i liði Frøygæ iRs.*

From these examples the most common basic pattern that emerges is personal pronoun + verb + prepositional phrase. The range of variation can be illustrated schematically as follows:

	fors			
	do			
hann	*ændaðis*		*i*	place name
saR	*fell*		*a*	personal name
es		*drepinn*	*með*	other condition
	vaR			
		dauðr		
	varð			
		svik(v)inn		

Exceptions to this pattern are few, for example:

U258 (Fresta kyrka): *hann drapu norrmænnr a knærri AsbiarnaR.*
U338 (Granby, Orkesta sn.): *hanum va at Vigmundr.*
U1161 (Altuna kyrka): *baðiR fæðrgaR brunnu.*

Often the additional information in the inscriptions concerns the family relationships of the dead and is merely an extension of formulations of the type *boanda ÆrnfriðaR* or *sun JorunaR* found as part of the memorial formula. The pattern is familiar, as can be seen from U862 (Säve, Balingsta sn.): *hann vas arfi GuðbiornaR.* This pattern is broken only rarely, as in U98 (Rotsunda, Sollentuna sn.): *Ragnarr het broðiR hænnaR.*

Closely allied to questions of relationship are clarifications of inheritance rights, in which cases rune stones may do service as legal documents. Thus, U332 (Vreta, Markims sn.) informs the reader that Inga, who had the monument erected in memory of her husband, *kvam at arfi barns sins.*

Other examples of information about the deceased may be summarized briefly. There are references to ownership, as in U212 (Vallentuna kyrka): *hann atti æinn Tæby allan.* Similarly, additions may relate where the person who is commemorated lived, as in U114 (Runby, Eds sn.): *þæiR byggu i Runby ok bo attu;* or where he is buried, as in U170 (Bogesund, Ö. Ryds sn.): *hann eR grafinn i kirkiugarði.*

Besides these monuments with additional information about the dead, there is a handful of inscriptions that append information of a rather different sort. The onlooker may be exhorted to read or interpret the runes, as in U328 (Lundby, Markims sn.): *Rað þessi!* In a similar vein U203 (Angarns kyrka) adds *rett es ristit.*

THE SIGNATURE

As has been noted, there are almost two hundred Upplandic monuments that reveal the name of the artist who executed the memorial.[10] Most of these signatures are formulated in terms of a simple pattern:

	risti	*stæin*
N. N.	*hiogg*	*runaR*
	markaði	*mærki*

[10]A few of these are cases in which Wessén refuses to accept the signature at face value, speculating that *let,* or *letu,* is to be understood. See, for example, U948 and U1011.

This pattern may be incomplete, as in the common formulation *N. N. risti*. In an extreme form the signature consists of a single word—the name of the carver. (These usually occur late in the century with Öpir and his followers.) On the other hand, the pattern may be augmented by a preceding conjunction (*en* or *ok* 'and, but'), an adjective (e.g., in *runaR rettaR*), an adverb (*hiogg val*), or a demonstrative pronoun (*stæ in þenna, runaR þessaR*). Table 2.3 illustrates the scope and frequency of the signatures. It should be remarked that of the twenty cases of *en* or *ok*, fourteen are by Öpir, and that all signatures with *markaði* are by Asmund.

TABLE 2.3

Expression	Total and Percentage	Conj.	Demonstr.	Adv.	Adj.
risti	51 (28%)	6	—	0	—
risti runaR	51 (28%)	8	16	1	0
hiogg	22 (12%)	2	—	0	—
hiogg runaR	17 (9%)	0	7	2	2
hiogg stæin	10 (5%)	0	5	0	0
risti stæin	8	0	3	0	1
markaði	6	1	—	0	—
N. N. only	6	2	—	—	—
markaði runaR	3	1	1	0	2
hiogg mærki	2	0	0	0	0
markaði stæin	1	0	1	0	0
gærði	1	0	—	0	—
reð	2	0	—	0	—
bað N. N. rista runaR	3	0	1	0	0
bað N. N. haggva	1	0	—	0	—
	184	20	34	3	5

In order to counteract the impression of complete uniformity, mention should be made of several inscriptions that are poorly or uneconomically formulated and defy the patterns analyzed above. Thus, U284 (Torsåker, Hammarby sn.): *Svæinn risti runaR þessaR. Kætill* [?] *let haggva ok Manni* [*Mani*]. *Þæ iR letu haggva æftiR Gunna, faður sinn* could have been formulated more succinctly by combining the two memorial formulas to read: *Kætill ok Manni* [*Mani*] *letu haggva æftiR Gunna, faður sinn.* Similar is U91 (Vible, Järfälla sn.): *Gunvar* [?] *ok Kætil-*

frið[r let]u ræisa stæin. Holmstæinn ok Holmi ræistu [stæ]in a[t] Frøy-stæin...Also atypical is the formulation of U958 (Villinge, Danmarks sn.): *ÆftiR Signiuta es þetta. Gærði sunn hans Sigviðr runaR. Þorgautr risti.* These anomalous inscriptions illustrate by virtue of their rarity the strength of the formulaic patterns that have been described in this chapter.

3. Design

The runic monuments of Uppland have long been regarded as prime examples of late Viking ornamental art, and the term "Upplandic" has, above all, been associated with elaborate and sophisticated zoomorphic design. Several artistic traditions exist in Uppland, which can be identified chronologically and geographically.

There have been many studies of rune-stone art, but none of any value has been exclusively concerned with Uppland.[1] Much of the effort of the art historians has been directed toward the question of origins (which does not concern us here), and one of the results has been the identification of a great many "styles" in late Viking art, a common division being Jelling-style, Mammen-style, Ringerike-style, Rune-stone-style, and Urnes-style. Many alternative names and divisions have been proposed, and there is still widespread disagreement about the nature, origin, chronology, and geography of the various styles.

In 1959 the Swedish scholar Hans Christiansson attempted to overcome these difficulties by analyzing the ornamental art of the rune stones as a set of stylistic features (line-rhythm, geometric forms, etc.) that together make up a "stilcomplex."[2] Although Christiansson's book, as the title *Sydskandinavisk stil* suggests, deals primarily with the

---

[1] Bengt Bergman's *Uppländsk run- och bildstensristning* treats the province we are concerned with, but it is unfortunately of little use as a piece of scholarship.

[2] Hans Christiansson, *Sydskandinavisk stil*, pp. 48–50. This type of analysis takes B. Almgren's "kurvaturteori" as its starting point, as Christiansson acknowledges.

rune-stone areas to the south of Uppland, he makes many valuable observations concerning "Middle Scandinavia" as well. Especially useful are his general characterizations of the two styles. South Scandinavian style, he finds, is composed of "severely arched and angular lines that are often cut off by crossing lines or that give the illusion of being 'truncated' by abruptly meeting lines."[3] Its structure is additive, asymmetrical, and "self-contradicting."[4] In contrast, Middle Scandinavian style is characterized by "shaping in terms of the whole and a dislike of broken lines."[5] Christiansson sums up the Middle Scandinavian style under five points: "(1) The text band is completely zoomorphic; (2) the text band and the beast's head are organically combined; (3) the construction of the pattern is clear and distinct, and the figural representations unambiguous; (4) a soft, pliant rhythm of line is sought; (5) one line serves as a border only for one surface within the pattern and has no intrinsic value of its own."[6]

Although Christiansson's observations serve well as an introduction to Swedish rune-stone art, his method is not of much value in the study of Upplandic runography. Part of the difficulty is his refusal to permit any chronological considerations, even when these are clearly called for.[7] Furthermore, since according to Christiansson some Upplandic masters could work in both styles, it is difficult to use his style features to identify carvers. Christiansson unwittingly proves this himself, when he is led by an analysis of Fot's style to ascribe to him U186 (Gillberga, Össeby-Garns sn.), an attribution not substantiated by an examination of orthography and rune forms.

There are a great many ways to describe the design on Upplandic runic monuments, and for our purposes a typological categorization based on the number and structure of the rune animals or text bands will suffice. Following this, other ornamental features (e.g., the cross) can be described.

[3]Ibid., p. 48.
[4]Ibid., p. 51.
[5]Ibid., p. 49.
[6]Ibid., p. 148.
[7]Christiansson is right in maintaining (p. 46) that "the ornamentation is in part too general and in part too individual to permit a narrow classification or a more exact dating." It is clear, however, that a broad chronology, roughly along the lines established by von Friesen, is justified. For one thing, chronology would explain why Christiansson is able to find South Scandinavian features in the Middle Scandinavian area but little or no Middle Scandinavian traits in the southern rune stones.

Two types of Upplandic design may be described only briefly. The first of these, von Friesen's "unornamented stones," makes no attempt to be zoomorphic, but is instead composed of a text band that runs up and down along the contours of the stone, forming rounded arches at top and bottom. U617 (Bro kyrka) exemplifies a common variant of this type. The second type, common in southwestern Uppland (Balli, Tiŏ-kumi), is composed of a closed, non-zoomorphic text band that forms a kind of frame inside of which appears zoomorphic ornamentation (e.g., a standing quadruped seen in profile). U692 and U716 may serve as illustrations of this type.

Most of the remaining Upplandic monuments can be classified into three basic types.[8] In Type A the text band is composed of one rune animal whose head and tail are juxtaposed and whose body, in following the contours of the stone, forms an arch. There are three subcategories within Type A, depending on whether the rune-animal's head and tail (1) diverge, (2) cross, or (3) diverge and then cross. (See figure 3.1.) In addition, Types A-2 and A-3 can be broken down into subgroups according to the patterns that the head and tail make when crossed. (See figure 3.2.)

The rune animal of Type A is by far the most common design on the Upplandic monuments, representing some 64 percent. Type A-1, with 23 percent, is well attested throughout Uppland. Type A-2 is less common (14%) and is often associated with Fot (although not limited to him). Type A-3 (26%) is especially frequent in southeastern Uppland and is found commonly on slabs (cf. U80, U102). In an extreme form (A-3c) it is a favorite of Öpir and his followers (cf. U104).

Type B shares with Type A many stylistic features but differs structurally by having a text band composed of two rune animals. The two animals may be juxtaposed head-to-head or head-to-tail, and may cross each other at one, both, or none of these junctures. (See figure 3.3.) Rune animals of Type B make up 12 percent of the corpus. Type B-1 is familiar as the typical design of the Jarlabanki-stones (e.g., U212), while Type B-2 can be seen in works by Asmund (L1049), among others. Type B-3 is often attested in Balli's work (U690).

While both Type A and Type B use the arch as a fundamental structural element, Type C takes as its basis the figure eight. It is a much freer form than A or B and occurs in many variations, defined by the number, position, and relative size of the figure eights. (See figure 3.4.)

[8]I exclude almost 300 stones that are too fragmentary or otherwise unfit for analysis.

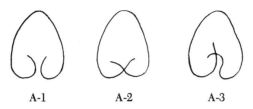

Figure 3.1. Type A rune animals

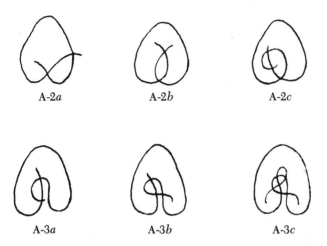

Figure 3.2. Subgroups of Type A rune animals

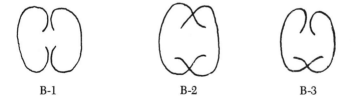

Figure 3.3. Type B rune animals

Figure 3.4. Type C rune animals

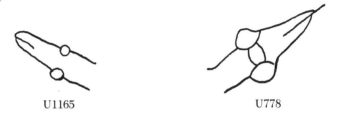

U1165   U778

Figure 3.5. Heads of rune animals

Type C rune animals represent about 15 percent of the material, most of the examples coming from the latter half of the century. Öpir especially makes use of the figure-eight pattern, as in U279.

About 90 percent of the Upplandic stones can be accounted for by these three types, and most of the remaining 10 percent are recognizable as the unornamented and frame types described briefly above. There remain a few scattered monuments that in some way escape the above classifications. Some of these (e.g., U114) are composed of two or more rune animals that wander freely about the stone; a few are ambiguous in their zoomorphism, such as U186, which Christiansson discusses as a South Scandinavian type.

The shape and position of the rune-animal's head and tail affect the apparent structure of the entire design and thus play an important role in defining a carver's style. In rune animals of Type A-1 the head is most commonly found on the left, facing away from the center of the stone. On Type A-2 it is most frequently on the right, also facing away from center. The heads of Type B rune animals are usually found at the base of the stone, those of Balli's carvings being important exceptions.

The head may be seen in profile or from above. The latter (see figure 3.5) is not very common; its occurrence may be especially noted in southwestern Uppland, on stones associated with Æskil and Æirik. Heads seen in profile illustrate a great deal more variation, depending not only on proportion (length versus width) but also on the shape of such features as snout, jaws, eyes, ears, and combs. (Heads can also be distinguished by the absence of some of these features.) In terms of proportion, heads may be short, normal, or elongated. The snout may be outfitted with a lobe, sometimes folded or elaborately woven. The jaw may be open or closed, occasionally appearing to "bite" a part of the text band. Eyes appear in round, almond, oval, and tear-drop form. Ears and combs (structurally equivalent) occur pointed and rounded, long and short.

Figure 3.6 illustrates a variety of types. In figure 3.6*a* is seen the short head with round eyes, stubby snout, and comb. (The comb is rare in Uppland, with about fifteen occurrences.) The head of 3.6*f* is of "classical" proportions: its ear is small and rounded, and its eye is slightly tear-shaped. A curving lobe arches its way over the snout. The ears of 3.6*h* (Balli) and 3.6*i* (Þorfast) are pointed, while 3.6*j* lacks ears altogether. In 3.6*k* the typical elongated head with tear-drop eye is pictured. This type is especially common in designs of Type A-3. Figure 3.6*m* shows an eyeless head by Öpir; 3.6*n* illustrates a head with an extended lobe terminating with a rolled effect by means of a spiral. The head of 3.6*o* belongs to a large standing quadruped by the carver Lifstæin.

The Upplandic rune animal may terminate in a tail or, less frequently, something resembling a claw, hoof, or paw. Figure 3.7 illustrates the (not necessarily historical) development of the tail from a completely unornamented stage (3.7*a*). The tail of 3.7*b* terminates in a knob, and 3.7*c* adds a lobe. In 3.7*d* the lobe is lengthened and the knob emphasized by means of a spiral. Figure 3.7*e* shows a fully developed tail elaborately ornamented according to the principle of interlace. A claw of the Öpir variety is seen in 3.7*f*.

The rune animal is occasionally found with additional ornamentation, such as wings (U107, U295, U305, U887) or haunches (U177, U337, many others). The logical extension of an animal with haunches is the standing quadruped of Lifstæin, Tiðkumi, and Balli.

The bodies of rune animals of Types A and B are frequently joined at the bottom or top by a knot or buckle (the "irisk koppel"). Three of these are shown in figure 3.8.

In addition to the rune animal, which usually serves as the text band, there often appears a number of smaller serpents that fill the stone in an

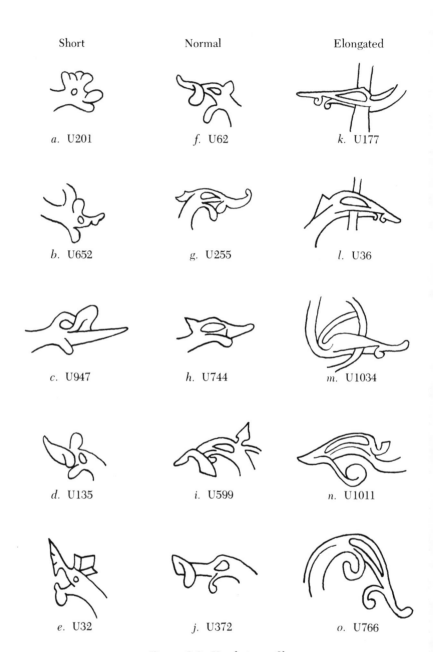

Short	Normal	Elongated
a. U201	*f.* U62	*k.* U177
b. U652	*g.* U255	*l.* U36
c. U947	*h.* U744	*m.* U1034
d. U135	*i.* U599	*n.* U1011
e. U32	*j.* U372	*o.* U766

Figure 3.6. Heads in profile

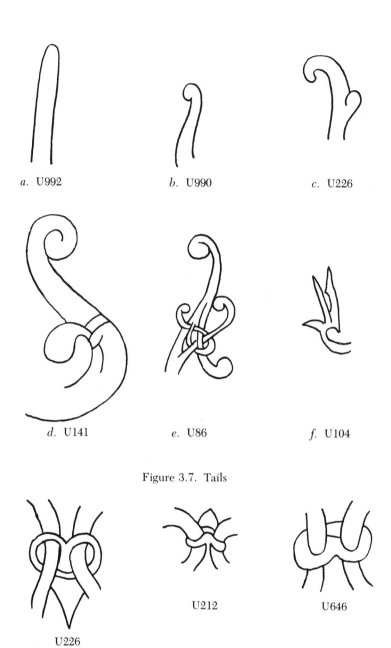

a. U992   b. U990   c. U226

d. U141   e. U86   f. U104

Figure 3.7. Tails

U226

U212   U646

Figure 3.8. Knots on bodies of rune animals

interlaced manner and give the design a lively play of line. The figure
eight is a dominant pattern. The heads of these serpents are characteristically viewed from above. (See figure 3.9.)

A common ornament of the Upplandic rune stones is the cross. This
Christian symbol can be found on about 64 percent of the monuments;[9]
in contrast, no verifiable pagan symbols (Thor's hammer, etc.) occur in
Uppland. Although the cross appears in a great variety of shapes, there
is a limited number of structural types, and about 71 percent of the Upplandic crosses are made up of only three types. A typology of crosses can
be seen in figure 3.10. The basic form of Type A is a St. George cross; by
the addition of rings or "rays" (pointed in figure 3.10, but occasionally
found rounded) or both a variety of subtypes is formed. The same holds
true for Type B, whose base form differs from that of A in that the arms of
the cross are not connected. Type C is an overlapping cross, fastened by
a ring. Type D is a so-called woven cross, and Type E a crossed cross.
Type F is a simple Latin cross.

The various types break down, according to frequency, in the following manner:

Type	Occurrences	(%)
A	200	(32.8)
B-4	163	(26.7)
B-1	70	(11.5)
E	25	(4.1)
A-1	22	(3.6)
A-5	21	(3.4)
B-2	16	(2.6)
D	16	(2.6)
C	13	(2.1)
A-3	8	
B-6	7	
F	7	
A-6	6	
B-5	5	
B-7	4	
B-3	3	
A-2	3	
A-4	2	
B	2	
A-7	1	
Misc.	16	

[9]Of 909 monuments that can be checked, I count 610 crosses on 581 stones.

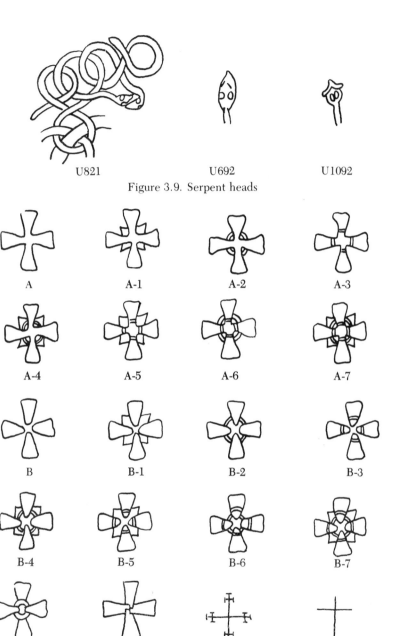

U821   U692   U1092

Figure 3.9. Serpent heads

A   A-1   A-2   A-3

A-4   A-5   A-6   A-7

B   B-1   B-2   B-3

B-4   B-5   B-6   B-7

C   D   E   F

Figure 3.10. Crosses

There are a number of other decorations that, like the cross, are not integral parts of the zoomorphic design. These include depictions of human beings (e.g., U855, U1163) and animals (U860, U904), some of which are no doubt illustrations of mythological and legendary lore (e.g., U1161). Decorations of a purely geometric sort are the so-called "*repstav*," common in northern Uppland (e.g., U887, U894, U907, U910, U919, U1047, U1051, U1057), and the triquetra (U484, U937, U1172). The lattice-like motif of U519, it may be noted, is unique.

4. Rune Forms

The runes of the Upplandic inscriptions are not structurally uniform, but exhibit considerable variation in physical shape. The standard rune forms that are illustrated in the handbooks are in reality convenient fictions, or graphemes; on the runic monuments themselves, only allographs appear. The study of these allographs is an important part of runographic investigation, for the style of a carver is to a great extent defined by his rune forms.[1]

Since the length of a stroke, the degree of an angle, and the fullness of a curve can be varied infinitely, the possible forms of a single rune are theoretically limitless. Thus, although it is possible to isolate a few basic types of each rune, it is perhaps methodologically sounder to analyze allographic variation in terms of a limited number of distinctive features, such as angularity and proportion, instead of attempting a strict typology. Some general features may be discussed first, before treating variation in the individual members of the futhark.

Two general features that do not affect the internal structure of a rune are direction and position. A rune may be said to be reversed (Swedish *vändruna*) when it appears as the mirror image of the normal (i.e., most frequent) form. Thus, ᛉ is a reversed rune, occurring rarely in comparison with the normal ᚹ Runes that by virtue of symmetry

[1] Otto von Friesen has briefly analyzed rune forms in *Runorna*, pp. 225–228. Bengt Loman has explored the rune forms of a more limited corpus (but with interesting results) in "Rökrunorna som grafematiskt system," *ANF* 80 (1965): 1–60. See also Jansson's discussion of some runic variants under U1151.

cannot be distinguished with respect to direction are ᚼ **h**, ᛁ **i**, ᛏ **t**, ᛘ **m**, and ᛦ **R**. A reversed **n**-rune is indistinguishable from a normal ᛆ **a** (and vice versa). It is somewhat arbitrary, though probably convenient, to view the forms ᛋ **s** and ᚬ **o** as reversed runes, since they occur with much greater frequency than other reversed forms.

A rune varies in position by appearing upside down, for example, the ᚠ **f** of **ifR** in U124 (Swedish *stupruna*). In the runes ᚼ **h** and ᛁ **i**, which are symmetrical along both a horizontal and a vertical axis, this distinction is neutralized; the same is true of ᚦ **þ**, ᚬ **o**, ᚾ **n**, ᛆ **a**, and ᛒ **b** if variable direction is taken into account. The runes ᛦ **m** and ᛘ **R** are distinguished only by position.

Reversed and upside-down runes appear relatively infrequently in Upplandic inscriptions. Only U193 and the now-missing U1103 are completely executed in reversed runes. All but the last eleven runes of U344 are reversed; on U884 reversed runes appear only in the outer text band on the back of the stone. The entire right side of U1107 is in reversed runes, creating a mirrored effect in relation to the left side. On Asmund's stone at Järsta in Gästrikland (L1053), all three **b**-runes are reversed.

It is more common to find reversed runes that are at the same time upside down, especially at the beginning or the end of an inscription. The reason for this lies in the nature of Upplandic design: in rune animals of Types A and B (see chapter 3), the reverse bends at head and tail render the runes topsy-turvy to the eyes of the onlooker. The carver corrects this by reversing the direction of the runes and placing them on the outer line of the text band, instead of the inner as is normally the case.[2] The inscriptions U22, U173, U311, and U1041 begin in this manner; in U901 it is the conclusion (the prayer) and in U210 only the final rune. Both the beginning and the end of U1047 are executed in inverted and reversed runes. On U1034 Öpir has used this technique to separate his signature from the inscription that precedes it; the carver of U913 seems to have attempted likewise. Conversely, on U887 the signature is in normal runes, while those of the memorial formula are inverted and reversed. The position and direction of runes are often varied in inscriptions that are not linguistically meaningful (the works of illiterate carvers), for example, U522 and U596.

[2]Thus, *stuprunor* should perhaps be defined as "standing on the outer line." They are "upside down" not in relation to the reader, but in relation to the other runes in the inscription. In U924, however, *all* runes stand on the outer line and are thus technically upside down.

Related to position and direction is the "fit" of the rune to the text band. Generally the runes extend from one line of the text band to the other, but there are cases in which a rune may touch the text band at only one extremity or not at all. The second **u** of **bruþur** in U948 is connected to the text band only at the base, as is also the case with the final r-rune of U1144. In U94 none of the four t-runes reaches the text band at the top, nor does the final l. The same is true of Öpir's signature on U36. In many inscriptions by the runographer Viseti (whose f-rune is typically ⊩) runes are totally or partially disconnected from the text band, which is illustrated in U74 and U208 by his signature on the arms of the cross. On U337 the runes "float" where the text band grows broad, at the haunch of the animal, and on U862 near the head of the rune animal. Two of the i-runes of U614 are connected only at one end, while one is completely free.

The runographer Ulf (i Baristam) also shows a tendency to free the runes from their frame in his works U160 and U328. In these two stones, separation occurs in areas of interlacing text bands. Finally, the inscription U689 may be mentioned, in which more than half the runes fail to reach the text band at their bases.

The angle at which the runes stand in relation to the text band may also be considered an aspect of fit. As a rule, Upplandic runographers strove to carve mainstaves perpendicular to the lines of the frame, so that the angle of intersection approximated 90°. There are, however, numerous deviations from this ideal, many of which can no doubt be attributed to the inexperience of the carver or to the nature of the material (crevices, flaws, veins in the stone). In the work of Þorbiorn Skald there is a conscious tendency away from perpendicular runes, so that non-parallelism of mainstaves must be viewed as an integral part of his style. The a- and n-runes, particularly, are inclined at widely differing angles (see, for example, U29).

By proportion is meant the relationship between the height of a rune and its width. (One may imagine a rectangle into which the rune can fit.) Some carvers, such as Lifstæin, Balli, and Fot, are characterized by their broad runes. The first **u** of Fot's U177, for example, is one of the rare examples of a rune whose width (5.5 cm.) exceeds its height (5 cm.). Asmund's runes, on the other hand, are consistently narrow.

Runes may also be described in terms of the round versus angular contrast. The r's of U309 and the þ's of U1127 are characterized by angularity, while the k's of U600 are extremely rounded. These features, it should be noted, are not restricted to a few runes, such as **r** (ᚱ ᚱ)

and **k** (ᚴ ᚴ), but apply as well to some runes generally thought to lack any curvature at all. Thus, the **l**'s and **t**'s of U665 are rounded in most cases, as is the final **s**-rune on side A of U1039.

Except for ᛋ **s** and ᛁ **i**, all runes are composed of a mainstaff and one or more branches or bars (or arcs), and the manner in which these lines intersect is an important feature of the structure of a rune. The point(s) of intersection may vary considerably along the length of the mainstaff, as the allographs ᚠ ᚠ ᚠ illustrate; with some runes (**u**, **þ**, **r**, **t**, **b**, **l**) the branches may fail to touch the mainstaff altogether, appearing to emerge from the text band, for example, ᚢᚦᚱᛏᛒᛚ. The angle(s) of intersection can also be subject to variation. The **a**-rune ᛆ is distinguished from the **n**-rune ᚿ by the angle of intersection alone, and in purely theoretical terms this could be said of **u** and **k** (ᚢ and ᚴ) and **m** and **R** (ᛘ and ᛦ).

In the case of some runes, the number and length of the branches are features of allographic variation. The "Swedish-Norwegian," or "short-branched," runes may be mentioned as primary examples of this condition.[3]

Variation within each rune may now be discussed with reference to the allographs illustrated on pages 41–45. These forms are taken from photographs and are identified below by the number of the inscription and the number of the rune in that inscription. It should be noted that the charts do not offer an exhaustive survey of runic variants, but only some typical, distinctive, or otherwise noteworthy forms.[4]

The f-rune: (i) U308:24. Overrounded branches that meet the mainstaff on either side of the midpoint. Not uncommon, cf. U583, U597. (ii) U650:3. One of Balli's broad and rounded **f**'s. (iii) U49:18. An **f** of normal proportions, but with lower branch meeting mainstaff at unusually low point. (iv) U1018:33. Here the lower branch meets the mainstaff at the frame-line. Rare. (v) U186:35. Narrow but otherwise not unusual. (vi)

[3]Although Swedish-Norwegian runes are attested in quite a few Upplandic inscriptions, few stones are executed completely in this alphabet, namely, U4, U5, and perhaps U9 and U752. (See Ingrid Sanness Johnsen, *Stuttruner i vikingtidens innskrifter*.) For this reason, and since the relationships among the various younger alphabets have yet to be explained to the satisfaction of all, my discussion of rune forms will simply treat Swedish-Norwegian runes as allographs without regard for alphabetic systems.

[4]The i-rune is omitted, being simply a vertical stroke. (It may, of course, be somewhat rounded or disconnected from the text band.) Also omitted are Uppland's two inscriptions in the older futhark (U877 and U1125).

U73:44. Viseti's typical f-rune, with abbreviated lower branch. Occurs occasionally in works not attributable to Viseti, cf. U92, U947, U1160. (vii) U15:9. An extremely unusual form. Straight branches, neither of which touches the text band. (viii) U420:17. Broad with straight branches. (ix) U29:72. An f-rune of normal structure, but standing askew in relation to the text band. Þorbiorn Skald.

The u-rune: (i) U309:69. A common form, gently arched with intersection of mainstaff and branch just below top of rune. (ii) U814:6. With unusually low intersection. (iii) U80:68. Overround, a distinguishing characteristic of the entire inscription. (iv) U226:11. Here the roundness is carried to such extremes that the rune becomes indistinguishable from some forms of the þ-rune. Rare. (v) U177:5. A broad and rounded u by Fot. See also those on Lifstæin's U1152. (vi) U112:58. The branch is straight and emerges from the text band rather than the mainstaff. Not uncommon, see U86, runes 34 and 36. (vii) U22:1. The carver has rounded both mainstaff and branch. Not very frequent, but compare U29 and U79. (viii) U455:69. An "unfinished" u-rune, resembling an l. Branch from text band. Unique.

The þ-rune: (i) U719-64. Rounded more than is usual, with branches meeting mainstaff on either side of midpoint. (ii) U35:39. Branch at top emerges from the junction of the text band and the mainstaff. (Also quite low at bottom.) Fairly frequent. (iii) U164:23. Here the lower end of the branch meets text band, while the upper hits mainstaff. Also rather frequent. (iv) U922:11. Both ends of branch emerge from text band. Öpir. (v) U322:4. Narrow variant. Common. (vi) U1127:36. Angular. Rare, but consistently so in this inscription. (vii) U1160:3. Lifstæin's four-cornered angular þ.

The o-rune: (i) U104:2. The most frequent short-branched variant, common as both /a^n/ and /o/. Öpir. (ii) U1095:37. Reverse of the previous form. Not very common. (iii) U459:43. Resembles the a-rune of the older futhark. Rare. (iv) U173:66. Öpir. Not very common, but see U811 (a nonsense inscription) and U1097. (v) U945:69. Fot. Extremely common form of the long-branched variety. Rare as /a^n/, but compare Asmund's U356 and U540. (vi) U663:1. Frequent, and not uncommon as /a^n/; see U912, U947, U990, U1007, U1011, U1151. (vii) U641:14. Here the branches are somewhat extended. (There is much variation in this respect.) (viii) U124:10. With horizontal branches. Typical of Lifstæin.

The r-rune: This rune, with its wealth of possible variants, is often highly distinctive of a carver. (i) U948:39. A very common form. Angular at the top, rounded gently at the bottom. The branch is composed of three parts that form two joints, the lower one about half-way down (but not touching) the mainstaff. (ii) U104:102. An Öpir-r, completely angular. It has been made with four straight strokes (two of which were carried too far), and its branch has parallel upper and lower sections. (iii) U43:29. A totally rounded form. The branch is composed of two smooth arcs. Also common. (iv) U750:7. Like the previous form, but with branch extending from text band instead of from mainstaff. There is no danger of confusion with the b-rune, which with this carver (Balli) is unorthodox and highly distinctive. (v) U1172:44. Similar to the preceding one. By Æirik, and almost indistinguishable from his b-rune. (vi) U897:35. The joints here are almost imperceptible, and the rune is periously close to a u. Not altogether uncommon. (vii) U240:30. Asmund's characteristic r (although also found elsewhere; see U258, U328, U335). The upper stroke is almost horizontal, the lower almost vertical, making the angles formed by their intersections widely disparate, in contrast to those of, say, Öpir's r (see [ii] above). (viii) U911:41. As the upper section approaches the text band it tends away from, rather than toward, the mainstaff. Not altogether infrequent. (ix) U519:46. Rounded with an unusually high joint. (x) U17:13. Narrow, with a short mid-section and an unusually low joint. (xi) U35:29. Even the mainstaff is rounded here. Consistently thus throughout the inscription, but rare otherwise. (xii) U296:9. A rounded variant with all parts of the branch touching the mainstaff. Infrequent (U440, U641, U642, U1127) and perhaps influenced by the Latin R.

The k-rune: (i) U1048:12. A typical form. The intersection of (rounded) branch and mainstaff is at about mid-height, and the width of the rune is about half its height. (ii) U80:56. Overround. Not uncommon. (iii) U177:3. Broad. Fot. (iv) U293:10. With a straight branch, i.e., angular. (v) U1012:8. Narrow and with a straight branch. (vi) U201:24. The mainstaff is not straight, but arches slightly, mirroring the branch. Not uncommon in Gunnar's work; see U226.

The h-rune: (i) U429:9. A frequent type, nearly symmetrical. (ii) U948:40. Short bars render this h narrow. (iii) U23:21. Broad, with long bars; compare U49, U50, and U450. (iv) U1003:4. The bars intersect to the right of the mainstaff. Very few h-runes are perfectly symmetrical, but most come closer than this. (v) U1018:43. The bars are unusually low. (vi) U911:9. Incomplete. The lower right bar is lacking.

The n-rune: (i) U130:117. The normal short-branched variety. (ii) U795:7. With horizontal (and rather extended) short branch. Lifstæin.

(iii) U36:2. With unusually high branch. Öpir. (iv) U924:14. Branch points upward. Transliterated in *Runverket* as a, which, however, the carver keeps distinct. (v) U104:35. Here the branch extends slightly on the left side as well. Öpir. (vi) U1028:7. The normal long-branched n. Branch intersects mainstaff at about midpoint. (vii) U937:42. The branch rises from left to right as in the normal a-rune (but transliterated in *Runverket* as n). (viii) U29:135. Þorbiorn Skald's n-rune with inclined mainstaff.

The a-rune: (i) U117:28. The normal short-branched a. (ii) U719:54. Lifstæin; with horizontal branch. (iii) U780:26. Also Lifstæin. Infrequent. (iv) U179:20. Öpir. A rare form. (v) U179:8. Branch abbreviated on left side. Öpir; compare the fifth n above. (vi) U802:49. The normal long-branched a-rune. Intersection at midpoint. (vii) U49:19. Extremely long branch results in wide rune. (viii) U322:24. Intersection uncommonly high. Rare. (ix) U937:22. The branch is almost horizontal. (x) U946:23. An unusual form, by the awkward Grim Skald.

The s-rune: There is a great range of variation, often highly characteristic, with this rune. (i) U945:26. Probably the most common form. Angular, middle bar rises at an angle of about 30°. (ii) U135:14. A reversed version of the preceding. Quite common. (iii) U177:50. Broad, by Fot. (iv) U948:28. Unusually narrow. (v) U167:2. This variant is slightly rounded. Not very common. (vi) U45:4. With horizontal bar. Frequent. (vii) U130:50. With falling middle bar, typical of Asmund (among others). (viii) U956:65. A reversed Asmund-s. Fairly frequent. (ix) U946:3. A narrow variety of the s with falling bar. Grim Skald. (x) U382:25. Unfinished. Characteristic of the carver Svæin (cf. U321). Rune 100 of Asmund's U932 is a reversed example of this. (xi) U642:19. A "chair-s," narrow and with rising bar. Not infrequent, and typical of U642. (xii) U903:22. A chair-s with horizontal bar. (xiii) U238:13. The same with incomplete mainstaff. Viseti. (xiv) U903:1. This strange form could be interpreted as an inverted chair-s with horizontal bar. (xv) U49:20. A wide, unorthodox form. (xvi) U1053:34. A common Gotlandic form, but rare in Uppland. (xvii) U74:13. The "Swedish-Norwegian" type, not uncommon in Uppland. Very frequent in Viseti's work, for example.

The t-rune: (i) U188:10. A common type. The branches meet the mainstaff just below the frame-line. (ii) U179:17. Branches emerge from frame. Öpir. (iii) U104:39. Also Öpir. Unusually low branches; see also rune 71 of U821. (iv) U50:6. Long branches, wide rune. (v) U665:23. Rounded branches, typical of this carver. (vi) U201:36. Gunnar's t-rune with almost horizontal bar; compare U226. (vii) U636:7. Left bar longer than right. (viii) U859:64. Asmund. Left branch is slightly lower than right. (ix) U74:14. No branch on right side. Swedish-Norwegian.

The b-rune: Along with s and r an extremely variable rune, of great value in making attributions. (i) U407:13. An elegant, symmetrical rune of great frequency. (ii) U32:73. With branches meeting mainstaff at a distance from text band. Also common. (iii) U466:18. Here the loops are not joined. Not unusual. (iv) U409:34. Similar to the preceding, but with branches emerging from text band. Þorfast's typical form. (v) U179:40. Öpir. Similar to a Latin R (but distinct from Öpir's). (vi) U708:24. Balli's well-known b, like a Latin K. (vii) U212:6. A narrow variety with loops that are joined but do not touch the mainstaff. (viii) U1154:31. Not unlike the previous form, but with branches from text band. Scarcely distinguishable from the carver's (Æirik's) r-rune. (ix) L1053:78. The angular and reversed b-rune on Asmund's Järsta-stone. (x) U1160:27. Lifstæin's angular rune of a different shape. (xi) U719:53. Another Lifstæin b, resembling a þ-rune with a cross-bar. (xii) U1146:27. The Swedish-Norwegian b-rune. Occurs elsewhere in Uppland only on U4 (ᛒ) and the lost U585 (once as ᛰ , once as ᛒ).

The m-rune: (i) U112:32. The most common form. Gently rounded branches, meeting mainstaff at or slightly above midpoint. (ii) U600:12. Overround, typical of this inscription. (iii) U735:27. Balli's broad and rounded m. (iv) U91:46. With uncommonly high junction of branches and mainstaff. (v) U951:18. Grim Skald's asymmetrical form. (vi) U323: 168. Narrow, angular variant (with straight branches).

The l-rune: (i) U177:6. Fot's l with slightly elongated branch, joining mainstaff at text band. (ii) U948:45. Branch coming from text band. (iii) U946:5. An extremely long branch. Grim Skald. (iv) U508:17. Branch almost horizontal. (v) U665:32. Rounded branch. Characteristic of this inscription, but otherwise infrequent. (vi) U438:80. The branch is quite low on this form, indistinguishable from some forms of the n-rune.

The R-rune: In general the variants are similar to those of the m-rune, above. (i) U255:24. The most frequent type. (ii) U80:67. Overround. (iii) U723:6. Broad; Balli. (iv) U485:32. With high intersection of branches and mainstaff. (v) U394:48. Narrow, with low intersection. (vi) U394:56. With straight branches. (vii) U678:85. Branches are straight and low. Necessitated in this case by lack of space.

Most of the inscriptions in Uppland employ some kind of word divider, which may serve to set off groups of words as well as individual words and which can occasionally be found in the middle of a word. The most frequent types are ×, • , and **⦂**. Not uncommon are ' and + . The forms **⦂**, ` , - , ⦙ , and ⤬ are found only occasionally. Some carvers use the word divider in an artistic way, enhancing the design with a harmonious distribution of these markers.[5]

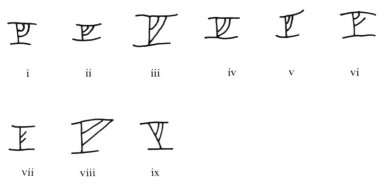

i   ii   iii   iv   v   vi

vii   viii   ix

Figure 4.1. The f-rune

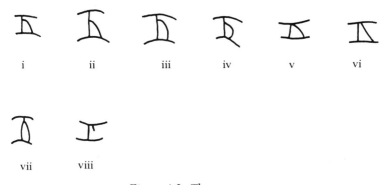

i   ii   iii   iv   v   vi

vii   viii

Figure 4.2. The u-rune

[5]In *Die Ornamentik der Runensteine*, Friedrich Plutzar has seized upon this relatively simple matter of aesthetics and carried it to extremes, finding not only symmetry but also number magic in the distribution of word dividers. As with most scholars who share this hobby-horse (unfortunately Plutzar has several), it is an easy matter to "discover" what one has decided in advance to find.

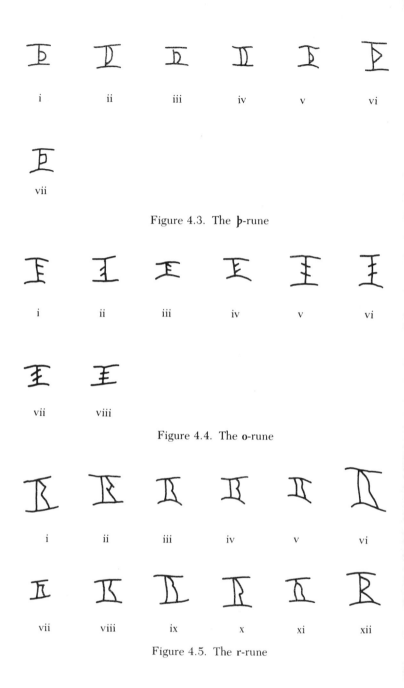

Figure 4.3. The þ-rune

Figure 4.4. The o-rune

Figure 4.5. The r-rune

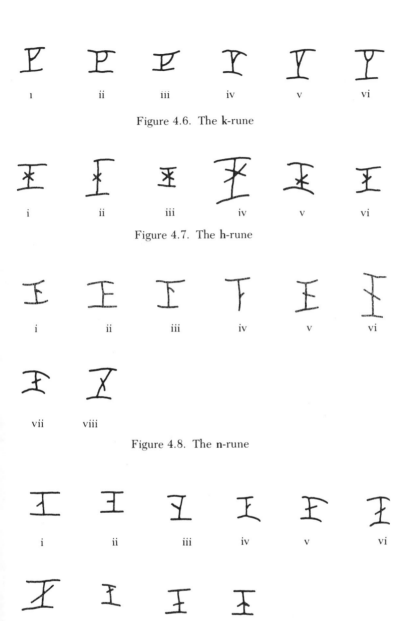

Figure 4.6. The k-rune

Figure 4.7. The h-rune

Figure 4.8. The n-rune

Figure 4.9. The a-rune

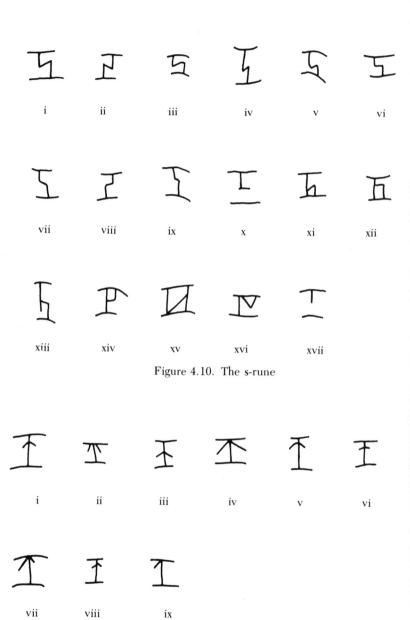

i	ii	iii	iv	v	vi
vii	viii	ix	x	xi	xii
xiii	xiv	xv	xvi	xvii	

Figure 4.10. The s-rune

i	ii	iii	iv	v	vi
vii	viii	ix			

Figure 4.11. The t-rune

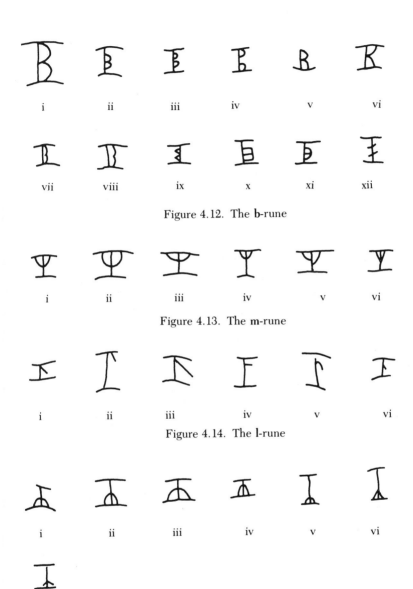

Figure 4.12. The b-rune

Figure 4.13. The m-rune

Figure 4.14. The l-rune

Figure 4.15. The R-rune

Dotted runes are well attested in Uppland, but few inscriptions are composed in a completely dotted alphabet. These few are typically grave slabs (U15, U64, U799) or mason's signatures (U219, U220). On the other hand, the dotted runes ᛂ g, ᛁ or ᛏ e, and ᚼ or ᚽ y are found sporadically in typically commemorative inscriptions on raised stones throughout the eleventh century. They are, to be sure, most common with Öpir and his followers. The carver Drosboi, probably influenced by Öpir, uses a ᛏ d in U216.

Bind-runes are infrequent in the Upplandic monuments.[6] U595 is an extraordinary inscription with its dotted runes, bind-runes, and a depiction of an early church tower. The newly found Kummelby-stone has two bind-runes, ᚿ u͡l and ᛦ a͡r.[7] The latter also occurs on U799. Other stones on which bind-runes occur are U60 and U106.

There are occasional occurrences of strange rune forms that resemble bind-runes but do not function as such. In U163 and U313, extra branches and unorthodox runes seem intended only to baffle the reader; the inscriptions can be interpreted reasonably well by ignoring them. (See the discussion of cryptographic orthography in chapter 5.)

Related to the use of bind-runes is the practice of employing an ornamental line as the mainstaff of a rune. Though infrequent in Uppland as a whole, this technique is common in the works of Öpir (e.g., U36, U142, U687, U1063) and Asmund (e.g., U356, U859, U998). In Asmund and Svæin's Söderby-stone (L1049, now in Gävle), part of an overlapping text band is used as the upper branch of an r-rune.

In general an attempt is made to space the runes in an elegant manner, so that the runes are approximately equi-distant. In a number of inscriptions, notably those of the runographer Lifstæin (cf. U795), the runes are widely spaced, while in others (e.g., U130) the length of the inscription prohibits such wide spacing. Symmetrical spacing is occasionally destroyed by the addition of a previously omitted rune, as in U844 and U945, or as a result of poor planning that made it necessary for the carver to crowd the concluding runes into a small space.

[6]Hugo Pipping, in his "Gömda bindrunor," believed that an i-rune could be found (where needed) in the mainstaff of an adjacent rune.

[7]See *Fornvännen* 48 (1953): 262–266.

5. Orthography and Language

Since a writing system, such as the runic alphabet of eleventh-century Uppland, attempts to supply visible representation for spoken sounds, an analysis of orthography necessarily involves a discussion of language. What is the nature of the language conveyed by the runes on the monuments of Uppland? Although linguistic studies treating the Rune-Swedish period are not lacking,[1] it is fair to say that our knowledge of this language, because of several difficulties, is somewhat incomplete. The first of these difficulties is that, strictly speaking, runic inscriptions are the only source of our knowledge.[2] Moreover, the number of linguistic forms attested in the inscriptions is surprisingly small, considering the size of the corpus (a result of stereotypical formulations; see chapter 2). Finally, and perhaps most seriously, the sixteen to twenty runic graphemes could not provide an adequate fit with the far more numerous phonemes that must have existed in eleventh-century Swedish, so that the linguistic details of the forms attested in the inscriptions cannot always be ascertained with the desired exactitude.[3] For these reasons studies of

[1]The period is treated in a general way in Adolf Noreen, *Altschwedische Grammatik mit Einschluss des Altgutnischen;* Axel Kock, *Svensk ljudhistoria;* Otto von Friesen, "Om de uppländska runstenarnas och upplandslagens språk," in *Uppland: Skildring af land och folk,* II, 491–504.

[2]The only primary source. There is, of course, comparative evidence as well.

[3]On the development of the younger futhark and the motivation behind its reduction of graphemes, see Harry Andersen, "Det yngre runealfabets oprindelse," *ANF* 62–63 (1947

interesting linguistic questions have occasionally refrained from treating the Rune-Swedish period.[4]

Furthermore, since a runographic study is concerned, above all, with features that distinguish or identify carvers, schools, geographic areas, and periods of time, language plays a role only insofar as it is capable of variation. What is of interest to runography is the dialect (or idiolect) illustrated by an inscription or set of inscriptions. In the corpus with which the present study is concerned, linguistic variation is very limited. The province of Uppland is a relatively unified linguistic area; isoglosses do exist within Uppland, but the major linguistic boundaries are between larger areas, such as Svealand and Götaland. Moreover, linguistic change through time can rarely be observed when the period in question is only two or three generations.

Though there is undeniably some variation in the Upplandic inscriptions from the eleventh century, it is necessary to question this variation on two points. First, do the differences in the forms on the Upplandic monuments really represent differences in language, or are they merely orthographic, that is, differences in spelling? Second, if there is indeed linguistic (as well as orthographic) variation, is this variation significant? Are the runographers consistent in their use of linguistic variants, so that we may use language to distinguish them?[5]

The difficulty in determining whether a difference in orthography represents a difference in language may be illustrated by the following problem. As is known, the Proto-Scandinavian diphthongs /ai/, /au/, and /øy/ appear in modern Swedish as the monophthongs /e/ and /ö/. This monophthongization is largely complete by the time of the earliest Swedish manuscripts, so that the situation in Rune-Swedish is of particular interest. Now, in the eleventh-century inscriptions we do indeed find alternation in such words as **raisa/risa** 'raise, erect' (modern Swed-

---

−1948): 203–227; Elmer H. Antonsen, "The Proto-Norse Vowel System and the Younger Futhark," *Scandinavian Studies* 35 (1963): 195–207; Einar Haugen, "On the Parsimony of the Younger Futhark," in *Festschrift für Konstantin Reichardt*, ed. C. Gellinek, pp. 591 −597; Jørgen Rischel, *Phoneme, Grapheme, and the "Importance" of Distinctions: Functional Aspects of the Scandinavian Runic Reform.*

[4]For example, Gösta Bergman, *Utvecklingen av samnordiskt ē i svenska språket: En dialektgeografisk undersökning*, p. 8: "The omission of the Rune-Swedish period is due to the phonetically inexact designation of the e-sound and the ä-sound on the younger rune stones."

[5]Here we must also assume that the language of the inscription represents that of the carver, rather than that of the person who commissioned the memorial.

ish *resa*), **tauþr/tuþr** 'dead' (modern Swedish *död*), and **may/mu** 'maiden' (modern Swedish *mö*), the diphthongal spelling occurring with about twice the frequency of the monophthongal.[6] The circumstances of this alternation, however, do not agree very well with our expectations; we do not, that is, find diphthongal spellings in the older stones and monophthongal ones in the later stones. Instead, monophthongal spelling occurs with greatest frequency in inscriptions that are reckoned among the earliest and is in fact a primary characteristic of von Friesen's "unornamented" stones. As the century progresses, diphthongal spelling increases in frequency and dominates until late in the century, when monophthongs again make their appearance, on grave slabs and the like. In view of these circumstances, the situation cannot be described as purely linguistic but must be treated as an orthographic question. Thus, von Friesen interpreted "the runic spellings i and ai as representing an actual pronunciation $\bar{e}\mathit{i}$, and u and au the pronunciation $\bar{o}\mathit{u}$, with $\bar{e}\mathit{i}$ and $\bar{o}\mathit{u}$ indicating an approximation to the present-day pronunciation $\bar{e}$ and $\bar{ø}$." The alternations in spelling, he writes, "are merely more or less successful attempts to render a pronunciation that, to be sure, is still diphthongal, but in which the first element $\bar{e}$, $\bar{ø}$ is lengthened and the second *i*, *u*, *y* is reduced."[7] Wessén, too, views the problem as primarily an orthographic one: "We must, however, reckon with traditional spelling also in runic writing." He notes, further, that "the conservative writing tradition that must have existed makes it difficult, even at this early stage, to draw conclusions concerning pronunciation from the written forms."[8] Wessén agrees with von Friesen that the eleventh century is a period of transition from diphthong to monophthong (in Uppland), but he explains the monophthongal spellings on early stones in a different way, regarding them as an orthographic borrowing from southern Sweden and Denmark, where monophthongization was already carried out. "Presumably monophthongal spellings in Uppland in the beginning of the eleventh century are due to models from the south. Little by little the actual pronunciation becomes dominant (**stain, tauþr**), and only toward the end of the century are the monophthongal spellings,

---

[6]The statistics for *ræisa* 'raise' are as follows: monophthongal, 150 occurrences, or 33% (117 with **i**, 13 with **e**, 20 with **a**); diphthongal, 298 occurrences, or 67% (277 with **ai**, 21 with **ei**). For *stæinn* 'stone' the proportion is closer to 60–40.

[7]Von Friesen, "Om de uppländska runstenarnas och upplandslagens språk," II, 495.

[8]Elias Wessén, *Svensk språkhistoria*, I, 28.

more and more frequent, an indication that the transition has now taken place in the Middle Swedish spoken language."[9]

While the monophthong-diphthong alternation is not, therefore, a truly linguistic phenomenon, it is nevertheless quite distinctive runographically. Some carvers can be described and distinguished by the ways in which they spell *ræisa stæin, dauðr,* and so forth.

There are, on the other hand, some types of variation in the Upplandic inscriptions that are undoubtedly linguistic but that do *not* facilitate the identification of runographers. In the accusative plural of the feminine demonstrative pronoun *sāRsi* 'this', for example, there is an alternation between forms ending in *-a(R)* and those ending in *-i*.[10] Thus, U519 **runaR þisi** *runaR þessi,* but U148 **runaR þisaR** *runaR þessaR* 'these runes'. However, instead of constituting a dialect difference that might distinguish one carver from another, these forms may both occur within the works of a single carver. In U707 Balli writes **þisi** *þessi* and in U740 **þisam** *þessaR* (the **m** is an upside-down **R**).

Another example of a linguistic difference that is runographically nondistinctive is the alternation between *vas* and *vaR* 'was'. In this case the two forms not only occur within the work of a single carver, but also are found together in the same inscription (U112).

To be sure, a number of orthographic variations do reflect linguistic differences and at the same time provide criteria for runographic analysis. One of the most striking of these is the loss of initial /h/ before vowels, as in U201: **kuþ ialbi ot ans** *Guð hialpi and hans.* To be understood best, this phenomenon should be seen in its historical and dialect-geographical context.

By the eleventh century, Swedish had lost /h/ entirely in medial and final positions (**slahan>slā, *slōh>slō*), and was in the process of losing

---

[9]Ibid., pp. 27–28. A perhaps more striking example of orthographic variation is *Assur/ Andsvarr,* indicating one and the same person. See the discussion under U276.

[10]The data are as follows: (1) *-aR:* þisaR U148, U257, U321, U884, U1114, U1139; þisar U251, U284, U308 (twice), U919; þesar U391; þisam U740; þisr U1064; isar U422; –isar U846; þøsar U799. (2) *-a:* þisa U59, U80, U337, U544, U887; þsa U760. (3) *-i:* þasi U43, U167, U758, U759; þas U1039; þisi U517, U519, U707. The problem is aggravated somewhat by inconsistent normalization in *Runverket.* While þisaR, þisar, þesar, etc. are regularly normalized as *þessaR* and þisi as *þessi,* þisa and þsa are normalized sometimes as misspellings of *þessaR* (U59, U80, U337, U544) and sometimes as *þessa* (U760). þisa in U887 is normalized on one page as *þessa* and on another as *þessaR.* Similarly, þasi is normalized as *þessi* in U43, U167, U758, and U759, but under U1039 Wessén writes *þasi,* "av ett äldre *þāR-si.*"

it initially before consonants (/l n r/).[11] In modern Swedish loss of /h/ initially before vowels can be noted in several dialects. In Uppland it is limited to an area in the east and southeast (notably Roslagen), extending as far north as Singö on the coast and as far west as the *härader* Långhundra and Seminghundra.[12] This area was considerably larger in the eleventh century, according to 115 Upplandic inscriptions that indicate loss of initial /h/ to a greater or lesser degree.[13] Because of the mobility of the various runographers, however, it is uncertain whether loss of initial /h/ was as widespread as the inscriptions testify. Otto von Friesen, for example, sought to minimize the difference between the modern and the eleventh-century isogloss:

> The phenomenon seems to have had a somewhat greater geographical distribution within eleventh-century Uppland than today: it comprised at that time roughly the so-called Attundaland. In Tiundaland historically incorrect use of the h-rune is rare and—of especial interest—almost exclusively limited to the carvings of Öper and his school... In Fjädrundaland loss of **h** occurs mainly in the works of Lifsten. Might there be a connection between this and the present-day loss of **h** in certain parts of Västmanland and Dalarne, or was Lifsten from Attundaland?[14]

[11]Among personal names with original /hr/ in the Upplandic inscriptions, there are eight cases of retention (versus eleven cases with loss). Thus, **hruþailfr** *Hroðælfʀ* U357, **hruþa** *Hroða* U429, **hru:muntr** *Hroðmundr* U692, **hrifnkR** *Hræfningʀ* U759 (?), **hrulf** *Hrolf* U793, **rhuþilfaR** *Hroðælfaʀ* U824, **hrafn** *Hrafn* U1144, and **hurulfr** *Hrolfʀ* U1155. Note also the historically incorrect restoration of /h/ in Þorfast's **hristi** and **hriti** *risti* 'carved' U629 and U599.

[12]Bengt Hesselman, *Sveamålen och de svenska dialekternas indelning*, pp. 38, 57; Elias Wessén, *Våra folkmål*, p. 32; E. Kruuse, "De lefvande folkmålen," in *Uppland: Skildring af land och folk*, II, 537–552 (with map). Standard Swedish has lost /h/ before semi-vowels; cf. *hjärta*, *vad*.

[13]I count 73 inscriptions with definite loss of /h/ before vowels, 32 in which the loss is only indicated before semi-vowels, and 10 in which the only evidence of loss is the restoration of unetymological /h/. (The number would, of course, be greater if one included all the inscriptions of carvers known to have shown loss of /h/ in at least one of their works.) I have excluded as uncertain the following cases, many of them lost and known only through old or unreliable readings: U44 **hystin** (misread or miscarved *a*); U317 **imlauk** (name uncertain); U527 **in** (misread for hn?); U582 **huk** (misread for auk?); U615 **ans** (misread for hns?); U653 **huk** (orthographic eccentricity); U688 **auk** (misread for huk?); U773 **hunef** (not the name *Onæf* but rather *Honæf*); U813 **oais** (misread *h*); U843 **arþkaiR** (misread?); U894 **ulbiarn** (name uncertain); U940 **hont** (interpretation uncertain); U954 **hut** (misread for aut); and U984 **huikaiR** (name uncertain).

[14]Von Friesen, "Om de uppländska runstenarnas och upplandslagens språk," II, 497.

It is evident, however, that von Friesen's argument is seriously flawed by both oversimplification and circularity. The frequency of loss of /h/ in Attundaland[15] can be at least partially explained by the fact that runic inscriptions are most numerous in that area. It is unfair, moreover, and no doubt incorrect, to suggest that Lifstæin was a native of southeastern Uppland in order to prove that loss of /h/ is restricted to that area. In addition, there are not a few inscriptions outside Attundaland that lack initial /h/ but that cannot be linked to either Öpir or Lifstæin.

The map on page 53 illustrates the extent of this phenomenon both in the eleventh century and in modern times. The modern isogloss is taken from the dialect map in *Uppland: Skildring af land och folk*. The shaded portion on the map constitutes Attundaland and its *rod*. The three symbols indicate, respectively, inscriptions that show loss of /h/ (1) before vowels (an *hann* 'he'), (2) only before semi-vowels (ialbi *hialpi* 'help'), and (3) only by virtue of unetymological restoration of /h/ (hut *ut* 'out, abroad'). Loss of /h/ is perhaps the most prominent linguistic feature that is of runographical importance. Most other variation in the inscriptions can be considered orthographic.[16]

CONSONANTS

Deriving the consonant phonemes of Rune-Swedish from the Upplandic runic inscriptions presents few difficulties. While it is true that the inscriptions as a rule use a single rune to represent more than one consonant, there are enough inscriptions that make finer orthographic distinctions to permit a satisfactory derivation of almost all the consonants. The few Upplandic inscriptions that employ the completely dotted alphabet are of great value here, and, where these fail, the evidence of later (manuscript) Swedish and of related languages can be of assistance.

[15]Attundaland, with Tiundaland and Fjädrundaland one of the three "Folklanden" of Uppland, consisted of the following *härader*: Bro, Sollentuna, Vallentuna, Ärlinghundra, Seminghundra, Långhundra, Sjuhundra, and Lyhundra. Attundaland's *rod*, which von Friesen probably meant to include in his statement, consisted of Färentuna härad and the following *skeppslag*: Danderyds, Åkers, Värmdö, Frötuna-Länna, Bro-Vätö, and Väddö-Häverö. See Carl Gustaf Styffe, *Skandinavien under unionstiden*, pp. 261–308, for details.

[16]In the attributions of other scholars, language has rarely been cited as a criterion in the same way as design, orthography, formulation, technique, and rune forms. Moreover, when von Friesen, for example, writes of U904 (see article by Rutger Sernander, "Läby-Bron. En uppländsk brobyggnad från slutet af den yngre järnålder," *Upplands fornminnesförenings tidskrift* 5 [1905–1908]: 142–149): "The language and ornamentation refer us to Asmunder Karasun or his school," he undoubtedly has orthography in mind (the spellings ukarl *ok Karl*, ukirua *ok gærva*) rather than language.

It should be noted that consonant length is left unmarked in the runic inscriptions. The exceptions to this rule are U219 **þinna** *þenna* 'this' and U799 **brunnum** *Brunnum* (place name). The double **g**-rune in **iggeborg** *Ingiborg* (feminine name) on U15 represents /ng/.

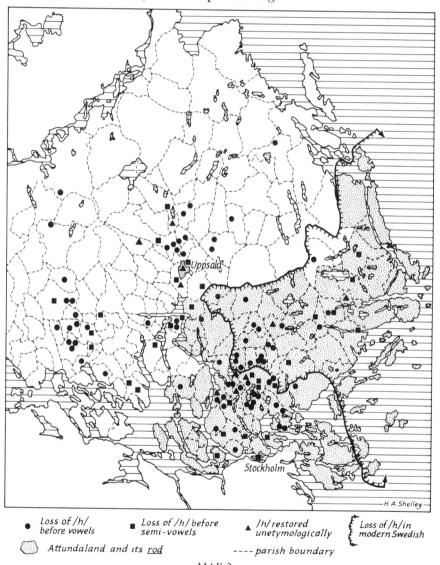

● Loss of /h/ before vowels	■ Loss of /h/ before semi-vowels	▲ /h/ restored unetymologically

Loss of /h/ in modern Swedish

Attundaland and its <u>rod</u>

---- parish boundary

MAP 2

In the same way, a single rune can represent two sounds separated by a morpheme boundary, in that the same rune serves as the final sound of one word and the initial sound of the next. The sounds signified by the rune need not be identical; compare Asmund's common spellings **ukuþs** *ok Guðs* 'and God's' and **þinabtiR** *þenna æftiR* 'this [stone] in memory of'.

/p/

This consonant phoneme is the only one in Rune-Swedish that is never distinguished by its own symbol.[17] Its existence may be inferred, however, from such forms as **baratis** on U160, which is clearly the loan word *paradis* 'paradise'. /p/ is always symbolized by the b-rune: **hialbi** *hialpi* 'help' U34 and, frequently, **mals[b]aka** *malspaka* 'eloquent' U1146. In the form **traþi** *drepinn* (?) 'slain' on U577 the b-rune was probably misread as **þ** by Rhezelius. On the spelling **abtiR** see /f/ below.

/t/

A Rune-Swedish phoneme /t/ may be derived from such spellings as U922 **til** *til* 'to' (cf. ON *til*, Ger *Ziel*). The normal representation of /t/ is the rune ↑ ; in U1161, a rare exception orthographically, the sound is written with ▷↑ and ▷ : **uifasþtr** *Vifastr* (name), **sþten** *stæin* 'stone', **ulfasþ** *Holmfast* (name), **fresþen** *Frøystæinn* (name), and **lifsþen** *Lifstæin(s)* (name).

/k/

Evidence of this phoneme in all positions can be observed in such spellings as **kuam** *kvam* 'came' U332; **skibi** *skipi* 'ship' U439; **sakaR** *sakaR* 'transgressions' U323; **miuk** *miok* 'much, very' U166. As in these examples, the k-rune serves to symbolize /k/. An exception is U15, which is clearly post-Viking age and writes the Latin word *iacet* 'lies' with a c-rune (ᚲ).

In **yg** *ok* 'and' on U1158 and in **sig** *sik* 'self' on U1011, the dotted k-rune (/g/) probably indicates the voicing of /k/ in unstressed position.

/b/

The Rune-Swedish phoneme /b/ is evident in such forms as **barstam** *Barista(þu)m* 'Bårresta' (place name) U161 and **bo** *bo* 'dwelling' U348.

---

[17]It is unlikely that the "dotted" b-rune of L1049 represents /p/.

/b/ is always written with ᛒ in the Upplandic inscriptions. In medial and final positions /b/ was a fricative [ƀ], which by Rune-Swedish times functioned as part of the /f/ phoneme (**sialfan** *sialfan*, etc.).

/d/

This phoneme can be safely derived from the few inscriptions that use a dotted rune (ᛡ , ᛏ) to distinguish /d/ from /t/. Thus, U15 **ermundi** *Ermundi* 'of Ermund' (in Latin), U216 **drosboi** *Drosboi* (name), U219 **andur** *Andorr* (name), and U220 **tælhdi** *tælghde* 'carved'. Otherwise /d/ is always written with the t-rune: **tauþr** *dauðr* 'dead' U29; **baratis** *paradis* 'paradise' U160; **lant** *land* 'land' U948.

/g/

Many inscriptions employ a special g-rune (ᚵ) to make the distinction between /g/ and /k/: thus, **guþ** *Guð* 'God' U1011. It is further evident from such spellings as the names **sihraif** *Sigræif* U746 and **uih** *Vig* U884 that in medial and final positions (except after /n/) the fricative allophone [ɡ] was found. While initial /g/ can be written with either the g-rune (**guþ**) or the k-rune (**kuþ**), the fricative allophone may be written with one of three possible runes:

1. ᚵ **birki** *bergi* 'save' U786; **mak** *mag* 'kinsman' U245.
2. ᚵ **helgi** *hælgi* 'holy' U391; **mags** *mags* 'kinsman's' U947.
3. ᛼ **berhi** *bergi* 'save' U440; **mah** *mag* 'kinsman' U90.

Of these the k-rune is most commonly used. Nevertheless, the g-rune is far more usual than the corresponding d-rune ᛏ , though perhaps less common than the e-rune ᛁ .

In **fira** *gæra* 'make' on U565, the k-rune has a superfluous branch, through either miscarving or misreading (stone now lost).

/f/

This phoneme may be derived from such spellings as **frenta** *frænda* 'kinsman' U973; **aft** *aft* 'after, in memory of' U4; **af** *af* 'of, from' U214. It is probable that medially in voiced environments the voiced allophone [v] (or [ƀ]) was found, but this is not indicated by a special symbol. Thus, **lifiR** *lifiR* 'lives' U114 (cf. modern Swedish *lever*). Such a spelling as U354 **arfua** *arfa* 'heir' suggests, however, that the carver was unsure of the distinction between the fricative [v] and the semi-vowel /u/. (The two eventually merge as /v/.) The f-rune is thus the standard representation of /f/, regardless of allophones.

In the word *æftiR* 'after, in memory of' the **b**-rune is used to spell /f/ in about 3 percent of the cases. The exact nature of the consonant thus represented is uncertain.[18]

In the spelling **kiþka** *fæ ðga* 'father's and son's' on U241, a branch has been left uncarved.

/þ/

A Rune-Swedish phoneme /þ/ is evident in such forms as **þikaliþi** *þingaliði* 'band of retainers [of Knut]' U668 (cf. the corresponding Icelandic term *þingmannalið*). As with /f/, a voiced allophone [ð] appeared medially in voiced environments, but this, too, is spelled with the **þ**-rune: **baþi** *baði* 'both' U854. It is possible that the voiced allophone is represented graphically on U799, for there seems to be a dot within the loop of the **þ**-rune (ᚦ) in the word *þæmma* 'this', indicating that the pronunciation was [ðæmma], the voicing a result of lack of stress.

In four inscriptions /þ/ is written with ᚦᛏ : U636 **þtin**; U776, U792 **þtina**; U785 **þtino** *þenna* 'this'.

It is possible that ᚼ stands for /þ/ in the form **siRa** on U592 (*þæiRa* 'their').

/h/

This phoneme is only attested in initial position and is lacking entirely in some inscriptions. When present it is always spelled with the **h**-rune ᚼ . Thus, **hualf** *hvalf* 'grave, tomb' U170; **hion** *hion* 'married couple' U1093.

Asmund has spelled the word *hialpi* 'help' **mialbi** on U356, no doubt a miscarving.

Nasals

There are only two nasal symbols, ᛘ **m** and ᛏ (ᚾ) **n**. Thus, **man** *man* 'man' U300; **kumo** *koma* 'come' U719; **krikium** *Grikkium* 'the Greeks, Greece' U431; **nu** *nu* 'now' U617; **henaR** *hænnaR* 'her' U808; **kuþan**

---

[18]Thus, **ibtiR** U322, **ebtiR** U30, **ebti** U59, **abtiR** U193, U409, U431, U438, U824, U859, U860, U903, U904, U956, U981, U986, U998, U1009, U1138, U1142, U1145, **abtir** U1101, U1146, **obtir** U372, **ybtir** U700, **bti–** U715, and **ebt**... on a newly found fragment at Sollentuna Church (see *Fornvännen* 54 [1959]: 250). It is uncertain to what extent this spelling reflects a pronunciation [æptiR]; see Noreen, *Altschwedische Grammatik*, par. 259, 2; Otto von Friesen, *Upplands runstenar*, p. 77; Wessén, *Svensk språkhistoria*, I, 39–40.

goðan 'good' U692. Before velars we may assume an allophone [ŋ], but this is represented by the n-rune: **trenk** *dræng* 'man' U143.

Before homorganic consonants the nasal is occasionally unmarked: **kubl** *kum(b)l* 'monument' U4; **at** *and* 'spirit' U793; **trik** *dræng* 'man' U610; **truknaþu** *drunknaðu* 'drowned' U455.[19]

/s/

Rune-Swedish /s/ is well attested in words like **sum** *sum* 'who' U489; **kristin[a]** *kristinna* 'Christians'' U1143; **furs** *fors* 'perished' U1016.

/s/ is always written with the s-rune except for a handful of spellings in which an i-rune precedes the Ⴑ, indicating that the carver has sounded the phoneme in isolation and thus reached a faulty analysis, producing the sounds /is/; spellings with |Ⴑ for /s/ occur in the word *sinn* 'his' on U41, U144, U152, U519; in the word *stæin* 'stone' on U152, U272, U367, U786, U800 (refound, see *Fornvännen* 1954 and 1955), and U803; and probably in the name *Sighvat* on U144 and U152.

/r/ and /R/

Both of these phonemes are evident in the inscriptions, and each has its own runic symbol, Ʀ **r** and ᚼ **R**. The distinction between the two seems to have been breaking down rather rapidly during the eleventh century, however, so that a variety of spellings is attested for each. As a general rule, one may say that the inscriptions seek to maintain the historical distribution of /R/, except that after some consonants it has become /r/. (In *Runverket* Wessén has chosen to normalize so that after dentals only /r/ occurs.) On the other hand, /r/ has become /R/ after palatal vowels, regardless of etymology.

The spellings are, then, as follows:

/R/ (1) ᚼ **uaRu** *vaRu* 'were' U626; **uR** *uR* 'out of, from' U736.

(2) Ʀ Not infrequent; thus, **uaru** *vaRu* 'were' U155; **þair** *þæiR* 'they' U2.

(3) Ⴑ In U61 **þais** *þæiR* 'they'; U126 **þisa** *þæiRa* 'their'; and U89 **ulmfris** *Holmfriðr* (name; pronounced /holmfriR/?). These interesting examples show the proximity of /R/ to /s/, its relation by Verner's law.

(4) ᚼƦ In **yfitiRr** *æftiR* 'in memory of' U616.

---

[19]On assimilation of nasals see Lennart Moberg, *Om de nordiska nasalassimilationerna mp > pp, nt > tt, nk > kk, med särskild hänsyn till svenskan.*

/r/ (1) ʀ Thus, **runaʀ** *runaʀ* 'runes' U346; **uarþ** *varð* 'became' U29;
              faþur *faður* 'father' often.

     (2) ⊹ Occasionally; thus, **faþuʀ** *faður* 'father' U512, U952; **bʀ–**
              bro (?) 'bridge' U102; **Risa** *ræisa* 'raise' U912.

     (3) ⋈ In **faþurʀ** *faður* 'father' U190, U191, U509, U571; **bru–**
              þurʀ *broður* 'brother' U509.

/l/

The Rune-Swedish phoneme /l/ is easily derived from common Germanic words attested in the inscriptions, such as **likr** *liggr* 'lies' U541; **alan** *allan* 'all' U164; **sal** *sal* 'soul' U940.

The **t** of **satu** *salu* 'soul' on U586 has an extra branch (probably a misreading). In **utu** *letu* 'let, authorized' on U759, the **u** would seem to be a miscarving or an unorthodox bind-rune for **li**.

SEMI-VOWELS

Two semi-vowels are attested in the runic inscriptions.

Consonantal /i̯/ is consistently written with the i-rune. Thus, **hialbi** *hialpi* 'help' frequently. Exceptions to this rule are rare: **eubern** *Iobiorn* (name) U121; **ranbRarn** *Ragnbiorn* (name) U590; **heabi** *hialpi* 'help' U644; and possibly **baorn** *Biorn* (?) (name) U1132. On omission of /i̯/, a not infrequent occurrence, see pages 66–67.

Consonantal /u̯/ is generally indicated by ᚾ **u** (**uaR** *vaR* 'was' U329; **tuar** *tvaR* 'two' U393), but it is evident that this sound was difficult for the runographers to analyze, possibly because it was moving from a bilabial semi-vowel to a labio-dental fricative (/v/, and normalized thus in *Runverket*). The evidence is found, on the one hand, in a few spellings in which ᚾ **u** indicates a fricative (**arfua** *arfa* 'heir' U354; **sikuast** *Sigfast, Sigvast* [name] U260; **kaitluastr** *Kætilfastr* [name] U1088) and, on the other hand, in at least one case in which ᚨ **f** indicates the semi-vowel /u̯/: **fita+faþum** *hvitavaðum* 'baptismal clothes' U896.

In a small number of inscriptions the o-rune is employed to represent /u̯/: **ohr** *vaR* 'was' U60; **hoita+uaþum** *hvitavaðum* 'baptismal clothes' U613; **oithafþ[a]** *Hvithaufða* (name) U622. Note also **kouikon** *kvikvan* 'alive' U1040. The spelling **yas** *vas* 'was' with the dotted rune ᚺ on U802 is an orthographic eccentricity that cannot be explained linguistically: the occurrence of the same rune in U1102 **oþyaken** *Oþva-*

ginn (name) is probably a misreading (stone now lost). On omission of /ų/, which occurs often after consonants, see page 67.

VOWELS

One can easily derive the three vowel phonemes /i/, /a/, and /u/ from the standard runic symbols ᛁ, ᚠ, and ᚼ. Nor is it difficult to derive /e/ and /o/, for a number of inscriptions employ the dotted symbol ᛁ e (uer-þa *verða* 'be, become' U323), and in all but the earliest inscriptions the old ansuR-rune may serve to symbolize /o/; thus, koþan *goðan* 'good' U703.

The other vowels are more difficult to derive. The dotted u-rune ᚼ symbolizes /y/ in by *by* 'farm, village' U331; ryþia *ryðia* 'clear (a road, etc.)' U101. The same rune may also stand for /ø/ in the frequent spelling bryþr *brøðr* 'brothers'. Only in U799, in the completely dotted alphabet, is /ø/ distinguished by its own symbol, represented by ᛆ in þøsar *þøssar* 'these' (the symbol for /o/ being ᛆ). The same inscription is also one of the few that distinguish /æ/ (written ᛏ) from /e/ (ᛁ); thus, þæma *þæmma* 'this'. U220 (tælhdi *tælghde* 'carved') and U595 (æftiR *æftiR* 'in memory of') also employ a separate rune (ᛏ) for /æ/. (All three inscriptions are post-Viking age.) The existence of a vowel phoneme /ǫ/, the u-umlaut of /a/, is now for the most part accepted, but it does not have its own symbol in the futhark, and the editors of the Upplandic inscriptions do not use it in their normalizations.

We may thus presume that Rune-Swedish had the following vowel system:

i	y	u		æi	øy	au
e	ø	o				
æ		ǫ				
		a				

All the simple vowels occur long, but length is not indicated in the inscriptions. Nor is nasality marked as a rule; only with /a/ and /aⁿ/ do some inscriptions indicate the nasal-oral contrast, by employing the symbol ᚠ as /aⁿ/ and ᛏ as /a/.

Although the handbooks state that the i-rune symbolizes /i/ and /e/, the a-rune /a/ and /æ/, and the u-rune all remaining vowels, this general rule is subject to so many exceptions that it is of little value in a runographic study (in which divergent spellings are of the greatest interest).

For this reason it is best to describe rather thoroughly the various ways in which the Rune-Swedish vowels are represented in the inscriptions:

/i/

(1) | This is by far the most frequent spelling. Thus, **sin** *sinn* 'his'; **þriR** *þriR* 'three' U214.

(2) | Not uncommon in the word *sinn* 'his'; thus, **sen** U2, U40, U61, U89, U143, U145, U515, U631, U663, U703, U723, U724, U727, U729, U735, U766, U794, U797, U838, U870, U918, U948, U1051, U1057, U1091, U1107, U1111, U1116, U1134, U1152, U1161, U1164. Otherwise infrequent: perhaps **ifteR** *æftiR* 'in memory of' U498; **mesku** *miskunn* (?) 'mercy' U1039.

(3) +   Occasionally: **san** *sinn* 'his' U573, U590, U593, U1137.

(4) || Thus, **sein** *sinn* 'his' U59, U931.

(5) +| In **sain** *sinn* 'his' U575, U578, U582, U896.

(6) |+   In **siena** *sina* 'his' U334.

(7) ⅄   Thus, **irfRkR** *ærfingi* 'heir' U60.

/e/

(1) | Most frequent. Thus, **li** *le* 'grant' U160; **miþan** *meðan* 'while' U114; **rit** *rett* 'correctly' U203.

(2) | The dotted rune makes its appearance quite early and is used frequently. Thus, **uerþa** *verða* 'be, become' U323; **ret** *rett* 'correctly' U11.

(3) +   Occasionally: **þana** *þenna* 'this' U1, U32, U135, U189; **þansa** *þennsa* 'this' U222; **maþ** *með* 'with' U439; **lat** *let* 'let, authorized' U136, U826, U1151.

(4) |+   In **kiatit** *getit* 'mentioned, remembered' U226; **ian** *en* 'but, and' U518. There has been considerable discussion of the linguistic character of such spellings.[20]

(5) ⅄   In **lRt** *let* 'let, authorized' U60, U590; **lRtu** *letu* 'let, authorized' U124, U573, U593.

(6) +| Thus, **raita** *retta* 'erect' U384.

---

[20]The problem is whether such forms illustrate breaking or are simply digraphic spellings of a monophthong. See Bengt Hesselman, "Några nynordiska dialektformer och vikingatidens historia," in *Ordgeografi och språkhistoria*, pp. 127–162; Lis Jacobsen and Erik Moltke, eds., *Danmarks runeindskrifter, Text*, Sp. 945, note 22; John Svensson, *Diftongering med palatalt förslag i de nordiska språken*.

/æ/

(1) ✝ Most frequent. Thus, anta**þ**is *ænda**ð**is* 'died' U136; kati *gæti* 'protect, care for' U478.

(2) ⊦ Often. Thus, enta**þ**is *ænda**ð**is* 'died' U140; heli *hælli* 'slab' U102, U146, U265.

(3) | Not infrequent: ita**þ**is *ænda**ð**is* 'died' U358; hili *hælli* 'slab' U130; hifan *hæfan* 'doughty' U289.

(4) |✝ Frequent in the word *gæra* 'make': kiara U45, U101, U114, U143, U267, U269, U279, U307, U310, U311, U312, U314, U330, U376, U377, U413, U434, U440, U456, U500, U505, U687, U914, U1133. Also in miarki *mærki* 'monument' U314. See also (4) under /e/, above.

(5) ⊦✝ In freantr *frændr* 'kinsman' U337; keara *gæra* 'make' U617.

(6) ⋏ In gRra *gæra* 'make' U947; Rftia *æftiR* 'in memory of' U742; R**þ**ti *æftiR* 'in memory of' U1161; Rfti *æftiR* 'in memory of' U771, U789, U791, U1152, U1160.
The first vowel of the word *æftiR* is spelled in a variety of additional ways, some of which may reflect differences in pronunciation:

(7) ⋔ Thus, U616, U700, U719, U734, U766, U767, U795, U803, U887, U905, U1015, U1018, U1024, U1025, U1039, U1040, U1042, U1057, U1065, U1069, U1111, U1119, U1133, U1135, U1164.

(8) ⊦ Thus, U194, U419, U524, U987, U1116, U1149. In some of these occurrences, the vowel is nasalized by an /n/ in the preceding word.

(9) ⋔ In U162, U662, U763, U764, U828, U982.

(10) ✝| In U235, U580, U762.

/a/

It is convenient to distinguish between oral and nasal /a/.

/a/

(1) ✢ Thus, knar *knarr* 'long ship' U214; at *at* 'in memory of' frequently.

(2) | Occasionally: fi**þ**ur *fa**ð**ur* 'father' U908; runiR *runaR* 'runes' U605, U740.

(3) ⊦ Mainly in the work of **Þ**orfast: fo**þ**ur *fa**ð**ur* 'father' U525,

U629; **þurfostr** *Þorfastr* (name) U599. Also, **roþi** *raði* 'read'
U887 (not by Þorfast).

/aⁿ/

(1) ᚠ(ᚯ) Thus, **onar** *annarr* 'other' U1087; **kuþon** *goðan* 'good' U760;
         ot, ont *and* 'spirit' often.
(2) ᛏ   Thus, **a[na]r** *annarr* 'other' U392; **kuþan** *goðan* 'good' U300;
         at, ant *and* 'spirit' often.
(3) ᛁ   Rare: **buenta** *boanda* 'husband' U84; **stenta** *standa* 'stand'
         U707.

The classical rule that states that inscriptions using the o-rune as /aⁿ/ are
older than those using it as /o/ is not without exception; cf. U844 and
U845.

/ǫ/

As has been noted, the evidence in Rune-Swedish for this vowel is
somewhat sparse, and the editors of *Runverket* do not use it in their normalizations.[21] Occasional spellings that indicate its presence are the following:

(1) ᚯ   Thus, **foþur** *faður* 'father' (presumably [fǫður]) U32, U34,
         U492, U644, U654, U661, U912, U990, U992.
(2) ᛏᚿ In **fauþur** *faður* 'father' U1142; **haukua** *haggva* 'hew' U130;
         aut *and* 'spirit' U617; **vaurþr** *vorðr* 'watchman' U617. Note
         also the spelling **hut** *and* 'spirit' U954.
(3) ᚿ   In U234 **fuþoR**; U479 **fuþu**; U341 **fuþur** *faður* 'father'.
(4) ᚯᚿ In **out** *and* 'spirit' U470.
(5) ᛂᚯ In **aot** *and* 'spirit' U889.

Note also the orthographic alternation in the name *Iofur* on U901 (**iafur**)
and U904 (**iufur**), both referring to the same person.

/o/

(1) ᚿ   Especially frequent in inscriptions that employ ᚠ as /aⁿ/;
         thus, **uþal** *oðal* 'inherited property' U130; **furs** *fors* 'perished'
         U201; **bru** *bro* 'bridge' often.

---

[21]See Axel Kock, *Umlaut und Brechung im Altschwedischen*, pp. 159–160; Harry Andersen, "Til u-omlyden i dansk," *APhS* 16 (1943): 258–286; Bengt Hesselman, *Omljud
och brytning i de nordiska språken*, pp. 15 ff.; Herbert Markström, *Om utvecklingen av
gammalt ā framför u i nordiska språk: Tilljämning och omljud*, pp. 120–125, 151–152;
and Wessén's comments under U479.

(2)   ᚦ Frequent. Thus, ro**þ** *Roð* (place name) U11; **forunki** *forungi* 'leader' U112; **bro** *bro* 'bridge' frequently. The employment of this rune (originally /a/, then /aⁿ/) has, since Hildebrand, been used to date inscriptions.

(3)   ᚼ In **ys** *oss* 'us' U942; **fyr** *for* 'went' U948.

(4)   ᛏᚼ In |**rauþur** *broður* (?) 'brother' U575; **kaūþan** *goðan* 'good' U435.

(5)   ᚦᚼ In **kouþan** *goðan* 'good' U727.

The spellings **han** for *hon* 'she' U332 and **bata** for *bonda* 'husband' U606 could be the result of misreading (both stones now lost).

/u/

(1)   ᚼ The most frequent spelling by far. Thus, **uku** *ungu* 'young' U169; **hu–tari** *hundari* 'district, hundred' U212; **kuþ** *Guð* 'God' frequently.

(2)   ᚦ Occasionally. Thus, **troknaþi** *drunknaði* 'drowned' U214; **son** *sun* 'son' U146; **lito** *letu* 'let, authorized' U618, U1111, U1116; **salo** *salu* 'soul' U828. The carver Viseti consistently writes **koþ** *Guð* 'God' as in U74, U237, U245, U293, U337, U351. The forms **moþor** *moður* 'mother' U92, U595; **tutor** *dottur* 'daughter' U861; **broþor** *broður* 'brother' U215 may indicate vowel harmony in the carver's language. The spellings **lity** *letu* 'let, authorized' in U713 and **bru-er** *broður* 'brother' U578 were perhaps misread. The form [k]u[i]þ for *Guð* 'God' in U860 is no doubt a miscarving.

/y/

(1)   ᚼ The most common spelling. Thus, **sustur** *systur* 'sister' U92; **ruþia** *ryðia* 'clear (a road)' U149; **buki** *byggi* 'dwelled' U160.

(2)   ᚼ Use of this dotted rune, like that of the corresponding e-rune, is fairly common: **systur•suni** *systursyni* 'nephews' U72; **ryþia** *ryðia* 'clear' U101; **byki** *byggi* 'dwelled' U57.

(3)   ᛁ Occasionally. Thus, **biR** *byR* 'dwelling, farm' U130; **biku** *byggu* 'dwelled' U508.

(4)   ᛏ In **sestr** *systr* 'sisters' U393.

/ø/

(1)   ᚼ Thus, **bruþr** *brøðr* 'brothers' U510.

(2)   ᚼ Thus, **bryþr** *brøðr* 'brothers' U92; **fyra** *føra* 'transport' U735.

(3) | Thus, **miþkin** *møðgin* 'mother and sons' U240; **firþi** *førði* 'transported' U395.

(4)   †   Thus, **b·reþr** *brøðr* 'brothers' U73; **bereþr** *brøðr* 'brothers' U237.

(5)   ⅄   In **stRþinkr** *StøðingR* (name) U948.

DIPHTHONGS

/æi/

(1)   ┤| Frequently, as in **raisa stain** *ræisa stæin* 'raise the stone'.

(2) | Frequent in early inscriptions: **briþ** *bræið* 'broad' U323; **suin-aR** *svæinaR* 'lads' U225.

(3)   †   Occasionally. Thus, **breþa** *bræiða* 'broad' U638; **suenaR** *svæinaR* 'lads' U323.

(4)   †| Especially characteristic of Viseti: **þeiR**, **ein** *þæiR*, *æinn* 'they, alone' U337.

(5)   †   In **þaR** *þæiR* 'they' U357; **stan** *stæin* 'stone' U212, U353, U421, U590, U599, U707, U724, U735, U739, U749, U770, U810, U829, U838, U873, U929, U1051, U1074, U1079, U1088, U1098, U1131; **rasa** *ræisa* 'raise' U109, U124, U166, U356, U409, U421, U573, U590, U599, U629, U699, U746, U749, U770, U1008.

(6)   ††   In **raesa istaen** *ræisa stæin* 'raise the stone' U803.

(7)   ╞   In **rosa** *ræisa* 'raise' U987.

(8)   †↑   In **rausa** *ræisa* 'raise' U521; **þauR** *þæiR* 'they' U394.

/øy/

(1)   ┤↑   Thus, **ḷausa** *løysa* 'freed man' U696.

(2)   †↑   Thus, **maytumi** *møydomi* 'maidenhood' U29.

(3)   ↑   Thus, **lusa** *løysa* 'freed man' U168.

(4)   ↑   Thus, **my** *møy* 'maiden' U169.

/au/

(1)   ┤↑   Most common. Thus, **hauk** *haug* 'mound' U269; **braut** *braut* 'road' U149.

(2)   ↑   In early inscriptions especially: **brutaR×kuml** *brautaR-kum(b)l* 'roadside monument' U323.

(3)   ††   Thus, **þaon** *þaun* 'they' U1053.

(4)   ‡↑   In **þou** *þau(n)* 'they' U540 (perhaps nasalized /au/).

In addition to the orthographic practices outlined above, there are many deviant spellings (i.e., misspellings) that are of runographic interest. They can be grouped into several categories:

I. Loss of consonant

   A. In initial position: **uþ** *Guð* 'God' U622; **in** *sinn* 'his' U1062.

   B. Intervocalically: **hiua** *haggva* 'hew' U305; **þeia** *þæiRa* 'their' U337; **ruar** *runaR* 'runes' U790; **faur** *faður* 'father' U884; **brur** *broður* 'brother' U932; **slyiastr** *sløgiastr* 'wisest, most able' U1011; **kea** *gæra* 'make' U1053.

   C. In final position: **ha** *hann* 'him' U1028; **mesku** *miskunn* (?) 'mercy' U1039; **se** *sinn* 'his' U1158; frequently final /r/ or /R/ is dropped: **hena** *hænnaR* 'her' U112; **muþi** *moðiR* 'mother' U241, U343, U435; **moþu** *moður* 'mother' U75; **bru[þa]** *broður* 'brother' U341; **faþu** *faður* 'father' U1018, U1042, U1051; **suni** *syniR* 'sons' U498; **runa, runo, runi** *runaR* 'runes' U41, U99, U112, U144, U229, U279, U287, U288, U308, U337, U544, U566, U742, U760, U767, U880, U884, U887, U926, U958, U1007, U1022, U1039, U1041, U1063, U1158, U1164.

   D. In clusters:

      1. Loss of /t/: **fusra** *fostra* 'fosterfather' U163; **kas** *gats* 'took pleasure in' U226; **ris[i]** *risti* 'carved' U122, U862, U873; **ausR** *austr* 'east' U636; **þis** *þet's* 'that, which, when' U344; **besta** *bæzta* 'best' U719 (cf. **batstr** U802).

      2. Loss of /þ/: **kos** *Guðs* 'God's' U74; **kus** *Guðs* 'God's' U126, U200, U276, U341, U354, U435, U539, U620, U670 (?), U945, U1033; **lis** *liðs* 'of the troop' U112; **miR** *meðr* 'with' U431; **nur** *norðr* 'north' U518.

      3. Loss of /r/: **laþbo** *laðbro* 'landing bridge' U114; **boþur** *broður* 'brother' U721; **tekr** *drængR* 'man' U729; **meki** *mærki* 'monument' U619; **kiaþi** *gærði* 'made' U1041; **kaþ** *gærði* 'made' U954.

      4. Loss of /l/: **hiabi** *hialpi* 'help' U381, U818, U947; **hiebi** *hielpi* 'help' U815; **hibi** *hialpi* 'help' U857; **heabi** *hialpi* 'help' U644; **miti** *mildi* 'merciful' U971.

      5. Loss of /d/ in /nd/: **bona** *bonda* 'husband' U390, U1116; **on** *and* 'spirit' U130, U987; **an** *and* 'spirit' U322.

      6. Loss of /k/: **merilit** *mærkilikt* 'stately, monumental' U773; **meri** *mærki* 'monument' U1104.

II. Loss of vowel

    A. In initial position: **ftiR** *æftiR* 'in memory of' U104, U842, U905, U1032.

    B. Medially

        1. Before or after /r/ or /R/: **brþur** *broður* 'brother' U90, U708; **totR** *dottiR* 'daughter' U112; **faþr** *faður* 'father' U43, U1084; **kˣrþi** *gærði* 'made' U200; **krþi** *gærði* 'made' U69; **rsti** *risti* 'carved' U208, U1040; **þisr** *þessaR* 'these' U1064; **atrfi** *ættærfi* 'family inheritance' U130; **fr** *fyr* 'for' U312, U489; **krkum** *Grikkium* 'the Greeks, Greece' U358; **kra** *gæra* 'make' U586, U1017; **hrþ** *harð* 'hard' U323; **rt** *retta* 'erect' U346; **sunR** *syniR* 'sons' U473, U503; **ur** *vaR* 'was' U527; **mrþan** *myrðan* 'murdered' U691; **runr** *runaR* 'runes' U707; **bruþr** *broður* 'brother' U954; **friR** *fyriR* 'for' U947; **mrki** *mærki* 'monument' U1053; **rta** *retta* 'erect' U1167.

        2. After /h/: **hkua** *haggva* 'hew' U90, U102, U116, U239, U244, U247, U249, U251, U277, U280, U284, U294, U295, U296, U304, U306, U313, U317, U320, U604, U771, U773; **hn** *hann* 'he' U180, U200, U371, U614, U636, U1016; **hns** *hans* 'his' U17, U200, U245, U293, U758; **hna** *hana* 'her' U395; **hn** *hon* 'she' U605; **hfila** *hæfila* 'bravely' U792.

        3. Before /n/ (see also *hann*, etc., above): **sn** *sinn* 'his' U158, U237, U293, U453, U511, U620, U622, U1010, U1018, U1019, U1023, U1042; **sna** *sina* 'his' U75; **mn** *mun* 'may' U729; **kuþn** *goðan* 'good' U634.

        4. Other: **þsa** *þessa* 'these' U760, U1158; **sk** *sik* 'self' U1040; **btr** *bætr* 'better' U758; **kþ** *Guð* 'God' U620; **kml** *kum(b)l* 'monument' U620 (?); **lt** *let* 'let, authorized' U771; **ltu** *letu* 'let, authorized' U620, U1053, U1127; **mls** *mals* 'of speech' U703; **þta** *þetta* 'this' U913; **þm** *þæim* 'to whom' U1167.

    C. In final position: **rist** *risti* 'carved' U179; **þtin** *þenna* 'this' U636; **ut** *uti* 'abroad' U698; **markat** *mærki at* 'monument in memory of' U1030. Some runographers (notably Öpir) occasionally omit several runes at the end of a word, preferably at the end of an inscription: **run** *runaR* 'runes' U181, U462, U1042; **ru** *runaR* 'runes' U262, U479, U687; **faþ** *faður* 'father' U1047, U1160; **mu** *moður* 'mother' U341; **s** *sinn* 'his' U447.

III. Loss of semi-vowel

    A. Loss of /i̯/: **krikum** *Grikkium* 'the Greeks, Greece' U201, U446, U518; **lus** *lius* 'light' U160, U719. In the forms **berhi** U440 and

birki U786, both third-person singular present subjunctive of the verb *biarga* 'save', analogy (from the broken vowel of the first-person singular) has not been carried out; they should therefore be normalized *bergi* rather than *biargi*. Note also the occasional occurrence of other unbroken forms, for instance, *helpi* (U620, U785, U954, U971) and *selfan* (U734, U766, U1011, U1114) beside the more usual *hialpi, sialfan*.

B. Loss of /u/: **haka** *haggva* 'hew' U146; **ahka** *haggva* 'hew' U162; **kouikon** *kvikvan* 'alive' U1040; **seik** *svæik* 'betrayed' U954. The form *gæra* without the semi-vowel does not represent a misspelling but is the normal form; it occurs sixty-eight times, while *gærva* (the older form) is attested eleven times.

IV. Intrusive vowels in consonant clusters: **kirikium** *Grikkium* 'the Greeks, Greece' U73, U140; **kariþu** *gærðu* 'made' U225; **hialub·i** *hialpi* 'help' U700; **ialibi** *hialpi* 'help' U701; **bereþr** *brøðr* 'brothers' U237; **buruþur** *broður* 'brother' U479, U651, U655, U689, U845, U864, U1153; **byryþr** *brøðr* 'brothers' U323; **baruþar** *brøðr* 'brothers' U579; **boruþur** *broður* 'brother' U616; **buruþr** *broður* 'brother' U676; **boroþur** *broður* 'brother' U862; **buroþur** *broður* 'brother' U1046; **biruþr** *brøðr* 'brothers' U1172; **buro** *bro* 'bridge' U475, U1046; **buru** *bro* 'bridge' U947.

V. Intrusive consonants in clusters: **þentsa** *þennsa* 'this' U385, U401, U457; **sint** *sinn* 'his' U642.

VI. Metathesis

  A. Of two consonants: **kusþ** *Guðs* 'God's' U160; **hieþli** *hielpi* 'help' U38; **ritsi** *risti* 'carved' U824; **osmunrt** *Asmundr* (name) U859, U969, U981, U986, U998, U1149.

  B. Of two vowels: **stian** *stæin* 'stone' U824.

  C. Of vowel and consonant: **broþra** *broður* 'brother' U1083; **be[rþur]** *broður* 'brother' U74; **kirkum** *Grikkium* 'the Greeks, Greece' U136; **kriki** *kirkiu* 'church' U687; **burnu** *brunnu* 'burned' U1161; **ahkua** *haggva* 'hew' U145; **ahka** *haggva* 'hew' U162; **ahns** *hans* 'his' U411; **ihar** *hiar* 'here' U559; **ihlbi** *hialpi* 'help' U319, U323, U338, U518; **fitiR** *æftiR* 'in memory of' U886; **haunar** *hann vaR* 'he was' U739.

CRYPTOGRAPHY

Cryptographic orthography is rare in Uppland, a circumstance easily understandable in light of the communicative, memorial nature of the inscriptions, which do not bear messages of magic, ritualistic, or heathen import (in contrast to, say, the Rök-stone). The only certain cases are the following five:[22]

1. U60: kirRþu þRir utr×lRt+rnesn×st͡nea+iftRr+bira fnþur+
   RkRkriþnr×hna×ohr×irfRkR uRþa×h...-...þ

   Assuming **R** = i, **n** = a, **a** = n, and **h** = a (once), the inscription reads:

   > kiriþu þiir utr×lit +raesa×st͡aen +iftir+birn faþur ikikriþar×
   > han×oar×irfiki uiþa×h...-...þ

   or: ... *Uddr let ræisa* 'stæin *æftiR Biorn, faður IngiriðaR. Hann vaR ærfingi Viða* ...

2. U163: k͡lamal a s͡au k͡a n͡s auk a i n͡f a a͡uk+farulfr+litu+rista×ili tf s͡l·
   fR+þuri+R͡u f ak þa u͡m r͡a s͡l in×auk×kamal×iftiR×fusra sin
   f–str×iaRk

   Wessén comments: "All of this strikes one as a game, a peculiar whim designed to confuse the reader, and perhaps this is also the correct explanation," but is able to decipher the inscription (mainly by ignoring certain runes or parts of bind-runes):

   > *Gamall ok Svæinn ok FarulfR letu rista hælli [æftiR] Þori, faður sinn, ok Gamall æftiR fos(t)ra sinn. –fastr hiogg.*

3. U313: Normal orthography except for the following series:
   iafa͡urkutfast·asbtuibu

   which can be read: *Iufurfast, stiupu* 'Iufurfast, step-daughter'. The similarity to U163 led Brate to attribute both to the same carver.

4. U321: Normal orthography except for the following series:
   siutasirin·marnu·maþsi

   The solution, first attained by Brate, rearranges the runes to read:
   suain risti·runaR·þisaR
   Svæin risti runaR þessaR.

5. U1165: Normal orthography except for the carver's name:
   airikr   *Æirikr*

   in *is*-runes.

---

[22]In addition, there are a few inscriptions that yield no sensible message and are quite probably non-linguistic, being the works of illiterate carvers and intended primarily for decorative purposes. The possibility that at least some of these bear cryptographic messages cannot, however, be totally excluded, especially in the case of some of the more professionally executed monuments, such as U811.

6. Technical Considerations

The runographers who executed the Upplandic monuments possessed not only artistic and linguistic sensibilities but also a technical proficiency in the craft of stone-working. That the degree of proficiency varied greatly among the carvers of Uppland becomes especially clear when one views such carvings as the adjacent U80 and U81 (Sundby, Spånga sn.), one the work of a polished master, the other the abandoned attempt of an amateur.

THE MATERIAL

Most of the runic inscriptions of Uppland are found on stones that were intended to be erected.[1] The overwhelming majority of these raised stones (ca. 70%) are of granite, which could vary in color (from dark grey to light red) and in texture (from fine grained to coarse grained). Next in frequency, yet far behind granite, comes sandstone with 14 percent. Gneis and gneis-granite make up 9 percent, limestone (so dominant on Gotland and Öland) less than 1 percent.[2] Not infrequently the beauty of a stone is enhanced by veins or infusions of a min-

---

[1]Generally by sinking the base of the stone into the ground, although a few stones (for example, U85 and U846) may have been propped up on the surface of the ground.

[2]The figures are based upon Wessén and Jansson in *Runverket*. Of 880 stones that they identify by type, 617 are of granite (283 grey, 150 red, 166 light, 18 dark), 120 of sandstone (78 red, 42 others), 47 of gneis-granite, 36 of gneis, 14 of *"gråsten,"* 5 of limestone, and 41 of miscellaneous or unclearly identified stone.

eral like feldspar or quartz, and it is likely that the carvers took these nuances of color into consideration when selecting a stone.[3]

Although it is possible to suggest that the "classical" Upplandic stone is of grey granite and that the typical Öpir-stone from the end of the century is of red sandstone, these are extremely vague trends and subject to important exceptions. The Häggeby-stone (U664), for example, which is dated to about 550, is of sandstone, as are several Asmund-stones (see chapter 8). The choice of stone is not so much a matter of chronology or of individual style as of geological circumstances. In areas of Uppland where sandstone is found under the soil, it will be represented in the rune stones.[4]

While nearby quarries probably account for almost all Upplandic rune stones,[5] there is evidence that stones were occasionally imported. A clear case in point is U414 (Norrsunda kyrka), a stone that, although long since fragmented and lost, obviously possessed the mushroom shape typical of the Gotlandic picture stones. The inscription reads in part: *Þæir fǿrðu stæin þenna af Gutlandi*. Wessén suggests that "no doubt it [the stone] was brought to the mainland in its finished shape by an Upplander to whom this form of grave monument appealed. The inscription, however, was certainly not carved until it reached Uppland."[6]

Since the quarrying, dressing, and transporting of stone were difficult and expensive, the cost of such a monument, about which we can only conjecture, must have been considerable. In a book on the mason of medieval England, Douglas Knoop writes that

quarrying must often have been hindered and not infrequently brought to a stop by difficulties which the greater resources of modern times have overcome with relative ease. One, clearly, was the inferiority of mediæval instruments as compared with modern machine-driven drills and saws. The use of explosives for detaching great quantities of rock was not, so far as we know, practised, and the quarrymen had to rely almost exclusively on picks, axes, chisels, levers, and wedges. Moreover, both mining and quarrying to any depth were impossible in the Middle Ages, because of the lack of effective means to get rid of water in excavations.[7]

---

[3]This can be observed as far back as the Möjbro-stone (ca. 400?); see Sven B. F. Jansson, "Möjbrostenens ristning," *Fornvännen* 47 (1952): 124–127. Color photographs have a definite superiority over black-and-white in runographic work.

[4]See the discussion of the geology of Uppland in *Uppland: Skildring af land och folk*, I, 8–13 (with map).

[5]The transport of the stone from the quarry (?) is occasionally mentioned in the inscriptions themselves; see U735 and the discussion there.

[6]Note also U1028, a limestone monument with design and prayer atypical of Uppland.

[7]Douglas Knoop and G. P. Jones, *The Mediæval Mason*, p. 8.

The expense of finished building materials, writes Knoop, led to a considerable traffic in second-hand stone, some of it stolen.

There is some slight evidence of a similar situation in eleventh-century Sweden. On the reverse of U203 (Angarns kyrka), for example, is the beginning of a presumably unrelated carving in runic style, indicating perhaps the use of second-hand stones. Similar evidence can be noted on U393 (Sigtuna, Borgmästarvreten). A much more striking parallel to the practices described by Knoop is, of course, the use of rune stones as building material for Sweden's first stone churches.[8]

Raised stones do not constitute the only medium for the runic inscriptions of Uppland. Runographers often took advantage of glacial slabs and large boulders that dominated the landscape and thus commanded as much attention as a raised stone. There are about fifty inscriptions in Uppland on natural slabs or cliffs (*berghäll* and *bergvägg*), and almost that many on stationary boulders (*jordfast stenblock*). Especially common in south-central Uppland (Seminghundra härad has 16, Sollentuna and Vallentuna härader 9 each), they are frequently ornamented with designs of Type A-3 and Type C.

Finally, the unique U436 (Arnberga, Husby-Ärlinghundra sn.) should be noted. What seems to be a typical memorial inscription has been executed on a sandstone pillar.

CUTTING AND DRESSING THE STONE

Once the raw stone has been quarried or otherwise obtained, it can be shaped and smoothed by the stonecutter. The Upplandic rune stones vary in size from a couple of feet in height to over ten,[9] but the average height is between five and six feet. In shape there is also much variation, and part of the esthetic merit of a monument depends on the success with which the shape of the stone and the design of the carving have been coordinated.[10] Nevertheless, there are clearly a few shapes, such as the arch, which attained some degree of popularity. While the two sides of the arch of U899 (Vårdsätra, Bondkyrka sn.), for example, are

[8]There has been an interesting feud on this subject. See Sune Lindqvist, "Jarlabanke-släktens minnesmärken," in *Nordiska arkeologmötet i Stockholm 1922*, p. 133; Wessén's discussion of U127 and U261; Sven B. F. Jansson, "Några okända uppländska runinskrifter," *Fornvännen* 41 (1946): 276–278; Sune Lindqvist, "Onaturliga runstenstransporter," *Fornvännen* 42 (1947): 50–51; and Jansson under U779.

[9]Stones of imposing height seem to have become especially fashionable in the area just southeast of Uppsala (Ärlinghundra härad); cf. U437, U455, U460, U462, U463.

[10]Toward the end of the century there is a tendency to reproduce on any and all surfaces, as if stamped by machine, the typical Öpir design (A-3c).

almost symmetrical, the symmetry in U945 (Danmarks kyrka) is disrupted by an angle on the right side of the stone, creating an interesting esthetic effect (not unlike that of the Rök-stone) which is in turn mirrored by the text band. Certain carvers, such as Fot, are particularly noted for their efforts to shape the stone carefully before carving.

In many cases the stones were further prepared by smoothing the surface that was to be inscribed. For this purpose (called "scrappling" in English) the stone ax or stone hammer was probably employed.[11]

Occasionally one finds on the surface of the Upplandic monuments small bowl-shaped hollows (*älvkvarnar*) in which offerings were made (*älvablot*). In the case of U875 (Focksta, Hagby sn.), these circumstances have been examined in detail by von Friesen as well as by Wessén. The carver has made no attempt to smooth the stone and has not avoided these depressions, but rather "allows his lines to go down into them freely, whenever it suits him." When raised the stone was thus unfit for its heathen use, and it is likely (as von Friesen suggested) that this was the conscious aim of the carver.[12]

CARVING

Except for a few works done in relief, such as Balli's U721 and U722, the Upplandic monuments were incised, with chisel and mallet. The ornamentation was probably executed before the runes, and the text band or the rune animal seems, as a rule, to have been carved first of all. Of this practice we possess some evidence in the form of incomplete or abandoned runic monuments. U728 (Tängby, Lund, Löts sn.) and U801

---

[11]I am unable to find adequate literature on the subject of tools. Jan Petersen's *Vikingetidens redskaper* treats equipment of various fields (riding, the smithy, cooking, carpentry, etc.) but neglects the tools of stonework. We may presume that the tools of this trade (like those of the smith) have changed little since Viking times, and would include stone axes, picks, stone hammers, mallets, and chisels.

In Gwyn Jones' recent *History of the Vikings* there appears (p. 344) a text figure taken "from a rubbing made by Søren Krogh" at Gjøl Church, North Jutland. From this picture Jones concludes that a "pointed hammer" was employed, rather than a chisel, to inscribe in stone. We may rather suppose that the worker is dressing the stone, not carving or inscribing it. Knoop writes (*The Mediæval Mason*, p. 78), for example, that both freemasons and roughmasons "frequently dressed stone with axes, either roughly with a view of its being finished with a chisel or in a relatively finished manner intended for immediate use."

[12]Seven centuries later, the stone having toppled over, these hollows were again used for offerings. For a complete account see Otto von Friesen, "Run- och offerstenen vid Focksta i Hagby socken," in *Uppsala Nya Tidnings Julnummer*, 1913.

(Långtora prästgård) are two examples of rune stones on which complete zoomorphic text bands have been executed but left empty of runes. Similar, but more elaborate, is U1171 (Axsjö, Vittinge sn.) with its rune animal of Type A-1, "Irish buckle," standing quadruped, and interlaced serpents. The text band is devoid of runes, and it has been speculated that the stone, which may be the work of Lifstæin, was abandoned when the top was broken off during the carving. On U747 (Kullinge, Husby-Sjutolfts sn.), with somewhat similar ornamentation, someone has incised a number of runes (or runelike symbols) as if the inscription were begun but left unfinished. The same can be said of U81 (Sundby, Spånga sn.), probably the work of an amateur who was unable to carry it to completion.

Further evidence that the design was executed before the inscription is that the runes are compressed at the end of some inscriptions (e.g., U686) or spill out of the text band onto the free surface (e.g., U792).

From the testimony of a number of carvings it is clear that the runographer did not execute his work in one stage, but made a shallow preliminary sketch on the stone that could be deepened later according to the carver's will. In this way a potential miscarving could be neutralized by leaving it shallow while hewing the other lines to greater depth. This practice, easily understandable in consideration of the interlace patterns alone, can perhaps be observed most frequently in the smaller serpents; on U866 (Björnome, Gryta sn.), for example, the interlace principle is occasionally violated by the intersection of two serpents, but, since one of them is traced with shallower lines, we may assume that the carver did not intend it to be visible. Similarly, ornamental lines on U1084 (Hämringe, Bälinge sn.) and U1089 (Marsta, Bälinge sn.) are often falsely sketched but not always deepened by the carver's chisel, and in those cases they are not painted in by the editors of *Runverket*. It is characteristic of Öpir to leave some of these sketched lines completely unfinished. The ornamentation of U973 (Gränby, Vaksala sn.) is often scarcely visible and in places is completely absent. The text band of U974 (Jädra, Vaksala sn.) is left largely undone.

The runes could also be sketched before final carving. On U859 (Måsta, Balingsta sn.) the carver seems to have mistakenly sketched a ᚾ for rune 73, but discovered the error and hewed only the mainstaff to greater depth, thus rendering (correctly) an i-rune. In U1140 (Burunge, Vendels sn.) the correction is not so neat. When the carver discovered that he was repeating rune 9 (f), he simply left it unfinished (resembling a k-rune) and began the intended rune to the right. In contrast, the carver of U844 (Viggby bro, Dalby sn.) omitted a rune and was forced to insert it after completion of the text, destroying the equality of spacing he had produced. It is a fact, then, that the principle of preliminary sketching was not always used to advantage.

An extremely interesting example of sketching is U884 (Ingla, Skogs-Tibble sn.), which Wessén discusses in some detail:

The carving surface on all three sides is very uneven and coarse. On side A there are clear traces of smoothing. The carving here is also very shallow. This is in particular true of the runes, which are in part extremely hard to read. Often the runes (or ornamental lines) can only be glimpsed as light changes in the surface, without noticeable penetration. Nevertheless, by careful observation a reliable reading can probably be had.—The carving on sides B and C is extremely shallow; in part it appears only as scraping on the stone surface, white against the red granite, without perceptible penetration. On side B only the runic frame is cut with a chisel, and shallowly. The inner field is filled with a sketch produced by scraping on the surface; it has never been carved deeply with a chisel... —On side C the ornamentation is shallow, only faintly visible in parts. On the left side within the runic frame are a few staves and at the top some runes. It is unlikely that there were ever any runes carved on the right side, perhaps just sketched there... —The rune boulder at Ingla is interesting and unparalleled inasmuch as it contains carvings that to all appearances were not finished but merely sketched and in part faintly incised.[13]

It should be noted that uneven depth of line does not always indicate preliminary sketching, but may simply be the product of an extremely untalented carver. It is usually an easy task, however, to distinguish the skilled from the unskilled, for the latter leaves his mark not only in uneven depth but also in a generally unsteady technique, a linguistic uncertainty, and an awkward artistic sense.[14] The editors of *Runverket* have made an attempt to describe the carvers' proficiency, using expressions like "*säkert, omsorgsfullt huggen*" ("carved with assurance and great care"), "*skickligt utförd*" ("skillfully executed"), and "*klumpig, o-säkert huggen*" ("awkward, unsteadily carved"), but without much regularity or consistency.

The lines of the Upplandic carvings vary not only in depth but also in

[13]Unmarked references to Wessén or Jansson indicate discussion of the inscription in question in the appropriate volume of *Runverket*.

[14]We may be grateful to Hans Christiansson, however, for his strictures against equating asymmetry and irregularity with lack of talent. See his *Sydskandinavisk stil*, p. 51.

width, according to the chisel employed. With a wide-tipped chisel the carver will produce broad lines; these are noted often by the editors of *Runverket*. Fine lines, in contrast, are the work of a narrow chisel and seem to be characteristic of the unornamented stones (e.g., U335, U336, U502, U504, U518, U539, some of which are no doubt by a single carver). Occasionally one finds a carving that contains both broad and narrow lines, such as U828 (Bodarna, Fittja sn.), of which Jansson writes: "The runes are as a rule carved with narrow, sharp lines, while the ornamentation and frame lines in many cases are carved with relatively broad, rounded lines. It is conceivable that the difference is due to the carver's use of two different kinds of chisel."

The type of chisel may also have a bearing on the relative smoothness of the lines; with a sharp chisel the bottom of the incision is often jagged.[15] Some runographers make an effort to smooth the lines left by their chisels; in Wessén's opinion, soft and rounded lines are distinguishing characteristics of Asmund and Fot, although not all the stones he attributes to them share this feature.[16]

On occasion extremely unorthodox techniques can be noted. The lines of U574 and U575 (Estuna kyrka) seem to have been "dotted," as it were, by a pointed chisel. Similarly, the runographer Þorbiorn (of the Sigtuna area) produces his dot-like symbol for word division and the points of his dotted runes by, in effect, drilling a hole into the surface of the stone (see U394).

---

[15]For example, U313 ("The lines are jagged, without softness"), U491 ("clear traces are visible from the blows of the tool"), U471 ("The carving has been done in notches that have not been smoothed"), U511 ("broad lines, uneven at the bottom; the chisel blows can be clearly seen and felt"), and U859 and 860 ("At the bottom the lines are bumpy, not softly rounded").

[16]Thus, under U379: "His chisel blows are sharp and clear but not very deep and not rounded at the bottom as are, for example, Fot's and Åsmund's." Under U539: "He has used a sharp, pointed tool, and his lines are therefore narrow, often uneven and not particularly deep; they lack the soft form, rounded in the bottom, which is so characteristic of especially Åsmund Kåreson and Fot." The attribution of U471 to Fot and U860 to Asmund is, however, done in violation of this observation.

7. Runographers, Attributions, and the Five Criteria

At this juncture we must consider the problems of attributing runic inscriptions to specific carvers and evaluate attribution criteria that have been discussed in previous chapters.

It is fair, first of all, to consider the meaning behind the formulaic expressions that we term "signatures." For the most part, it has been tacitly assumed that these expressions are equivalent, that there are no differences in the activities indicated by the messages "N. N. carved the runes," "N. N. hewed the stone," "N. N. made," and the like. In these cases we imagine a single artist who chooses and cuts the stone, formulates the inscription, plans the design, and alone executes the entire monument in his own orthography and his own characteristic rune forms. That the influence of those who commissioned the monuments was relatively slight seems clear. There is evidence, in the works of Viseti, for example, that the formulation of an inscription was largely the task of the carver. The sponsor probably played a small role in the formulation of the text, supplying little beyond the factual information (names, relationships, etc.) necessary for the inscription. Only rarely, as in U958, is there evidence of the sponsor's influence in the formulation; otherwise, Viseti's characteristic features (present tense of *lata*, word order *þenna stæin* and *faður sinn N.N.*) remain fairly constant regardless of the differing sponsors. A similar assumption is no doubt justified concerning the design, the orthography, and the execution of the memorial, for the artistic, linguistic, and technical training these tasks demand was probably not available to the ordinary eleventh-century Upplander. That there were amateur as well as professional carvers is, however, undeniable.[1]

The possibility that an apprentice executed an inscription according to plans laid down by his "master" must also be admitted. Evidence of this practice is found in a few inscriptions that employ the verb *raða* to indicate the activity of the master.[2] Thus, U896 and U940: *Reð runaR ØpiR*; U913: *Svæinn reð þetta*; and U961: *ok Igulfastr reð, en ØpiR*.[3] In these cases we hold the master responsible for the conception of the monument, the apprentice chiseling lines that are more or less predetermined. The extent to which the resulting memorial deviates from the style of the master depends, of course, on the technical proficiency of the apprentice and the degree of freedom he has been permitted.

A slightly different situation arises when we find stones signed by two carvers. In such cases we are not always able to determine the exact di-

[1]Note U353, carved by the sponsor. Wessén's own attitude regarding this question is somewhat ambiguous. Under U887, a stone bearing the signature *SialfR hiogg AurikR æftiR sinn faður*, he remarks on the artistic sensibilities of an amateur carver: "The ornamentation is executed with great skill, especially when one considers that *AurikR* can scarcely have been an experienced carver. As far as is known, he did not carve any other rune stone besides this one. This testifies to the very strong impression that rune-stone ornamentation must have made in its flourishing period, that it could call forth individual masterpieces from artistically sensitive people." A couple of years later, however, he rejects the signature *Þialfi ok Orøkia hioggu runaR æftiR broður sinn* of U948 on the grounds that the stone is too well done to have been executed by these unknown brothers: "One wonders whether it really could have been executed by a couple of men who just for this one occasion made a memorial to their brother, but nothing further. This is hard to believe." He thus assumes that *hioggu runaR* should be understood as *letu haggva runaR*, in the same way that *ræisti stæin* can mean *let ræisa stæin*.

[2]*Raða* in the sense 'plan, supervise' rather than 'interpret, read'. On the semantics of this term, see Wessén's excellent discussion under U940.

. .[3]In U961 the word *risti* is understood, as elsewhere with Öpir. According to Wessén this inscription indicates that Igulfast assisted the two female sponsors in the commissioning of the monument, whereas in the other examples *raða* signifies the planning and supervision of the carver's labor, as master to apprentice. This latter explanation should not, however, be denied U961; it is possible that this inscription has given us the name of Öpir's teacher. This somewhat bold assertion gains credulity in light of the discovery, in 1953, of a rune stone signed by a previously unknown carver named Igulfast. The similarities of this stone to the works of Öpir are very striking indeed, and in his report of the find (*Fornvännen* 48 [1953]: 266) Jansson remarks: "Igulfast, a hitherto unknown carver, is artistically related to Öpir." See C. W. Thompson, "Öpir's Teacher," *Fornvännen* 67 (1972): 16–19.

vision of labor, although scholars generally designate one carver (the more familiar one) as master and the other (usually unknown) as apprentice. The inscriptions themselves tell us nothing of these details.[4]

It is customary to explain the relationships between masters, assistants, and other carvers who share stylistic features in terms of "schools," although what is meant by a school is not immediately evident. It is possible that in the eleventh century the term *lið* 'retinue, troop, following' indicated the notion of a school. It appears that Balli and an otherwise unknown carver named Frøystæin[5] acknowledge themselves as pupils of Lifstæin on U1161, in the signature: *en þæiR Balli, Frøystæinn, lið Lifstæins ristu.* Such explicit testimony is, however, rare.[6]

Pupils do not necessarily inherit the most striking features of their master's style. Although Balli's artistic designs are clearly related to Lifstæin's, the pupil has not taken over the orthographic eccentricities of his teacher. Conversely, there are cases in which two carvers who cannot possibly have belonged to the same school exhibit many common features. It seems wise, therefore, to avoid overuse of the term "school," lest it become an easy method of solving problems that have no solution. As an abstract notion the term may be of some value, providing we recognize the limitations of our knowledge concerning the details of the teacher-pupil relationship.

If it is difficult to define precisely the idea of a runographer or of a school, the problem of finding a foolproof method for judging the accuracy of an attribution is even less easily solved. Attributions must be based on features that are significantly distinctive, as Erik Moltke has observed,[7] but the problems lie in determining the point at which a fea-

---

[4]In contrast, some stones outside of Uppland indicate the division of labor in the inscription, such as "*x* made the monument, *y* carved the runes." Or, as on the Eskilstuna sarcophagus (Sö356): *Tofi risti runaR a; Næsbiorn hiogg stæina.* See also G36, G113, and G136.

[5]Perhaps the son of Lifstæin, as Þorgaut of Fot? Note the so-called variation in the name (both with -*stæinn*).

[6]Note also the signature of U479: *Ulfkell hiogg ru(naR), Lofa liði,* which Wessén interprets, however, in a militaristic sense: "Ulvkel was a member of Love's *lið*, a warrior band whose leader was a man named Love."

[7]Lis Jacobsen and Erik Moltke, eds., *Danmarks runeindskrifter, Text,* Sp. 930–931: "Common features in the manner of carving cannot be taken as evidence that the inscriptions in question are executed by the same carver or at the same time, unless it is a matter of genuinely individual peculiarities. Conversely, inscriptions at considerable variance with one another can be by the same carver."

ture becomes sufficiently individual to exclude all other attributions. There is unfortunately no formula for determining this point with scientific precision; deviation can be shared.

These difficulties are augmented by the need to evaluate the five criteria that have been set up to determine authorship. In an article on a newly found inscription from Småland, Sven B. F. Jansson discusses some of the problems involved in basing an attribution on formulation:

How difficult it is to base a carver-attribution on correspondences in the linguistic formulation is strikingly illustrated by the immediate continuation of the Transjö-inscription [Sm5]: *eR a Ænglandi / aldri tynði*. For as it happens this couplet has an exact counterpart on another rune stone. The inscription on the Vist-stone in Västergötland (Vg187) concludes in the following way: **eR·aok· lanti·altri·tynþi**. The West Gautish stone exhibits otherwise no similarity with the Transjö-stone, and it is out of the question that the same carver has, in these cases, wielded the chisel. The alliterative couplet was clearly a piece of formulaic common property.[8]

It seems clear that an attribution founded mainly on formulation considerations is an extremely risky one. We must reckon not only with "formulaic common property" but also with the possibility that one carver has simply borrowed an expression from the nearby stone of another carver. At the same time we can make good use of extremely deviant details of formulation that are clearly individual: for example, Viseti's use of the present tense of *lata*.

Technical considerations, such as the manner of chiseling the lines or dressing the stone, probably carry even less weight than the criterion of formulation. The various types of stone no doubt responded to a carver's chisel in different ways. Nor can the possibility be dismissed that one carver used two or more (different) chisels in his work, creating a different impression with each. The results of weathering must also be taken into consideration.

Extreme divergences in the manner of carving that are shared by two rune stones may of course lend weight to an attribution, as is exemplified by the "pointed" technique of U574 and U575 (see page 75). On the other hand, when two stones that seem attributable to one carver (on other grounds) differ in technical execution, the evidence is not necessarily compelling but merely suggests that one look elsewhere for other differences. It is possible that one of the stones was planned by a master

---

[8]Sven B. F. Jansson, "Runstenen i Ryssby kyrka (Sm39)," *Fornvännen* 59 (1964): 234.

but executed by his apprentice. The hypothesis that a stone represents an early, youthful work of a runographer should also be taken into account.

Considerably higher priority is no doubt to be granted to orthographic features. There are a great many ways in which the spelling of an inscription may vary, and the runographers are fairly consistent in their orthographic habits. For instance, all the examples of the spelling **koþ**, **kos** for *Guð*, *Guðs* are signed by or attributable to Viseti. Intrusive runes, the sound value of the o-rune, and orthographic-linguistic traits, such as loss of initial /h/, can be especially telling features. Problems may occasionally arise, however, in brief inscriptions that contain no unusual spellings at all.

The design of a runic monument has traditionally been the standard yardstick in matters of attribution (see the account of previous studies in the Appendix). Emphasis on this criterion (the most obvious, striking feature of the Upplandic rune stones) has resulted in an overestimation of its value in determining authorship. Some of the mistaken attributions of Celsius, Brate, von Friesen, and even Wessén are the outcome of an overdependence on design.[9] Many of the artistic structures on the Upplandic rune stones were shared by large groups of runographers. Imitation, or borrowing, appears to have been common. U511, by Viseti, is a (mirror-image) copy of the nearby U510 of a generation earlier.[10] Even more striking is the similarity in the design of U1151 to works by Æirik (signed U1165). Despite the artistic correspondences, which extend to details, Jansson conclusively demonstrates the impossibility of attributing U1151 to Æirik.

Conversely, variation of considerable scope can be found among the designs of a single carver. Similarity in stylistic detail, it is true, can usually be observed, but in the case of U29 and U532, both signed by Þorbiorn Skald, not even this feature is apparent. On the dissimilarities of U29 and U532 Wessén comments (under U29): "Were it not for the explicit statement, surely no one would have come upon the idea of assigning these two inscriptions to the same master." It seems likely that a

[9]Celsius' attribution of U732 to Balli and of U1092 to Öpir; Brate's attribution of U1151 to Æirik; von Friesen's attribution of U11 and U77 to one carver; Wessén's attribution of U143 to the carver of U112.

[10]Viseti's primary artistic characteristic is his ability to imitate. He frequently, as here, uses Fot's basic structure (A-2). In U668 he is clearly imitating Balli (cf. U724, U735, U739), and in U449 he copies the beast of U428.

careful investigation of the rune forms on U29 and U532 would have indeed resulted in an attribution to the same master, even if Þorbiorn Skald had not signed them both. In both inscriptions one encounters the otherwise infrequent feature of "tilted" mainstaves; note particularly the **g**-rune of **sigruþ**, the **k** of **kara**, the **a**- and **n**-runes of **kara+buanta** and **hialbi+ant+hans** on U532, and the corresponding forms (e.g., in **raknfastr**) on U29.

The value of rune forms as a criterion can also be illustrated in the opposite situation, that of two inscriptions by different carvers sharing striking correspondences in design. Thus, U1151, with its consistent ᛏ ᛏ **t**, ᛚ ᛚ **l**, ᛅ **a**, ᚾ **n**, and ᛋ **s**, cannot be the work of Æirik, whose corresponding runes have the forms ᛏ, ᛚ, ᛆ, ᚿ, and ᛋ (see Jansson under U1151 for details). Since there is a clear and consistent correlation between runographer and rune form and since the corpus of allographs is advantageously large, it is reasonable to assign the highest priority to this criterion in problems of attribution.

Nevertheless, no criterion can be disregarded when its evidence speaks for or against an attribution. It is the cumulative weight of evidence from all runographic perspectives that should determine the final decision.

What degree of accuracy will such a decision have? Absolute certainty of attribution is prohibited by the very nature of the problem. There will be cases in which the evidence is not sufficiently positive or negative to permit a corresponding judgment. For these reasons it may be convenient to establish a scale of certainty, which, though somewhat arbitrary, will be of value if it is used consistently. We may set up a neutral point (which indicates that the evidence speaks neither particularly for nor against an attribution) with two degrees of certainty on either side (the positive and the negative). Thus, in determining whether stone *y* is the work of carver *x*, our decision can be emphatic or hesitant in either the affirmative or the negative direction. To say that *y* is "very likely" or "doubtless" the work of *x* is emphatically affirmative, but the statement that *y* is "likely" or "probably" the work of *x* is only mildly affirmative. Similar expressions will be employed negatively to indicate corresponding reluctance to assign a stone to a particular runographer.

8. Asmund Karasun

SIGNED ASMUND STONES

In treating the works of Asmund Karasun, it is wise to limit our initial
analysis to those carvings that are unambiguously signed by Asmund
alone. There are thirteen of these:

(1) U301 (Skånela kyrka). Now lost, presumably within the walls of the
church. Rhezelius is our only primary source of information:

· nsmar×li– ṛita · stin þi . . . þs muþiR · a osmuntr · kla markaþi

*Asmarr (?) let retta stæin þenna . . . (Gu)ðs modiR. Asmundr . . . mar-
kaði.*

(2) U346 (Frösunda kyrka). Like the preceding, this stone is now perhaps hidden in the church walls. Our information stems from Peringskiöld:

rahnfriþr · lit rt stain þino · aftiR biurno sun þaiRa kitilmuntaR · hon ·
fil a urlati · kuþ hialbi hons ant aukuþs muþiR · osmunr mar · kaþi
runaR ritar

*Ragnfriðr let retta stæin þenna æftir Biorn, sun þæiRa KætilmundaR.
Hann fell a Virlandi. Guð hialpi hans and ok Guðs moðiR. Asmundr
markaði runaR rettaR.*

(3) U356 (Ängby, Lunda sn.). A stone with almost the same inscription
as the preceding one:

rahnfriþr·lit rasa stain þino·aftiR biurn·sun þaiRa·kitil muntaR
kuþ mialbi hons ant aukuþs muþiR hon fil a uirlanti·in osmuntr
markaþi

Ragnfriðr let ræisa stæin þenna æftiR Biorn, sun þæiRa Kætilmun-
daR. Guð hialpi hans and ok Guðs moðiR. Hann fell a Virlandi. En
Asmundr markaði.

(4) U824 (Holms kyrka):
  iukiR auk·ifriþr·litūrita stian þinabtiR bruþur·rhuþilfaR·i u–
  rbhrki osmuntritsi runaR
  IogæiRR ok Afriðr (?) letu retta stæin þenna æftiR broður HroðælfaR
  i . . . -bergi. Asmundr risti runaR.

(5) U847 (Västeråkers kyrka):
  ·[oski. . .–––]islauh×litu ritu rita stin þinoto suni sino·atiarf·uk
  s[l]uþa·osmun[tr·]h[iu]ru[n]a[R]itaR þim·raþa skal ia·osmuntr
  –––aþi risti
  AsgæiRR (?) ok Gislaug letu retta stæin þenna at tva (?) syni sina
  Adiarf ok Sloða. Asmundr hio runaR rettaR þæim raða skal. En As-
  mundr . . . risti.

(6) U859 (Måsta, Balingsta sn.):
  fastbiurn·ukþurun·litu rita . . . bru kiruabtiR inkif[a]–. . . u̯anta sin
  kuþ hialbi hont·osmunrt risti runoR
  Fastbiorn ok Þorunn letu retta . . . bro gærva æftiR Ingifast, boanda
  sinn. Guð hialpi h(ans) and. Asmundr risti runaR.[1]

(7) U871 (Ölsta, Gryta sn.). Moved to Skansen by Hazelius in 1896:
  binrn·auþulfr k̨unor·hulmtis·–––u ri–o stin þino·iftiR·ulf·kin-
  lauhaR buanta in osmuntr hiu
  Biorn, AuðulfR, Gunnarr, Holmdis letu retta stæin þenna æftiR Ulf,
  GinnlaugaR boanda. En Asmundr hio.

(8) U956 (Vedyxa, Danmarks sn.):
  stniltr·lit·rita stain þino·abtiR·uiþbiurn·krikfara·buanta sin·kuþ
  hialbi hosalukuþs u muþiR osmuntr karasun markaþi
  Stæinhildr let retta stæin þenna æftiR Viðbiorn grikkfara, boanda

---

[1]In contrast to *Runverket*, I interpret **hont** as *hans and* rather than *and* with unetymological /h/. Asmund does not exhibit loss of initial /h/ but does contract words (cf. L1050,
U194).

sinn. Guð hialpi hans salu ok Guðs moðiR. Asmundr Karasun mar-kaði.[2]

(9) U969 (Bolsta, Vaksala sn.):
rahnuiþr · lit · rita st... · faþur sin · in osmunrt hiu
Ragnviðr let retta stæin...faður sinn. En Asmundr hio.

(10) U981 (Prästgården, Gamla Uppsala sn.). The stone has been missing since before Peringskiöld's visit in the early eighteenth century, and we possess no drawings of it:
ailif raisti stain þinso abtiR kalf buanta... iR+uifast+faþur+sin osmunrt risti
Æilif ræisti stæin þennsa æftiR Kalf, boanda (sinn)...(æft)iR Vifast, faður sinn. Asmundr risti.

(11) U986 (Kungsgården, Samnan, Gamla Uppsala sn.). Now lost:
+ali · auk sihualti · uk · inkifast · litu rita stin þino · abtiR · kanilf · buanta inkifastaR auk faþur ala osmunrt · risti
Ali (Alli) ok Sigvaldi ok Ingifast letu retta stæin þenna æftiR kanilf, boanda IngifastaR ok faður Ala (Alla). Asmundr risti.

(12) U998 (Skällerö, Marielund, Funbo sn.). Only the upper half of this stone is preserved. The inscription on the lower half is known through Rhezelius:
þurstin: auk ronti: [litu: raisa: stain þino: abtiR s–ar–hauf þ]a: br-uþur sin: kuþ hialbi honsalukuþs muþiR [osmun]rt · markaþi
Þorstæinn ok Randi letu ræisa stæin þenna æftiR Svarthaufða, bro-ður sinn. Guð hialpi hans salu ok Guðs moðiR. Asmundr markaði.

(13) L1053 (Järsta, Valbo sn., Gästrikland). As yet unpublished in the Swedish *Runverket*, this stone may be described fully as follows: Light red (Gävle) sandstone. A large stone, roughly rectangular. A break that separated the lower right-hand corner from the rest of the stone has been mended with little damage to the carving. (The same fissure is evident as early as Hadorph and Christofferson's woodcut in Bautil.) The surface of the stone is smooth and even. All the lines are extraordinarily deep and clear; there are no uncertain readings. An exceptionally well-executed stone.
þiuþkiR ukuþlaifr: ukarl þaR bruþr aliR: litu rita stain þino × abtiR

[2] I have restored the word divider between **sin** and **kuþ** (omitted in *Runverket*).

U29 Hillersjö, Hilleshögs sn. (H. Faith-Ell)

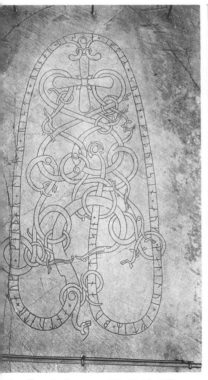

Sundby, Spånga sn. (H. Faith-Ell)

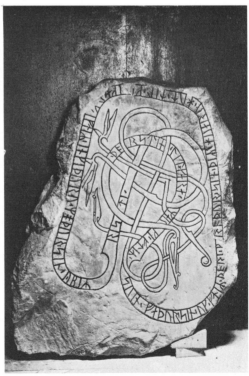

U104 Eds kyrka

U193 Svista, Össeby-Garns sn.

U194 Väsby, Össeby-Garns s

U203 Angarns kyrka

U240 Lingsberg, Vallentuna sn.
(H. Faith-Ell)

U241 Lingsberg, Vallentuna sn.

U279 Skälby, Hammarby sn.

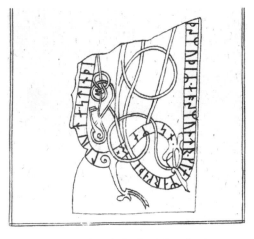

U301 Skånela kyrka (Rhezelius)

U322 Stensta, Skånela sn.

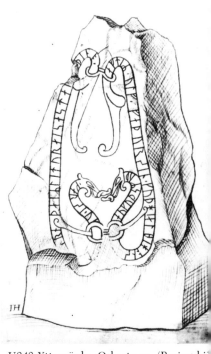

U343 Yttergärde, Orkesta sn. (Peringskiö

U344 Yttergärde, Orkesta sn. (H. Faith-Ell)

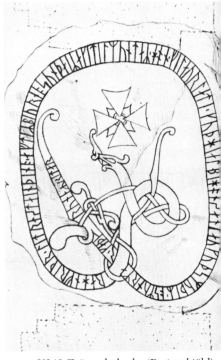

U346 Frösunda kyrka (Peringskiöld)

U356 Ängby, Lunda sn.

U357 Skepptuna kyrka

U367 Helgåby, Skepptuna sn., *front*

U367 Helgåby, Skepptuna sn., *back*

U372 Ånsta, Skepptuna sn.

U375 Vidbo kyrka

U409 Lövstaholm, St. Olovs sn.

U418 Brista, Norrsunda sn.

U419 Norslunda, Norrsunda sn.   U431 Åshusby, Norrsunda sn.

U438 Ekilla, Husby-Ärlinghundra sn.   U510 Mälsta, Kårsta sn.

U511 Mälsta, Kårsta sn.

U532 Roslags Bro kyrka

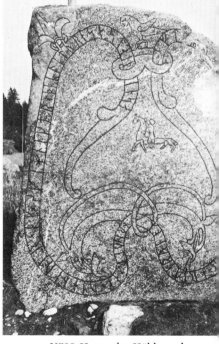

U540 Husby Lyhundra kyrka

U599 Hanunda, Hökhuvuds sn.

U617 Bro kyrka (Iwar Anderson)

U629 Grynsta backe, Svarsta,
Håbo-Tibble sn. (Iwar Anderson)

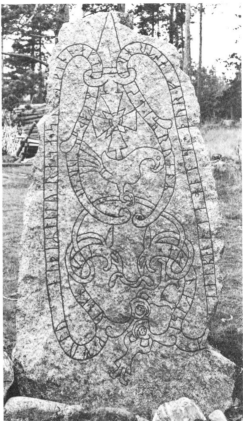

U645 Lundby, Yttergrans sn.
(Iwar Anderson)

U692 Väppeby, Arnö sn. (G. af Gejerstam)

U824 Holms kyrka (Nils Lagergren)

U846 Västeråkers kyrka

U859 Måsta, Balingsta sn. (Iwar Anderso

U847 Västeråkers kyrka

0 Måsta, Balingsta sn. (Iwar Anderson)   U866 Björnome, Gryta sn. (Iwar Anderson)

871 Ölsta, Gryta sn. (Iwar Anderson)   U875 Focksta, Hagby sn. (Iwar Anderson)

U884 Ingla, Skogs-Tibble sn., *side A*

U884 Ingla, Skogs-Tibble sn., *side B*
(Iwar Anderson)

U884 Ingla, Skogs-Tibble sn., *side C*

U885 Ingla, Skogs-Tibble sn. (Iwar Anderson)   U890 Österby, Ålands sn.

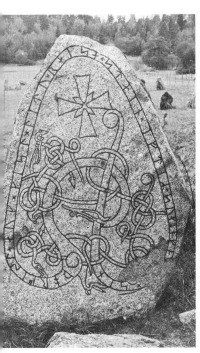

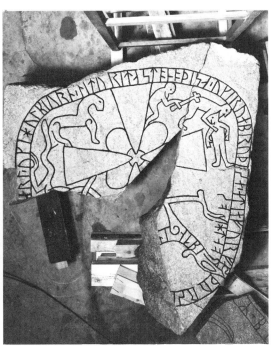

U899 Vårdsätra, Bondkyrka sn.   U901 Håmö, Läby sn.
(Iwar Anderson)

U903 Västerby, Läby sn.

U904 Västerby, Läby vad, Läby sn.

U932 Uppsala domkyrka, *side A*
(Iwar Anderson)

U932 Uppsala domkyrka, *side B*
(Iwar Anderson)

945 Danmarks kyrka (Iwar Anderson)

U956 Vedyxa, Danmarks sn. (Iwar Anderson)

59 Bolsta, Vaksala sn. (Iwar Anderson)

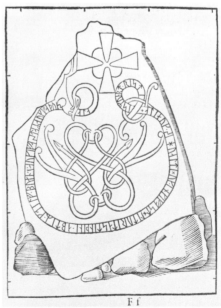

F f

U986 Kungsgården, Samnan, Gamla
Uppsala sn. (unsigned woodcut, B384)

U998 Skällerö (Marielund), Funbo sn.
(Iwar Anderson)

U987 Funbo kyrka (Iwar Anderson)

U1009 Yrsta, Rasbo sn. (Iwar Anderson)

U1012 Rasbokils kyrka (Iwar Anderson

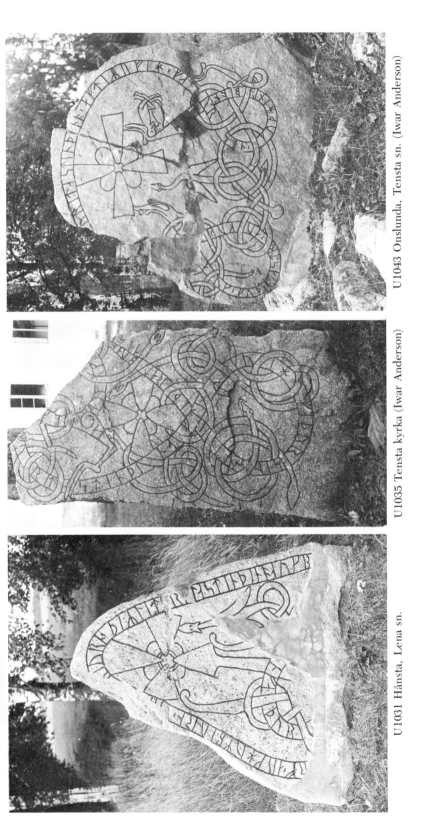

U1031 Hånsta, Lena sn.

U1035 Tensta kyrka (Iwar Anderson)

U1043 Onslunda, Tensta sn. (Iwar Anderson)

U1123 Tuna kyrka

U1132 Gimo, Skäfthammars sn.

U1142 Åbyggeby, Vendels sn.

U1144 Tierps kyrka

U1145 Ytterby, Tierps sn.

U1149 Fleräng, Älvkarlaby sn.

U1151 Brunnby, Frösthults sn.

U1165 Rotbrunna, Härnevi sn.

þiuþmunt ˙ faur sin ˙ kuþ hialbi honsalukuþs muþiR in osmuntr karasun ˙ markaþi × runoR ritaR þasataimunt

Þiuðgæi RR ok Guðlæif R ok Karl, þæi R brøðr alli R letu retta stæin þenna æftiR Þiuðmund, faður sinn. Guð hialpi hans salu ok Guðs moðiR. En Asmundr Karasun markaði runaR rettaR. Þa(t)'s at Æimund.

The only difficulty in this inscription, which is otherwise easily interpreted, concerns the runes in the text band directly under the cross: þasataimunt. Early interpretations were Brocman's *þa sat Aimunt* "then Emund placed (the stone, after it was carved)" and Kempff's *þas(a) at Aimunt* "this for Emund."[3] In 1896, however, Fredrik Sander rejected these and speculated that the expression *sitja á stóli* was to be understood in the following way: "The last words, *þa sat Aimunt*, must be translated 'then Emund sat,' and cannot be understood in any other way than 'then Emund was king,' then Emund occupied the throne!"[4] Sander then identifies this Emund with Emund the Old, who became king after the death of Anund Jakob and is presumed to have ruled for a short period of time during the 1050's.

Were it not for von Friesen's adoption and energetic support, Sander's interpretation would have gained little following. Von Friesen insists that a more reasonable interpretation has not been offered and cites the report of the Arab Ibn Fadlan that Swedish merchants carved their king's name on poles erected to commemorate the dead.[5] What is of greater interest to von Friesen is of course the dating of the inscription, which Sander's interpretation provides.

Erik Brate dismissed Sander and von Friesen's idea and interpreted þasat as an abbreviated spelling of þasaR at, translating the sentence "these in memory of Emund" (*"dessa efter Emund"*).[6] Presumably Brate views þasaR as feminine plural (nominative or accusative), in agreement with *runaR*. Not all of Brate's objections to von Friesen and Sander's interpretation are justified. While it is true that we would expect *þa* 'when, then' to be written þo (as in L1049: þo brusi. . .), Asmund

[3]Nils Reinhold Brocman, *Sagan om Ingwar Widtfarne*, p. 246; K. Hjalmar Kempff, *Söderby runsten vid Gefle*. Kempff's final proposal (in the "Efterskrift" to his work) is the verse: *Þa Asa / at Æimund.*

[4]Fredrik Sander, *Marmorlejonet från Piræeus med nordiska runinskrifter*, p. 44.

[5]Otto von Friesen, *Upplands runstenar*, p. 37; *Runorna*, p. 209.

[6]Erik Brate, *Svenska runristare*, p. 29.

has spelled the same word þa on U344 (to be attributed to Asmund). On the other hand, the lack of precedent in the runic inscriptions makes it difficult to believe that Asmund would date his stone with the statement: "At that time Emund was king." As far as we know, the idea of dating a memorial for the benefit of posterity was totally foreign to the eleventh-century Swede, and one might well ask why a carver would choose the past tense of the verb *sitja* ("*was* king, *sat* on the throne") if, as von Friesen and Sander thought, Emund was still ruling when the stone was raised. One is also reluctant to grant von Friesen his point that Asmund could have omitted, for lack of space ("*af brist på utrymme*"), the nominative ending of *Æimundr* and such an expression as (*KonungR*) *at Uppsalum*. One is, however, equally uncomfortable with Brate's interpretation, which yields a verbless sentence.

The reading of þasataimunt as *þat es at Æimund* offers a number of advantages. In keeping with the criterion of simplicity, it is more reasonable to suppose that **aimunt** is an accusative form than to assume that something has been omitted. More important are the precedents, both orthographic and formulaic, for this interpretation. The omission of the t-rune in þas *þat's* on L1053 finds an exact parallel in the form þis *þet's* on U344, a stone that all scholars attribute to Asmund. The difference in vowel between þis (U344) and þas (L1053) can be explained either as orthographic variation (Asmund has written /æ/ with the a-rune in other inscriptions, e.g., in the word *æftiR*) or, as is more likely, by assuming several pronunciations of this word, namely, *þat*, *þæt*, and *þet* (see Noreen, *Altschwedische Grammatik*, 508, 3). Note the occurrence of this word in Viseti's U337: þat×uaru×freantr þeia *þat vaRu frændr þæiRa*. A similar vowel alternation occurs in spellings of the demonstrative *þessa, þenna, þessi*, and so on.

Nor is the formulation *þat es at Æimund* without precedent. The memorial formula on U958 begins: *ÆftiR Signiuta es þetta*. U188, which belongs to a memorial consisting of several stones, reads simply: *Sasi es ok at IargæiR* "This [stone] is also in memory of IargæiR." U585, not fully interpreted, may contain a similar formula in the runes **sas:at: anutr** *Sa es at Anund*(?). Indeed, one can even cite the Karlevi-stone, with the formula: *Stæin sasi es sattr æftiR Sibba*.

"This is in memory of Æimund" is thus an additional commemoration, a message that was not incorporated into the main memorial formula. Exactly who Æimund was is difficult to say; a reasonable assumption is that he was a deceased brother of Þiuðgæir, Guðlæif, and Karl, and therefore the son of Þiuðmund, from whose name *Æimundr* derives its second element (as *Þiuðgæiʀʀ* its first), according to the Germanic name-giving principle of variation.

Distinguishing Features of Asmund's Style

By investigating the formulation, design, rune forms, orthography, and carving techniques of the thirteen signed stones, a number of features can be isolated that distinguish Asmund's runographic style.

Formulation

All the stones bear commemorative inscriptions, beginning with a familiar memorial formula. The following chart shows the distribution and order of each of the parts of the formulation (see chapter 2), as attested in the thirteen inscriptions that Asmund alone has signed:

Inscription	Memorial formula	Prayer	Addition	Signature
U301	1	2		3
U346	1	3	2	4
U356	1	2	3	4
U824	1			2
U847	1			2, 3
U859	1	2		3
U871	1			2
U956	1	2		3
U969	1			2
U981	1			2
U986	1			2
U998	1	2		3
L1053	1	2	4	3

A survey of the memorial formulas on the thirteen stones reveals considerable uniformity:

U301	NN	let	retta stæin	þenna.....	...
U346	NN	let	retta stæin	þenna æftiR NN	sun NN's
U356	NN	let	ræisa stæin	þenna æftiR NN	sun NN's
U824	NN ok NN	letu	retta stæin	þenna æftiR—	broður NN's
U847	NN ok NN	letu	retta stæin	þenna at(?) tva	syni sina
U859	NN ok NN	letu	retta (stæin) ok bro gærva	— æftiR NN	boanda sinn
U871	NN, NN, NN, NN	letu	retta stæin	þenna æftiR NN	NN's boanda
U956	NN	let	retta stæin	þenna æftiR NN	boanda sinn
U969	NN	let	retta stæin	....	faður sinn
U981	NN	—	ræisti stæin	þennsa æftiR NN	boanda sinn
U986	NN ok NN ok NN	letu	retta stæin	þenna æftiR NN	boanda NN's ok faður NN's
U998	NN ok NN	letu	ræisa stæin	þenna æftiR NN	broður sinn
L1053	NN ok NN ok NN, þæiR brøðr alliR	letu	retta stæin	þenna æftiR NN	faður sinn

Note that in U859 there is only enough room for the words *stæin ok,* and, thus, *þenna* did not occur. In U969 there is enough room for about ten to twelve runes. Thus, one could supply either *stæin þenna æftiR* or *stæin æftiR NN,* but probably not *stæin þenna æftiR NN.*

Except for U871, names of sponsors are linked with *ok* 'and'. In L1053 the summarizing formula *þæiR brøðr alliR* is added. The auxiliary verb *lata (let, letu)* is used in all inscriptions but one (U981), and the act of commemoration is indicated by *retta stæin* in ten out of the thirteen cases, the remaining three employing the verb *ræisa.* In one case (U859) the augmentation *ok gærva bro* is found.

In all but one or two inscriptions (U859, U969; see notes above), a demonstrative pronoun follows the word *stæin,* and except for U981 the choice is *þenna.* The expression "in memory of" is denoted by *æftiR* in all cases but one, and in this one (U847) the interpretation is not without some uncertainty.

Word order following *æftiR (at)* is usually *NN, sun (faður, etc.) sinn,* but in U847 this order is reversed and in U824 the name of the dead man is omitted. In U981 the sponsor commemorates two relatives. The formulation of U859 is somewhat illogical; *boanda sinn* would read better as *boanda ÞorunaR.*

Prayers for the soul of the deceased occur on seven of the thirteen stones (54%), or with about twice the frequency of Upplandic monuments as a whole. As Celsius observed (see Appendix), it is characteristic of Asmund to augment the basic prayer with *ok Guðs moðiR,* "modo spatium in lapide permitteret."

U301	probably:	(Guð hialpi hans and/salu	ok)	Guðs moðiR.
U346		Guð hialpi hans and	ok	Guðs moðiR.
U356		Guð hialpi hans and	ok	Guðs moðiR.
U859		Guð hialpi hans and.[7]		
U956		Guð hialpi hans salu	ok	Guðs moðiR.
U998		Guð hialpi hans salu	ok	Guðs moðiR.
L1053		Guð hialpi hans salu	ok	Guðs moðiR.

Only three of Asmund's inscriptions bear what I have termed an addition. Two of these (U346 and U356), which can be grouped together (constituting one memorial), follow the typical pattern: *Hann fell a Virlandi.* The third (L1053) contains an addition (an afterthought?) of a more unusual structure that is best considered as part of the memorial formula.

Asmund's signatures reveal a characteristic use of the verb *marka:*

U301		Asmundr.......	markaði.
U346		Asmundr	markaði runaR rettaR.
U356	En	Asmundr	markaði.
U824		Asmundr	risti runaR.
U847		Asmundr	hio runaR rettaR þæim raða skal.
	En	Asmundr.......	risti.
U859		Asmundr	risti runaR.
U871	En	Asmundr	hio.
U956		Asmundr Karasun	markaði.
U969	En	Asmundr	hio.
U981		Asmundr	risti.
U986		Asmundr	risti.
U998		Asmundr	markaði.
L1053	En	Asmundr Karasun	markaði runaR rettaR.

It is puzzling that U847 is signed twice, once with *risti* and once with *hio runaR rettaR þæim raða skal.*[8] The runes that follow the name *As-*

[7]See fn. 1.

[8]According to Lis Jacobsen and Erik Moltke, eds., *Danmarks runeindskrifter, Text,* Sp. 926–927, the use of the adjective *rettaR* to describe the runes goes back to magical practice.

mundr on U301 and U847 have thus far regrettably defied interpretation. A reference to or a modification of Asmund's name would be a matter of great interest.

In two inscriptions (U956, L1053) the name *Asmundr* is followed by the patronymic *Karasun* 'son of Kari'. The implications of this are discussed in the summary of the signed and attributed stones.

Design

From an artistic point of view, Asmund's signed works reveal considerable diversity. In his designs, all basically zoomorphic, rune animals of Types A, B, and C are attested. Unfortunately we know nothing of the design of U981.

    A-1: U956
    A-2: U301, U346
    A-3: U824, U847, U859, U871, U969
    B-1: U998, L1053
    B-3: U356
     C: U986

A characteristic of U346 and L1053 that differentiates them from the normal form of their respective types is the loop that the forepart of the animal makes when crossing over itself. Also characteristic of Asmund is the text band that runs up and down the middle of the design of U998.

All the heads of Asmund's rune animals are seen in profile, as can be observed on the chart on page 91. They are of normal proportions or slightly elongated, and all but that on U986 (which is unclear in the sources) have a nasal lobe that is folded over the snout. A small detail that appears to be characteristic of Asmund's rune animals is the bulb formed at the intersection of the snout and the nasal lobe.[9] The ears are typically rounded, although U871 and L1053 illustrate pointed ones. Eyes range from almond-shaped (U956, U998, L1053) to elongated teardrop forms.

Smaller serpents appear to a limited extent on U859, U969, and L1053; on U824, U847, U871, and U986 they play a much greater part in the artistic effect. They are lacking on U356, U956, and U998.

There are no crosses on U824 and U847; whether U301 contained one on its now-missing upper section is impossible to determine. Crosses of

[9]I owe to Börje Westlund the observation of this feature, which may be called the "Westlund bulb."

Type A occur on U356, U871, U998, and with a slight variation on U956.
Type B-4 is attested on U346 and U859, while Type B-1 occurs on U986
and probably on U969. The cross on L1053 is an interesting variation of
Type A-5. Although Asmund's crosses are of the most common types,
many of them are distinguished by rounded rays or blades between the
arms, rather than pointed ones.

Other features of ornamentation that deserve notice are the Medusa-
like head on U824 and the bearlike animal figures on U969.

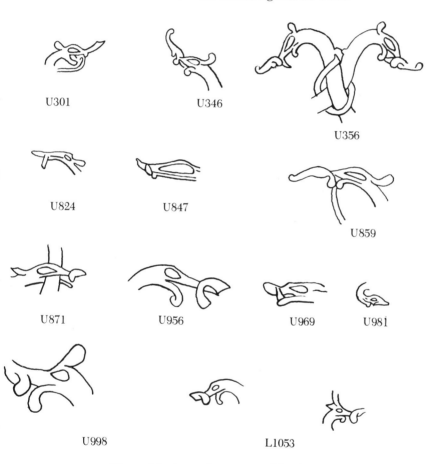

U301   U346

U356

U824   U847

U859

U871   U956   U969   U981

U998   L1053

Figure 8.1. Asmund rune-animal heads

Rune Forms

It is wise to exclude U301, U346, U981, and U986 from the investigation of rune forms, since they are known only through older sources, which are not always reliable in details.

Several reversed runes occur in Asmund's signed works—the þ-rune in **þino** on U956 and the three b-runes of L1053. The ᚦ **o** in **osmuntr** on U824 should perhaps, because of its rarity, be viewed as a reversed rune, and the ᚦ **n** of **stniltr** on U956 could be reversed and upside down, although possibly an a-rune was intended. Reading the first three runes of U871 as reversed is also possible, thus changing the misspelling **binrn** to the correct form **biarn**. The form ᚱ **s**, which is technically perhaps a reversed form, is quite frequent in Asmund's works, occurring some thirteen times (versus thirty-one "normal" forms) in carvings signed by Asmund alone.

Asmund's runes always extend from one line of the text band to the other, the mainstaves intersecting these lines at an angle approximating 90°. An exception would be the tilted f-rune of **atiarf** in U847.

A bind-rune occurs in **litūrita** on U824, but this is no doubt inadvertent, representing a correction (a previously omitted u-rune is added afterwards) rather than a planned ligature. There are no dotted runes in Asmund's signed inscriptions.

Asmund usually spaces his runes elegantly, although there are a few cases of "crowding" (e.g., runes 58–59 sm of U847). On U356 the last few runes could not find sufficient room within the narrowing text band and thus spill out onto the stone surface. Asmund makes a definite attempt to begin and end his inscriptions at equal height, so that the right and left sides are in balance. See, for example, U871 and U956.

An especially distinctive trait in Asmund's works is the use of an ornamental line as the mainstaff of a rune. Examples are the n in **ant** and the i in **muþiR** on U356, the r and s of **risti** on U859, the n in **hons** and the þ in **þurstin** on U998, the n in **hons**, the þ's in **muþiR** and **þas**, the r in **runoR** on L1053, and possibly the **iu** in **hiu** on U969 (the interlace is uncertain).

In terms of proportion Asmund's runes can be generally described as narrow; only rarely (an occasional f or r, the ᚠ **o** in **hons** on L1053) does one find a rune with a relative width comparable to Fot's or Lifstæin's. Asmund's runes may now be pictured and described briefly on an individual basis (damaged runes are not pictured).

In Asmund's f-rune the lower branch usually meets the mainstaff below its midpoint. Most of the branches are slightly rounded, although on U969 and L1053 straight ones occur.

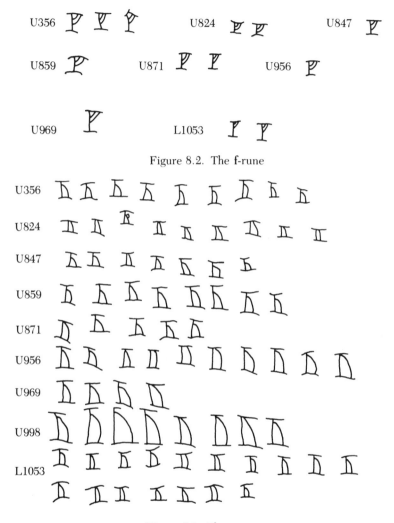

Figure 8.2. The f-rune

Figure 8.3. The u-rune

The branch of the u-rune characteristically joins the mainstaff at or below its junction with the text band. Note especially the "long necks"

(Brockman's term, see Appendix, fn. 44) on U356. Most branches are rounded; note the extreme curvature at the base of U356:7, U969:1, and L1053:1. In terms of proportion, Asmund's u-rune is distinctively narrow. The third rune of U824 is the bind-rune (a correction) ᚢᚱ.

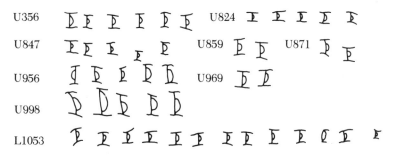

Figure 8.4. The þ-rune

The branches of the þ-rune tend to meet the mainstaff relatively close to the lines of the text band, but only once (U956:5) does a branch intersect with the text band itself. On rune 1 of U998 and runes 11 and 13 of L1053, an ornamental line serves as the mainstaff.

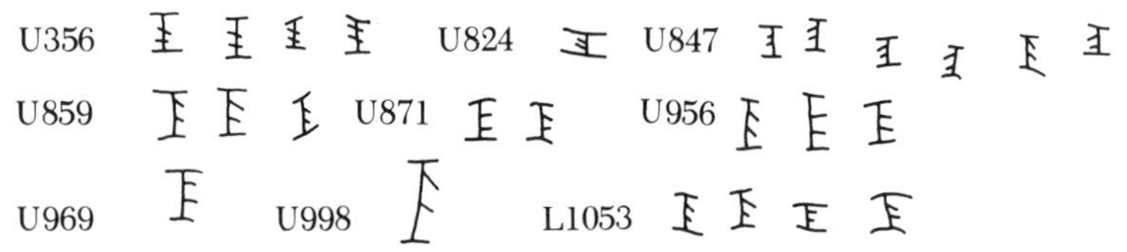

Figure 8.5. The o-rune

Typically Asmund's o-rune has falling branches on the right side. The o of U824 and five of the six on U847 are exceptions, having branches to the left of the mainstaff. On U356, all four o-runes are long branched, as are the first two of U871 (not pictured here because they are damaged).

The upper section of the r-rune most frequently touches the mainstaff below or at its junction with the text band. Occasionally the upper stroke is almost horizontal, the lower one almost vertical, giving the rune a distinctive appearance, for instance the last two runes of U356 and the fourth r of U859.

U356
U824
U847
U859
U871
U956
U969
U998
L1053

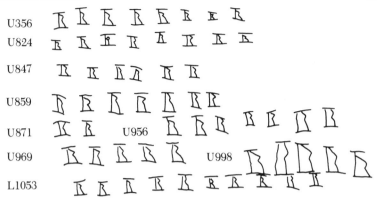

Figure 8.6. The r-rune

Not infrequently the branch of the **k**-rune is straight and is located relatively high on the mainstaff.

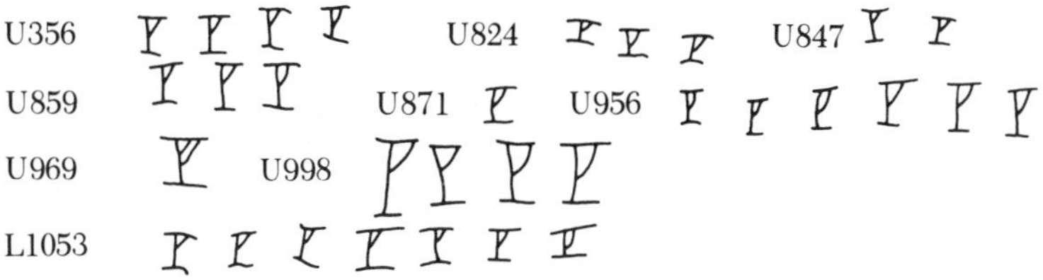

U356
U824
U847
U859
U871
U956
U969
U998
L1053

Figure 8.7. The **k**-rune

Asmund's **h**-rune is of a very common form, not particularly distinctive or individual.

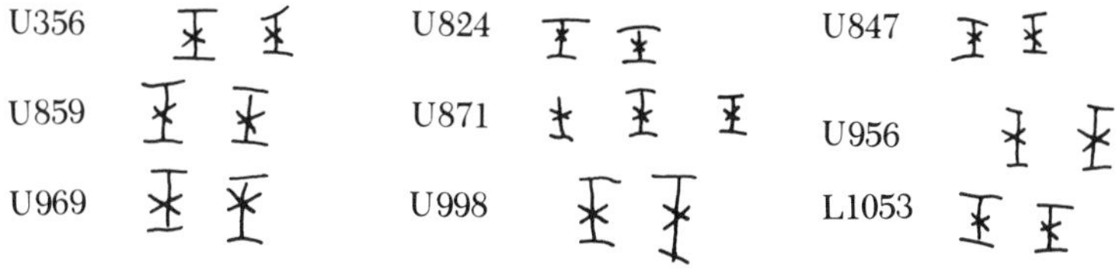

U356
U824
U847
U859
U871
U956
U969
U998
L1053

Figure 8.8. The **h**-rune

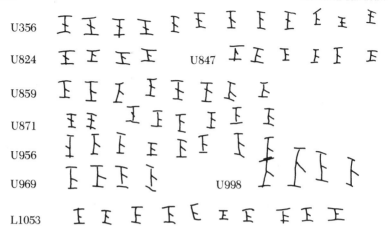

Figure 8.9. The n-rune

Like his **o-** and **a**-runes, Asmund's **n** is usually short branched, with a falling branch on the right side of the mainstaff. In U356 and U871, however, the long-branched variant dominates. (Note the similar situation with the **o-** and **a**-runes of these inscriptions.) The first **n**'s of U871 and U956 are unorthodox and may be interpreted as **a**-runes. Note also that in some of Asmund's **n**-runes the branch may slightly cross over the

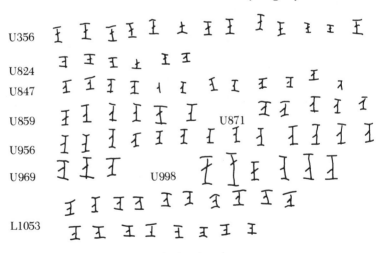

Figure 8.10. The a-rune

mainstaff, forming something between a long-branched and a short-branched **n**.

Asmund's **a**-rune has many of the characteristics of his **o**- and **n**-runes. Note, for example, the long-branched forms that dominate U356 and occur sporadically elsewhere, often with an abbreviated branch on one side.

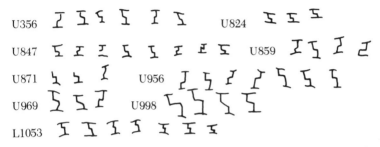

Figure 8.11. The s-rune

The **s**-rune is no doubt the most distinctive in Asmund's futhark. The angles between the vertical strokes and the short middle bar are never less than 90° and are usually larger. Note that the third **s** in U847 is not a "Swedish-Norwegian" form, as is suggested in *Runverket,* but consists of an upper (vertical) stroke and a bar to the left. The lower stroke, if there ever was one, has been worn away.

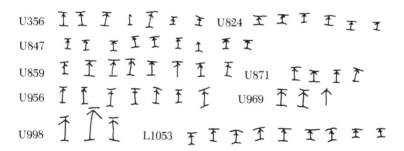

Figure 8.12. The t-rune

In the **t**-rune branches characteristically meet the mainstaff well below the text band. Unusual are the l-shaped **t** of U356 and the fourth **t** of U956 with an almost horizontal bar.

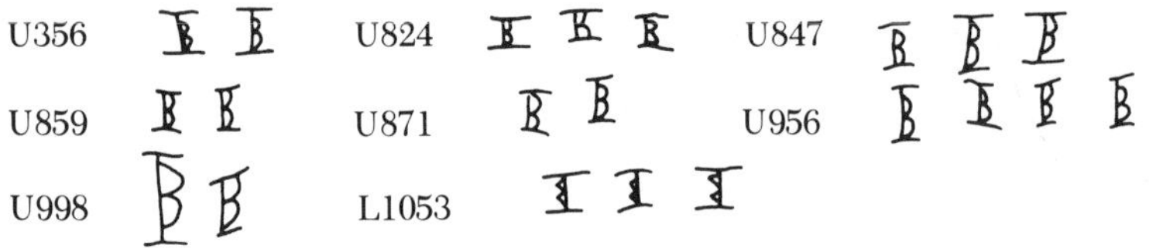

Figure 8.13. The **b**-rune

The loops of Asmund's **b**-rune are invariably joined in the middle, both to one another and to the mainstaff. At their opposite ends, the loops may intersect either with the mainstaff or with the text band. Asmund's **b** is often narrow and is rounded in all cases except the three highly unusual ones on L1053.

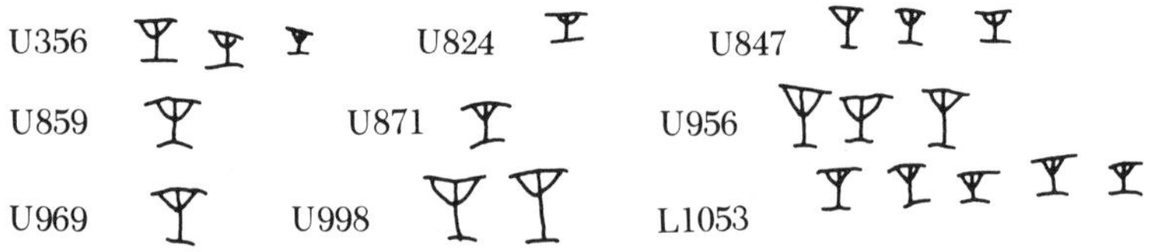

Figure 8.14. The **m**-rune

An angular variant (straight branches) of the **m**-rune occurs occasionally, notably in L1053. Both broad and narrow **m**'s are attested. The junction of branches and mainstaff is usually above the midpoint.

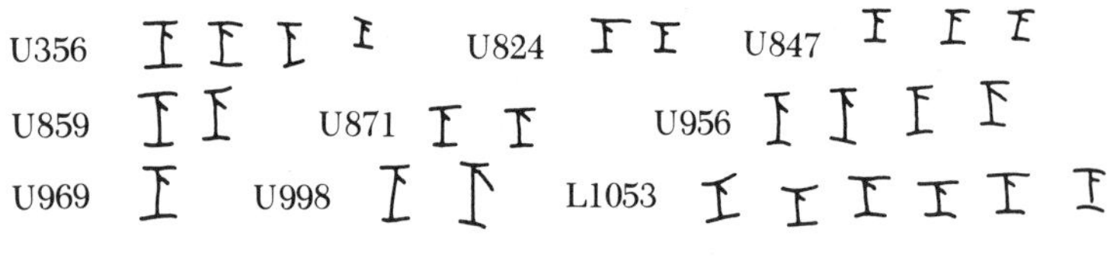

Figure 8.15. The **l**-rune

The **l**-rune shares with other Asmund-forms (**u, r, t**) the characteristic position of the branch—below the junction of mainstaff and text band.

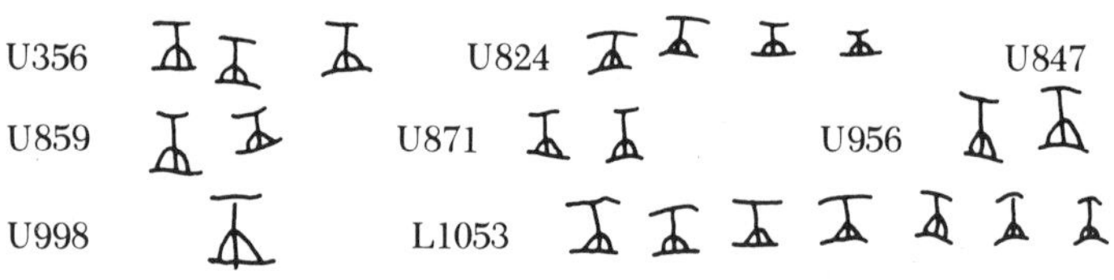

Figure 8.16. The **R**-rune

Asmund's **R**-rune, like the **m**-rune, is not very distinctive, occurring rounded and angular, broad and narrow. The junction of branches and mainstaff is generally at or below mid-height.

As a word divider, Asmund employs most frequently a short, vertical stroke, as can be noted in table 8.1.

Table 8.1. Word Dividers

	'	⁝	•	×	✕
U356	3		3		
U824			4		
U847	7			1	
U859	5				
U871	8				
U956	7		1		
U969	4				
U998	1	7			
L1053	4	2			2
Totals	39	9	8	1	2

According to the older sources that depict inscriptions now lost, a word divider of the less usual type + also occurred in Asmund's work.

Orthography and Language

Asmund renders the consonants of Rune-Swedish in a traditional manner, employing no dotted runes or cryptography. Thus, /p/ and /b/ are written with the **b**-rune (**hialbi, bruþur**), /t/ and /d/ with the **t**-rune (**risti, atiarf**), and /k/ and /g/ with the **k**-rune (**markaþi, kuþ**). Fricative /g/, on the other hand, is consistently written with the **h**-rune, an important feature of Asmund's orthography. Thus, **rahnfriþr** *Ragnfriðr* U346, U356, **rahnuiþr** *Ragnviðr* U969, **–islauh** [*G*]*islaug* U847, **kinlauhaR** *GinnlaugaR* U871, **sihualti** *Sigvaldi* U986.

/f/ and its voiced phone [b] are written with the **f**-rune, except in the word *æftiR* 'in memory of', which in Asmund's inscriptions is typically spelled with the **b**-rune. There are seven cases of **abtiR**, two cases of **aftiR**, and one case of **iftiR** in the stones signed by Asmund alone. /þ/ and its voiced phone [ð] are represented by the **þ**-rune; /h/ is written with the **h**-rune.

Asmund's carvings do not reveal loss of initial /h/ (see chapter 5), and in fact one of the rare examples of preserved /h/ before a consonant is attested in U824 **rhuþilfaR** *HroðælfaR* (with metathesis). The spelling hont on U859 does not represent an unetymological restoration of initial /h/, as one might suppose from the interpretation of *Runverket*, but in all likelihood it is a conflation of **hons** and **ant**. The spelling **stniltr** *Stæin-hildr* on U956 probably reflects the actual pronunciation of the name throughout Uppland. (The name is rare, but attested once in medieval Uppland [1316] in a Latinized form *Stenildis*, also without /h/.)[10]

Asmund writes /m/ with the **m**-rune, /n/ (and [ŋ]) with the **n**-rune; thus, **muþiR, runaR, inkifast** U986. Rarely are nasals omitted before homorganic consonants; Peringskiöld records the form **urlati** *Virlandi* on U346 (U356 has **uirlanti**), and the form **hos** *hans* occurs on U956.

The sounds /s/, /R/, /l/, and /r/ are symbolized, quite conventionally, by the **s**-, **R**-, **l**-, and **r**-runes. Asmund seldom reveals inconsistency in his use of palatal /R/ versus normal /r/, although the sounds were clearly similar, as the spelling **runaRitaR** *runaR rettaR* on U847 indicates. Asmund consistently writes /r/ after /f/ as well as after dental consonants; thus, **auþulfr** *AuðulfR* U871 and **kuþlaifr** *GuðlæifR* L1053. Only in the form **ritar** *rettaR* on U346 does Asmund betray an inconsistency.

One of Asmund's most distinctive orthographic habits may be seen in the form **runaRitaR** cited above. A single rune may do service as the final sound of one word and the initial sound of the next. The sounds need not be identical; thus **aukuþs** *ok Guðs* U346, U356; **þinabtiR** *þenna æftiR* U824; **osmuntritsi** *Asmundr risti* U824; **þinoto** *þenna at tva* (?) U847; **kiruabtiR** *gærva æftiR* U859; **hosalukuþs** *hans salu ok Guðs* U956; **honsalukuþs** *hans salu ok Guðs* U998, L1053; **ukuþlaifr** *ok GuðlæifR* L1053; and **ukarl** *ok Karl* L1053.

Asmund writes consonantal /i̯/ and /u̯/ with the **i**-rune and the **u**-rune respectively. Thus, **hialbi** *hialpi,* **kirua** *gærva.* Note that the latter word has the semi-vowel yet, in contrast to the more frequent *gæra.*

Asmund shows considerable vacillation in his representation of the diphthong /æi/, symbolizing it thirteen times digraphically and ten times with a single rune. Thus, **stain** U346, U356, U824 (with metathesis), U956, U981, U998, L1053; **kuþlaifr** *GuðlæifR* L1053; **ailif** *Æilif* U981; **raisti** *ræisti* U981; **raisa** *ræisa* U998; **þaiRa** *þæiRa* U346, U356. Monophthongal spellings are **stin** U301, U847, U871, U986; **þim** *þæim* U847; **iukiR** *IogæiRR* U824; **þiuþkiR** *PiuðgæiRR* L1053; **þurstin** *Porstæinn* U998; **rasa** *ræisa* U356; and **þaR** *þæiR* L1053. The diphthong /au/ is written digraphically in the three occurrences attested in the thirteen

---

[10]M. F. Lundgren et al., *Svenska personnamn från medeltiden,* cited by Wessén under U956.

inscriptions: **auþulfr** *AuðulfR* U871, **kinlauhaR** *GinnlaugaR* U871, and –**islauh** *(G)islaug* U847. The word *ok* 'and' is written **uk** in U847, U859, U956, and L1053, **auk** in U346, U356, and U824, and both ways in U986 and U998.

A noteworthy feature of Asmund's orthography is his use of the o-rune as nasalized /aⁿ/, as in **osmuntr** *Asmundr*, **þino** *þenna*, **hons** *hans*, **runoR** *runaR*, and **kunor** *Gunnarr*. (In three of the examples, the vowel is nasalized by a preceding sound.) On the other hand, the a-rune is employed in the forms **ant** *and* 'spirit' and *a* *a* 'on' in U346 and U356. The o-rune never symbolizes /o/, however, which is consistently written with the u-rune (**muþiR** *moðiR*, **bru** *bro*).

Asmund writes both /i/ and /e/ with the i-rune (**risti** *risti*, **lit rita** *let retta*), and he uses the u-rune to represent (in addition to /o/) the vowels /u/, /y/, and /ø/, as in **runaR** *runaR*, **suni** *syni*, and **bruþr** *brøðr*.

The vowel /a/ is written with the a-rune (thus **markaþi** *markaði*) except in the form **ifriþr** on U824 (presumably *Afriðr*). The vowel /æ/ is written with the i-rune in **kitilmuntaR** *KætilmundaR* U346, U356, **rhuþilfaR** *HroðælfaR* U824, **kirua** *gærva* U859, and **iftiR** *æftiR* U871, but with the a-rune in the nine remaining cases of the word *æftiR* (**aftiR**, **abtiR**).

Asmund uses the word divider not to separate individual words but to mark off larger semantic groups. There is not complete consistency in this matter; compare **lit·rita** U956, but **liturita** L1053.

Two linguistic forms that are typical of Asmund are *hio* 'carved' (preterite singular of *haggva*), rather than the otherwise ubiquitous *hiogg*, and *sala* 'soul', rather than the more usual *sial*.

Misspellings are not uncommon in Asmund's works. Omission of a rune or runes can be noted in **rt** *retta* U346, **osmunr** *Asmundr* U346, **urlati** *Virlandi* U346, **rasa** *ræisa* U356, **stniltr** *Stæinhildr* U956, **faur** *faður* L1053. Metathesis is also frequent, as in **stian** *stæin* U824, **rhuþilfaR** *HroðælfaR* U824, **ritsi** *risti* U824, and **osmunrt** *Asmundr* U859, U969, U981, U986, and U998.[11] The **u** of **kuþsumuþiR** *Guðs moðiR* on U956 and the **m** of **mialbi** *hialpi* on U356 must be considered miscarvings.

The runes **a** and **n** are confused in **ia** *en* U847 and **binrn** *Biorn* U871. A correction has been made in **liturita** on U824, but on U847 an error has been left untouched: **litu ritu rita**.

---

[11]There have been several "explanations" of this metathesis, especially that in the carver's own name. Hjalmar Kempff presumed *(Söderby runsten)* that the spelling **osmunrt** indicated a metathesized pronunciation. According to Magnus Olsen ("Ordblinde runristere," *Fornvännen* 48 [1953]: 327–329), such spellings can be interpreted as symp-

Technical Considerations

The monuments signed by Asmund alone are, with the exception of U956 (a rock of unusual shape), raised stones. Like 70 percent of the Upplandic rune stones, the typical Asmund stone is of granite; three are grey (U824, U871, U956), two are light grey (U859, U998), one is blue grey (U969), and one is red (U847). U356 is of grey gneis-granite, and L1053 is of light red sandstone, of which there is a great supply in the area around Gävle. The type of stone of U301, U346, U981, and U986 is not known.

Many of these monuments are of imposing size; of eleven for which we possess measurements, seven are over two meters in height. Six are approximately rectangular, three of them quite large (U847, U986, L1053) and three of more modest proportions (U346, U824, U998). The breadth of U301, U356, and U956 is small in comparison with the height. Some of the stones (U871, perhaps U301 and U969) are rounded at the top or arched.

Of unusual shape are U859 and U956. The former is a carefully shaped trapezoid, the smaller end forming the base. U956 is a rectangular rock with two flat surfaces that meet to form an obtuse angle, giving the impression of a broken slab (which it was considered to be by some early scholars).

All nine of the stones accessible at present are characterized by a generally smooth and even surface. Two of these (U824 and U847) may owe this feature to their positions as a church doorstep and a threshold, but in most of the others it is evident that the surface has been worked. In addition, the left edge of U871 was probably shaped with a tool.

On several of Asmund's works there is evidence of preliminary sketching. Thus, double-crossings (of smaller serpents especially) can be noted on U824, U847, U871, and perhaps U998. (In most cases one line is shallower than the other and not painted in for photographic purposes.) In U859 the first i-rune of **risti** has the branch of a u-rune, shallow and clearly an error that was discovered after the sketching. In U969 a large part of the carving (notably the runes and the animal's head) gives the impression of being an unfinished sketch. Wessén comments: "Fre-

---

toms of dyslexia or dysgraphia, and should be examined systematically by a runologist in collaboration with a neurologist (!). Wessén comments on the spelling **osmunrt** under U859: "Perhaps a mere oversight, but also perhaps intentionally, so that the two r-runes would not collide?" This explanation fails to account for the same spelling before **hiu** in U969 and **markaþi** in U998, and is contradicted by the spelling **osmuntritsi** in U824.

quently only light scraping can be observed, no noteworthy depth of line."

In contrast, the lines of most other stones are fairly broad and deep, though definitely less so than, say, Fot's. On U998 and L1053 they may be described as quite deep. Although Wessén considers it characteristic of Asmund to smooth the bottom of his incisions, there is not much evidence of this in the stones under consideration here, and Wessén himself observes of U859 that "in the bottom the lines are bumpy, not softly rounded."

In general Asmund shows himself to be a skillful technician as well as a talented artist. His lines are sure and straight, sometimes (e.g., in U871 and L1053) executed with extraordinary care. On the other hand, Asmund occasionally exhibits a tendency to be careless in some awkward or clumsy rune forms. In the case of U824, Wessén considers the technical execution of the work of such poor quality that he is reluctant to ascribe it to Asmund at all, despite the signature: "The carving lines are uneven, flat, and carved with a striking lack of assurance." He suggests that Asmund's preliminary sketch was carried to completion by an assistant or apprentice. In the absence of such information, however, it is probably best to conclude that Asmund's signed works reveal a carver who generally labors with care and precision but who is not immune to an occasional lapse in his execution.

POSSIBLE SIGNED ASMUND STONES

There are two additional inscriptions that are possibly signed by Asmund alone but cannot be regarded with absolute certainty:

(14) U368 (Helgaby, Skepptuna sn.). A fragment known only from older sources. According to Bautil (No. 34) the inscription reads:

... – ·ukautu– –aiR litu... ntr·mark– – ...

which Wessén reconstructs:

...(þ)æiR letu...(Asmu)ndr mark(aði)...

It is of course risky to interpret **ntr** as the final runes of *Asmundr* when names in *-mundr* are quite common in Upplandic inscriptions (*Guðmundr, Auðmundr, Sigmundr, Kætilmundr*, etc.). The fragmentary nature of the inscription does not permit the discovery of distinctive features of design or orthography, and we know nothing of the technical details. Yet the runes **mark**– – can scarcely be interpreted as anything but *markaði*, and this verb is especially distinctive for Asmund.

When, in addition, the characteristic feature of using an ornamental line as the mainstaff of a rune is noted (the a- and r-runes of **mark––**), the attribution to Asmund becomes fairly safe.

According to Brate the fragment U367 is part of the same stone as U368. Wessén rejects this notion: "U367 can scarcely have been carved by Asmund Karesun." Such a rejection is somewhat overhasty, however; there are features on U367 that are undeniably reminiscent of Asmund, and the two pieces appear to fit together, so that the fragmentary memorial formula and perhaps the cross on U367 complete that of U368. However, since U367 is carved on both sides, and our sources do not report the same of U368, it is perhaps best to consider the two fragments independently. See the discussion of U367 on pages 121–122.

(15) L1050, B1100 (Lund, Valbo sn.). The other stone in question is located at Valbo Church in Gästrikland but was formerly located at Lund in the same parish. It is as yet unpublished in the Swedish *Runverket* and may here be fully described: A tall rectangle of Gävle sandstone. The stone has been broken in two at the base and was in this condition at the time of the woodcut in Bautil. Extensive flaking around the area of cleavage has added to the damage, so that the most interesting part of the inscription has been lost. The surface is smooth and the lines fairly deep and clear.

iþalora×lit rita stin þino+abtiR ibiurn sun sin×þaR uaRu... ×–uain×
auk arnfasta aukai̩l...þaiR ua...–uþ hialbi honsalukuþs muþiR×
runoR ritaR husmsr

iþalora *let retta stæin þenna æftiR Æibiorn, sun sinn. ÞæiR vaRu...*
Svæin(n) ok Arnfasta ok Æil(if(R))...þæiR va(Ru)...Guð hialpi
hans salu ok Guðs moðiR. RunaR rettaR hio Asmundr (?).

iþalora is an unknown name, probably masculine. Brate interpreted it as "Idal of Rå," citing an eighth-century German *Idalus* (masculine), *Idala* (feminine), and viewing **ora** as *ā Rā* "which is also unknown in the district." *Æibiorn* is attested, but rarely; see Sö255 and U176.

þaR uaRu is no doubt the beginning of a sentence giving additional information about **iþalora** and Æibiorn. Bugge's assumption that **þaR** represents "a younger form, synonymous with *sáR*"[12] is untenable. Asmund writes **þaR** for *þæiR* on the nearby Järsta-stone (L1053), and the rune that follows **uaR** cannot be **þ** (as in *varð*) or **h** (as in Bautil), but

[12] Erik Brate and Sophus Bugge, *Runverser*, p. 133.

rather Ո **u**, Ռ**r**, /**i**, or Ր **l**. Of these the u-rune is most likely. Unfortunately we shall never know what followed *þæiR vaRu*, not because the reading in Bautil contains "several errors," as Brate thought, but because all the runes found on the lower part of the stone in B1100 are completely invented. The stone was not whole, as pictured in Bautil, but was in the same condition as it is today. The fragment that actually constitutes the base of the stone may be seen in B1100 depicted to the left of the restored stone, with the runes **þaiRu––**on it. And since B1100 is unable to follow the ornamental line on the lower right side of the stone any farther down than is possible today, we may assume that none of the runes in Bautil (which are far too numerous for the space allotted) may be used to supplement our reading. Brate's efforts to wrestle a meaning from them (*vann Øysilaland alt*, for example)[13] must be considered in vain.

The names that follow *þæiR vaRu* are grammatically ambiguous. **suain** can be nominative *Svæinn* or accusative *Svæin*. **arnfasta** is either an oblique form of a masculine name *Arnfasti* or the nominative of a feminine *Arnfasta*. These weak forms are unattested, although the strong masculine name *Arnfastr* is not uncommon. *Arnfasti* would stand in relation to *Arnfastr* as *Sigfasti* on U193 to the more common *Sigfastr*. Note also the *Signiuti* of U958, probably referring to the same person as the *Signiutr* of U945. Also frequent are the names *Fasti* and *Fasta*, abbreviated forms of names like *FastulfR*, *Fastlaug*. The third name is incompletely preserved; one might expect some form of *Æilif* (feminine) or *ÆilifR* (masculine), both attested in Uppland. If the second occurrence of *þæiR vaRu* on L1050 refers to the three names just discussed, one may safely assume that the masculine forms are called for.

The runes in B1100 that occur immediately before the prayer constitute a complete fabrication. They seem to suggest the words *gærði kumbl at Æibiorn ok* **iþalora**. In this connection see U585, with a similar series of runes.

The puzzling sequence **husmsr** was first interpreted as *hio Asmundr* by Bugge with subsequent support from Brate.[14] Since the stone would probably be attributed to Asmund even if unsigned, and since the expressions *hio* and *runaR rettaR* are characteristic of Asmund's signatures, Bugge's interpretation is probably valid. The misspelling is nevertheless impossible to explain rationally.

[13]Ibid., p. 66.
[14]Ibid., p. 34.

SIGNED ASMUND STONES WITH CO-RUNOGRAPHERS

There are six remaining monuments that bear Asmund's signature but differ from the preceding in that Asmund's name occurs not alone but in combination with others, indicating that each work is the product of a collaboration of two or more carvers. One must exercise great caution in drawing conclusions about Asmund's style from these stones.

(16) U884 (Ingla, Skogstibble sn.):
Side A: hulmkaiR·auk si[k]riþr————fatsr·þahl...o·aftiR uih·faur
hulmkiRs
Side B: osmuntr·s———...R markaþu þisaR runo
Side C: ...þaR u...

HolmgæiRR ok Sigriðr...–fastr, þau l(itu)...(þenn)a æftiR Vig, faður HolmgæiRs. Asmundr...markaðu þessaR runa(R)...þaR v(aRu)...

(17) U932 (Uppsala, Domkyrka). Now erected in the Universitets-plantering:
Side A: muli·u...————————...–ita stin þino·aftiR·suarthþa brur
sin osmuntr ·inkialt
Side B: muli·aukuni...a——ih...–astr·au——————...–·þ——h   litu
rita·stin þino·aftiR suarthaf–... k–suþrbi

Muli...(r)etta stæin þenna æftiR Svarthaufða broður sinn. Asmundr. Ingiald(r?). Muli ok...Igulfastr (?) ok...þ(au) letu retta stæin þenna æftiR Svarthauf(ða by)gg(i i) Suðrby.

(18) U1142 (Åbyggeby, Vendels sn.):
fastulfr lit rita stino·abtiR· huit·haufþa·fauþur sin·osmuntristi
[·]uk uihmar+

FastulfR let retta stæina æftiR Hvithaufða, faður sinn. Asmundr risti ok Vigmarr.

(19) U1144 (Tierps kyrka):
·kaiRfastr [auk hunifraR auk hrafn] ·auk ·fulkbiurn · auk þuriR·
litu rita stino·aftiR·kaiR[a] f[a]þur sin·kuþ hialbi an– hons·
osmuntristi·ukhiriaR·

GæiRfastr ok HonæfR ok Hrafn ok Folkbiorn ok ÞoriR letu retta stæina æftiR GæiRa, faður sinn. Guð hialpi and hans. Asmundr risti ok hiriaR. [15]

---

[15] I have changed the reading **hnns** of *Runverket* to **hons**, since the rune in question is more likely to be an o-rune (ᚮ) with the upper branch lost than an n-rune.

(20) U1149 (Fleräng, Älvkarleby sn.):

þurbiurn᛫auknutr᛫þaiR litu rit<u>au</u>stain þinoftiR᛫kaiRmunta faþur sin kuþ hialbi honsalukuþs muþiR᛫ suain ouk osmunrt markaþu stin þino

Þorbiorn ok Knutr þæiR letu retta stæin þenna æftiR GæiRmunda, faður sinn. Guð hialpi hans salu ok Guðs moðiR. Svæinn ok Asmundr markaðu stæin þenna.

(21) L1049, B1101 (Söderby, Hämlige, Gävle). Now in the Church of the Trinity, Gävle. The final stone that bears Asmund's signature is, like L1050 and L1053, from Gästrikland, and not treated as yet in the Swedish *Runverket*. A thorough discussion is therefore in order: Red (Gävle) sandstone. The stone lacks the upper right-hand corner and a large piece of the left side. The latter was still intact when the woodcut in Bautil was made, so that only an insignificant part of the inscription is lost. The surface is smooth, the runes fairly deep and clear.

× brusi lit rita s–. . . –b̦tiR a̦hil ß brur sin:in h–n̦ uarþ tauþr a tafsta lonti × þo brusi furþi lanklans᛫abtiR b[r]ur sin hon fur m̦iR fraukiRi kuþ hialbi hosalukuþș m̦u[þiR suain᛫uk osmunrt þau markaþu]×

Brusi let retta s(tæin þenna æ)ftiR Ægil, broður sinn. En hann varð dauðr a Tafæistalandi, þa Brusi førði lanklans æftiR broður sinn. Hann for meðr FrøygæiRi. Guð hialpi hans salu ok Guðs moðiR. Svæinn ok Asmundr þæiR(?) markaðu.

There would seem to be room for Asmund's usual formula **stin þino** in the lacuna. The strange symbol ß, resembling a dotted b-rune, is best understood as a correction; after discovering that the **b** of *broður* had been carved twice, the runographer "erased" the first by carving two dots as a word divider (only these dots would then be painted). To read ß as /p/, as Kempff did, would be unprecedented and would yield an unknown and uninterpretable name. The name *Ægill* is frequent in West Norse sources (*Egill*) but less common in the East Norse area; see Sm148. On the name *Tafæistaland* see U467.

There is some uncertainty about the ordering of the clause beginning *þa Brusi . . .* , but even more difficult is the interpretation of the passage. Hjalmar Kempff was the first to break with the older view that **furþi**-

---

The name *HonæfR*, uninterpreted by *Runverket*, is found on U773 (**hunef**) and on a newly found inscription from Södermanland; see Sven B. F. Jansson, "Ännu några runfynd från senare år," *Fornvännen* 54 (1959): 266, and "A Newly Discovered Runic Stone from Västerljung, Södermanland," in *Nordica et Anglica: Studies in Honor of Stefán Einarsson*, pp. 115–120.

lanklans was to be read *for til Ænglands* 'went to England' and recognized the form *førði* as preterite singular of the verb *føra*. He then interpreted **lanklans** as *"lands ledung"* ("land's levy") and arrived at the following translation: "Brusi then led the land's levy: after his brother." Otto von Friesen adopted this interpretation and considered it a statement of inheritance; Ægil was without offspring, so that after his death his brother Brusi inherited the position of military leader for Gästrikland: "Then Brusi (Egil's brother) led the levy of the land (= Gästrikland) after his brother." Brate differs from von Friesen only in translating *þa* as *"när"* ("when") rather than *"sedan"* ("then"), but this is a crucial distinction. The word order *þa* + noun + verb prohibits the interpretation of *þa* as "then." Von Friesen's translation would demand word order **þa førði Brusi...*, as in U29 *þa fingu þau sun* 'then they had a son'. Thus, *þa* must mean "when" and the passage must be subordinate to a main clause, as in U614 *hann vas siokR uti, þa þæiR giald toku a Gutlandi*.

Kempff's interpretation of **lanklans** as *"lands ledung,"* accepted by von Friesen and Brate, must also be subjected to scrutiny. What Kempff had in mind was no doubt a Rune-Swedish equivalent to Old Icelandic *leiðangr* 'levy of ships and men' and Medieval Swedish *leþunger (ledhonger)* 'warlike expedition with appropriate equipment' (Söderwall). **lanklans** could then be read as **læiðang lands* and the omitted þ-rune explained by Asmundic spellings like **faur** *faður*, **brur** *broður*. A difficulty, however, is that in the word *leiðangr* the final *-r* is part of the root, so that the Rune-Swedish equivalent should be accusative singular *læiðangr*. (On the other hand, the Medieval Swedish word *leþunger* does not retain the *-r*; thus, Upplandslagen *Nu biuþer konongr liþ ok leþung ut*.)[16] One wonders whether Asmund could have written **lank** for **laiþankr**, thus omitting four of the eight runes that would normally be employed.

Another objection to the idea that Brusi "led the land's army" is that, in contrast to modern Swedish *föra*, Rune-Swedish *føra* does not mean "lead" but rather "bring, take, transport." It occurs in this way three times in the Upplandic inscriptions (**firþi** U395, **fyrþu** U414, **fyra** U735), twice with specific reference to transporting stone for the memorial, and once (U395) somewhat uncertainly interpreted as taking a bride from her paternal home to her new husband's.

---

[16]Sam Henning, ed., *Upplandslagen enligt Cod. Holm. B199 och 1607 års utgåva*, p. 66.

The fourth and last occurrence of the word *føra* in the Swedish inscriptions is from a stone in Småland (Sm52): *Hrólfr ok Áskell reistu stein þenna eptir Lífstein, fǫður sinn, es varð dauðr á Skaney í Garðstangum, ok førðu á Finnheiði.* Kinander writes: "The inscription thus tells of two men from Forsheda whose father fell at Gårdstånga, whereupon they brought his remains home to Finnheden." Although it is tempting to suggest that Brusi, too, "brought back the remains" of his brother, the interpretation is unfortunately untenable.

The meaning of **lanklans** must remain unclear. As much as one would like to discover the simple words "lɒng" and "land's," it is impossible to reconcile them grammatically. (**lank** would be feminine nominative singular or neuter nominative-accusative plural *lǫng*; **lans** could be nothing but genitive singular of the neuter noun *land.*)[17]

The form *þau*, referring to Asmund and Svæin, is puzzling. It is hard to believe that ᛁ ᛦ could have been misread as ᚢ. The possibility is more likely that ᚱ would have been, but Asmund always uses palatal /R/ in the word *þæiR*.

The six monuments signed jointly by Asmund and other carvers may now be discussed systematically.

Technical Considerations

Five of the monuments are raised stones; U884 is a stationary boulder with the approximate shape of a cube. The shape of U1144, a rough square, is somewhat unusual. U1149 and L1049 are, like L1050 and L1053, of red Gävle sandstone; the remaining four are of reddish granite. Two of the monuments, U884 and U932, are distinguished by being carved on three sides.

[17]An interesting speculation is that of Professor Einar Haugen (private communication), who would view **lanklans** as *lag (lǫg) lands* 'law of the land', explaining the **n** of **lank** as anticipation of the **n** in the next word (**lans**). Since *fœra* can mean, in certain cases, "to speak" (Fritzner), Haugen would interpret *førði lag lands* as "took over the position of law speaker." "The context strongly suggests that this is the object of *førði* and that this was something he [Brusi] did after his brother had left to go to Tavastaland." A difficulty in Haugen's interpretation (in addition to the assumption of a miscarving) is that *fœra lǫg* is nowhere attested with precisely this meaning. On the other hand, Fritzner has it in the sense "change the law": *Íslendingar höfðu fœrt lög sín ok sett Kristinn rétt.* Could it be that L1049 tells us something of the Christianization of Gästrikland? This type of information has precedents in the inscriptions; cf. the Greater Jelling-stone in Denmark and the Frösö-stone in Jämtland.

The surfaces of the sandstone monuments are very smooth. Less so are those of U1142 and U1144, but weathering (U1142) and wearing (U1144, formerly before the church door) obscure the original conditions to a certain extent. U932 has been worked on three sides, but side A is not without some unevenness. The surfaces of U884 show traces of smoothing but are nevertheless somewhat rough.

The remarkable fact about U884 is its unfinished condition. As has been noted in chapter 6, most of the lines of the carving have not been hewn to normal depth but are instead merely traced on the surface with a sharp tool, a clear case of sketching. Similarly, the occasional double-crossings and the shallow lines of U1142 are evidence of sketching, a practice noted previously on U969. Except for the unfinished lines on U884 and U1142, the incisions are fairly deep (where preserved). Those on sandstone, a naturally soft medium, are extraordinarily deep.

Most of the lines are carved with a sure hand, but some of the work on U884 (e.g., sides B and C) and U1144 appears somewhat shaky. This fact may well be attributable to Asmund's co-runographer, assuming that he was less experienced than Asmund.

Formulation

All the inscriptions on these six monuments contain a conventional memorial formula, and U932 has two of them. The features of these memorial formulas are largely those found in works by Asmund examined previously, as, for example, the dominating formulation *let retta stæin þenna æftiR*.

Three of the six stones bear prayers. Those on U1149 and L1049 have the characteristic addition *ok Guðs moðiR*, while that on U1144 is a simple *Guð hialpi and hans*. The word order *and hans* has not been attested heretofore in Asmund's work.

Additional information is provided on L1049 (manner of death), U932 (dwelling place), and probably on U884 (*þaR v[aRu?]*).

The signatures are remarkable in that Asmund is not the only carver named. Svæin is named on L1049 and U1149, Vigmar on U1142, and a carver whose name is spelled **hiriaR** on U1144. These signatures use *marka* or *rista*. Whether the **inkialt** on U932 is to be viewed as a fellow-carver with the name *Ingialdr* is not entirely certain. Signatures consisting of a mere name are not unknown, it is true (see chapter 2), but there are also cases in which such names constitute additions to the memorial formula, such as the *DisælfR* on U917. The lack of a nominative ending *-r* on **inkialt** is especially puzzling.

It is most unfortunate that the names of the carvers who worked with Asmund on U884 cannot be read. As Wessén notes, there is room in the text band for two names, in addition to Asmund's.

Design

In terms of design, the six rune stones under consideration illustrate a rich variety of artistic patterns, some of which have not yet been encountered. The text band of U1144, for example, is not zoomorphic at all, but is rather a kind of frame inside of which appear animals and ornamental serpents. This type of design, described in chapter 3, is otherwise characteristic of southwestern Uppland, where it is associated above all with Balli and Lifstæin. Another interesting design is that of U1142, which combines features of Type A-2 and Type A-3. The rune animal crosses itself at the base of the stone, as in Type A-2, but the head then rises and forms a loop around the tail, as in most varieties of Type A-3. Also unorthodox is the knotted circle on side B of U884, but as the design is unclear and probably unfinished it does not offer reliable evidence.

Designs of Type A-2 occur on U884 side C and U932 side A, the latter much like that of U301. The designs of U884 side A and U932 side B are of Type A-3, the former agreeing quite well with what has been seen previously, for example, U824, U847, and U871, all from neighboring parishes. The two sandstone monuments (U1149 and L1049) are, like the nearby Järsta-stone (L1053), of Type B. On U932 and U1144, part of the text band runs up the middle of the stone, a characteristic feature noted on U998.

While the heads of the rune animals are comparable to those in Asmund's other signed carvings, there are several features worth noting. The head on side C of U884 is not seen in profile but from above, in the manner of those on the usual smaller serpents. Conversely, the heads of the ornamental serpents of U1144 are seen in profile and are in fact as developed zoomorphically as in the usual rune animal. A variety of smaller serpents appears on four of the six stones, but only in one case (U884) do they exert a dominant effect on the whole pattern. Interesting are the winged serpents on U1142, an unusual decoration that will be found on other (unsigned) Asmund stones.

Crosses appear on all but L1049, and except for the one on U1149 they are adorned with characteristic rounded rays. The crosses of U884 and U932 are of Type B-1 and are located on a surface different from the main inscription. Crosses of Type B-4 occur on U1142 and U1144.

The cross of U1149 is the somewhat less common A-5, a variation of which was noted on L1053.

Animal figures of some similarity are found on U884 side B and U1144; they bear little resemblance, however, to those on U969.

Rune Forms

Reversed runes, which we have noted sporadically in previous works (U956, L1053), occur extensively on side B of U884. A related phenomenon is the position of the runes on side B of U932; they stand on the outer edge of the text band instead of on the more usual inner line.

There are no dotted runes in the six works considered here. The ᛒ of L1049 is most certainly not to be read as /p/, but is rather a correction. Another correction is found in the series aũs on U1149; like the ũr of U824, it does not qualify as a true bind-rune. The first two runes in the second occurrence of **brusi** on L1049, however, could be viewed as a bind-rune.

The spacing is quite even on U932 side A, U1142, U1149, and L1049, but there are sections of uneven distribution on U884, U932 side B, and U1144. Some of this unequal spacing results from poor carving surfaces that had to be avoided.

An ornamental line serves as the mainstaff of a rune in U1142 (the r of **fastulfr** and the a of **rita**), U1144 (the þ of **kuþ**, the i of **risti**), U1149 (the þ of **þurbiurn**, the k of **kuþ**), L1049 (the r of **rita**, the u of **brusi**), and perhaps U884 (the i[k] of **si[k]riþr**?). On L1049 an ornamental line forms part of the branch of the r-rune in the second occurrence of *Brusi*.

The word dividers found on these six stones are familiar: the single vertical stroke ᛫ (36 times), a large cross ✕ (twice; cf. L1053), and the less common ⁞ , ⦂ , and + (once each).

It was noted earlier that narrowness is a general characteristic of Asmund's runes, and there are many examples of narrow rune forms in the six works in question here (e.g., the runes of **hulmkaiR** in U884, the f- and b-runes of U1144). It is therefore a matter of great interest to discover a series of rune forms in which this characteristic feature is conspicuously and consistently absent. The differences between these rune forms and those we recognize as Asmund's can best be observed by comparing the right and left sides of the Fleräng-stone (U1149). Note on the left side the forms ᚦᛒᚼ versus the forms ᚦᛁᛌ on the right side.

Nor is fullness the only difference between the runes on either side of U1149. While the right side of the stone reveals the familiar Asmund-forms ᚱ ᛌ ᚭ ᛁ ᛏ , the corresponding runes on the left side have the forms ᚱ ᚼ ᛏᛏ. The inescapable conclusion is that the runes on the left are not Asmund's but those of the other carver named in the signature: Svæin.

Having established a clear distinction between the rune forms of Asmund and those of Svæin, we can distinguish each carver's contribution to the inscription on L1049. Asmund is responsible for the initial section **brusi lit rita s–. . . ḅtiR ahil ᛒ brur sin** and for the series **þo brusi furþi lanklans abtiR ḅ[r]ur sin**. In contrast, Svæin executed the sentences in **h–ṇ uarþ tauþr a tafstalonti** and **hon fur miR fraukiRi**, as well as what remains of the prayer.

Unfortunately, it is a much more difficult task to discover the division of labor on the other four stones that have multiple signatures. The unfinished condition of U884 makes it risky to draw conclusions of this sort, and even some of the awkward forms on side B, which one would like to attribute to another carver, have correspondences on works signed by Asmund alone. The ⟩ᛁ **r** in **markaþu** on U884, for example, has a counterpart in the first r-rune of U871.

Similarly, U932 reveals little that cannot be the work of Asmund. The unusual s-rune of **stin** on side B, which lacks a lower stroke, has a parallel in the s of **sino** in U847. U1142 contains two s-runes with the uncharacteristic (for Asmund) shape ᚼ, but typical Asmund-forms are found throughout the inscription, as in the a-runes with branch slightly piercing the mainstaff, familiar from U859 and U871. It is therefore somewhat bold to assume that Vigmar did the occasional uncharacteristic rune. The same can be said of U1144 with its ᚼ-runes in **stino** and **sin**. Whether **hiriaR** had a hand in their formation is difficult to say.

Orthography

Many of Asmund's characteristic orthographic traits reappear in the six works that he has signed jointly with other carvers: the mixture of monophthongal and diphthongal spellings (both **hulmkaiR** and **hulmkiRs** on U884), the spelling of **abtiR** with the a- and b-runes, the use of the o-rune as nasalized /aⁿ/ (but not in *a* 'on' in L1049; cf. the same word on U346 and U356), and metathesis (**osmunrt** U1149, L1049; **–fatsr** –*fastr* U884). The use of a common rune for two adjacent words is a practice Asmund shares with Svæin; for instance, **auknutr** *ok Knutr*, **þinoftiR** *þenna æftiR* U1149.

A heretofore unattested spelling is the representation of /y/ with the i-rune, in **suþrbi** *Suðrby* 'Söderby' U932. Asmund writes fricative /g/

with the **h**-rune in **uih** U884, **uihmar** *Vigmarr* U1142, and **ahil** *Ægil* L1049; but he employs the **k**-rune in **si[k]riþr** *Sigriðr* on U884, if the older reading is reliable.

A noteworthy form is the spelling of the neuter plural pronoun *þau(n)* 'they' (masculine + feminine) with a final **h**-rune: **þah** U884, **þ--h** U932. This spelling, one of Asmund's trademarks, has not received adequate treatment hitherto. Brate attempted to explain it by the curious notion that ᚼ should be read /n/ and "could quite properly be an ornamental decoration of ᚽ, perhaps occasioned by a long-standing alternation between ᚼ and ᚾ in the meaning *a*."[18] Otto von Friesen misinterpreted the runes **þouhlitu** on U540 as *þau hlitu* and thought the /h/ of *hlitu*, which he also observed on U375 and U932, was unetymologically restored: "Here **hlitu** should no doubt be analyzed as a historically incorrect spelling of *litu* (= West Norse létu)."[19] Wessén, on the other hand, terms the **h**-rune in **þauh** on U375 "miscarved for **n**."

None of these explanations is satisfactory. The final **h**-rune is no doubt a result of Asmund's pronouncing the word *þau* in isolation. The extra aspiration that accompanied this pronunciation created an illusionary fricative phoneme that Asmund then spells with the **h**-rune. That carvers frequently analyzed words by pronouncing a sound or sounds in isolation is clear from such misspellings as **is** for /s/ and the occurrence of intrusive vowels in consonant clusters. It is possible, in fact, that a pronunciation /þauh/ or /þaug/ actually existed in Asmund's speech, for such has developed in Modern Icelandic, which has a colloquial neuter nominative and accusative plural pronoun *þaug*. Similar forms are attested in Norwegian (cf. Noreen, *Altisländische und altnorwegische Grammatik*, par. 305, note 3).

Other orthographic characteristics are the misspellings in the six stones under consideration here, especially the omission of a medial **þ**-rune, as in **miR** *meðr* 'with' (showing subsequent palatalization of /r/) on L1049, **faur** *faður* U884, and **brur** *broður* L1049 (twice). It is possible that the **fauþur** *faður* of U1142 represents a corrected misspelling of this sort, rather than an umlauted form as Jansson suggests.

The spelling **ouk** *ok* 'and' on U1149 is not a "miscarving," as Brate assumed, but a result of nasalization from the final sound of the preceding word (*Svæinn*).

[18]Brate and Bugge, *Runverser*, note p. 192.

[19]Otto von Friesen, "Hvem var Yngvarr enn viðfǫrli?" *Fornvännen* 5 (1910): 203.

In keeping with the orthographic practice evident in **auþulfr** *AuðulfR* U871 and **kuþlaifr** *GuðlæifR* on L1053, Asmund spells the name *Fast-ulfR* on U1142 with final ᚱ rather than ᚼ .

This examination of the runic monuments signed by Asmund with other runographers has strengthened some of the conclusions drawn from those works which Asmund signed alone. At the same time, the number of stylistic features characteristic of Asmund has been enlarged to include such things as the frame design of U1144, the winged serpents of U1142, and the representation of Rune-Swedish /y/ with the i-rune in U932.

The influence of the carvers whose names appear with Asmund's in U884, U932, U1142, and U1144 was found to be relatively slight. Such meager evidence as could be discovered indicated that the contribution of the co-signers was probably limited to the more-or-less mechanical matters of technical execution or to the shape of a couple of runes.

In the case of U1149 and L1049, however, the contribution of the co-runographer (Svæin) was seen to be considerable: at least half of the labor bears his stamp.

UNSIGNED RUNIC MONUMENTS WITH ASMUNDIC FEATURES (part 1)

It is now possible to review a large number of unsigned runic monuments that share some of the features found in Asmund's signed work, determining the nature of the runographic relationships and, if possible, indicating the extent to which various monuments can be ascribed to this master. The corpus to be considered is largely composed of those inscriptions which scholars have traditionally connected with Asmund's name; yet there are several that bear an unmistakable connection but have hitherto gone unmentioned in previous discussions.[20]

(22) U130 (Nora, Danderyds sn.):

biurn· finuiþaR sun lit· haukua· hili þisa· aftiR ulaif bruþur sin· hon uarþ suikuin o finaiþi· kuþ hialbi on hons · iR þisi biR· þaiRa uþal uk atrfi finuþaR sun o ilhiastaþum

Biorn, FinnviðaR sunn, let haggva hælli þessa æftiR Olæif, broður sinn. Hann varð svikvinn a Finnhæiði. Guð hialpi and hans. ER þessi byR þæiRa oðal ok ætt(æ)rfi, FinnviðaR suna a Ælgiastaðum.

[20]References to Brate in what follows are drawn from his discussion in *Svenska runristare;* an unmarked von Friesen attribution is to be found in *Upplands runstenar.* As mentioned in chapter 1, references to Wessén and Jansson are to be found under the numbers of the stones in their discussion in *Runverket.*

Brate and von Friesen do not treat this inscription, but Wessén notes a resemblance to Asmund's works: "In several respects it is reminiscent of Asmund Kareson's works and is probably contemporary with them." It is difficult to understand this reluctance to attribute U130 to Asmund. Nothing in the technical execution (which is excellent) or in the formulation prohibits such an attribution. While it is true that the design of the rune animal (an unorthodox variant of A-2) does not correspond precisely with any of those on Asmund's signed works, it bears great similarity with the smaller serpent on the right side of U1144 and with the rune animal of U969; in all three cases the animal is arched backward, its snout crossing part of its body. The head, with its "Westlund bulb," is reminiscent of those on U346, U356, and U859. Perhaps it is the form of the cross, which lacks the characteristic rounded blades, that has discouraged the attribution; yet striking parallels can be found in the crosses of L1050, U1149, and to a certain extent L1053. The first two of these share the additional feature with the cross on U130 of appearing to hang from a part of the rune animal.

When the runes on U130 are examined, most remaining doubts are dispelled. Here we find the familiar narrow f's, b's, and þ's, the short-branched o-, a-, and n-runes, the u-, l-, and t-runes with branches below the frame-line, and especially the distinctive forms ᛦ, ᛆ, and ᚼ. Ornamental lines serve as the mainstaves of runes 5 (n), 24 (u), and 108 (u), and the word divider is always a short vertical stroke.

Orthographic traits of U130 found in Asmund's works include the use of the o-rune for /a^n/, the u-rune for both /u/ and /o/, and the h-rune for fricative /g/. The spelling **biR** *byR* is paralleled by the **suþrbi** *Suðrby* on U932 and the spelling **haukua** *haggva* by **fauþur** *faður* on U1142. The omission of a rune in **atrfi** *ætt(æ)rfi* and in **finuþaR** *FinnviðaR* can be compared with similar omissions in **rt** *retta* and **urlati** *Virlandi* on U346. As in works signed by Asmund, the word divider is used sparingly, to set off word groups rather than words.

For these reasons U130 can be attributed to Asmund with an especially high degree of certainty.

(23) U193 (Svista, Össeby-Garns sn.):
    kuno auk inkialtr iluhi þoh litu ritu rita stin abtiR sihfasta buanta ku–u
    Gunna ok Ingialdr, Illugi, þau letu rettu retta stæin æftiR Sigfasta, boanda Gunnu.

Brate's attribution to Asmund by virtue of similarities with U1144 is emphatically rejected by Wessén ("completely out of the question") on the basis of technical considerations ("unsteady workmanship").

There is no denying the poor workmanship evident in the execution of the carving; the surface of the stone is coarse and uneven (much more so than is evident on the photograph), and the shallow runes are difficult to read. It is nevertheless unfair of Wessén to dismiss the similarities of U193 to works by Asmund as "actually very insignificant." The formulation with *retta stæin*, the band running up the middle of the stone (here only tentative, and without runes), the rune-animal's head, the form of the cross (B-1 with rounded blades), and the animal figure to the left of the cross are all familiar from works signed by Asmund. The rune forms are not unlike Asmund's, and orthographic features evident in **kuno** *Gunna* (the o-rune as /a^n/), **iluhi** *Illugi* (h-rune as fricative /g/), **abtiR** *æftiR*, and **þoh** *þau* are well known in his works. An especially striking characteristic is the mistake **litu ritu rita**, which has an exact correspondence on U847.

The connection is further strengthened when U193 is compared with side B of U884. There we find not only the same unsteady workmanship (in that case a result of the unfinished nature of the carving), but also the reversed runes, which occur on U193. It is therefore reasonable to assume that U193 is related to Asmund in much the same way as U884, which is an unfinished work signed by several carvers. It is possible that Asmund delegated the labor of carving U193 to a less skillful assistant.

(24) U194 (Väsby, Össeby-Garns sn.):
alit raisa stain þinoftiR sik sialfan ᛫ hon tuknuts kialt anklanti᛫ kuþ hialbi hons ant
Ali (Alli) let ræisa stæin þenna æftiR sik sialfan. Hann tok Knuts giald a Ænglandi. Guð hialpi hans and.

(25) U203 (Angarns kyrka):
ali lit−. . .−in þino ᛫ aftiR ᛫ ulf sun sin ᛫ faþur ᛫ fraikirþaR ᛫ i uisbi ᛫ rit is ristit
Ali (Alli) let (ræisa st)æin þenna æftiR Ulf, sun sinn, faður FrøygærðaR i Vesby. Rett es ristit.

Through a misinterpretation of the inscription on U203, Brate assigned both stones to the non-existent runographer "Frögärd i Ösby."

Wessén attributes (under U203) both works to Asmund "or at least to a carver who stood very close to him."

Wessén's attributions are no doubt correct. Despite the dissimilarity between the two rune animals, the works are very likely by the same carver, and both exhibit features characteristic of Asmund's style. The design of U203 can be compared to that of U956. U194 has a vertical text band in the middle of the stone. The expression *rett es ristit* is reminiscent of *runaR rettaR* on U346, U847, L1053, and L1050. Of the many familiar rune forms, the **a**- and **n**-runes with branches that slightly pierce the mainstaves (ᛆ ᚾᚾ ᚽ) may especially be noted. The orthographic peculiarity on U194 by which **alit** stands for *Ali let* has a near parallel in the spelling **hont** *hans and* on U859. In common with **suþrbi** on U932 (and **biR** on U130), the word *Vesby* is spelled with a final **i**-rune.

(26) U240 (Lingsberg, Vallentuna sn.):

tan auk husḳarl+auk suain+auk hulmfriþr×þaun ṃịþkin litu rita stin þino×aftiR halftan+faþ̣ur þaiRa tans·auk humf̣riþr at buanta sin

Dan ok Huskarl ok Svæinn ok Holmfriðr, þaun møðgin letu retta stæin þenna æftiR Halfdan, faður þæiRa Dans, ok Holmfriðr at boanda sinn.

(27) U241 (Lingsberg, Vallentuna sn.):

ntan auk huskarl·auk suain·litu rita stin aftiR·ulfrik·faþurfaþur sino·hon haf þi onklanti tuh kialtakit+kuþ hialbi þiRa kiþka salukuþs muþi

En Dan ok Huskarl ok Svæinn letu retta stæin æftiR Ulfrik, faðurfaður sinn. Hann hafði a Ænglandi tu giald takit. Guð hialpi þæiRa fæðga salu ok Guðs moðiR.

Like U194 and U203, these two stones are clearly by the same carver; the inscription is continued from U240 to U241. They have both been attributed to Asmund by von Friesen, Brate, and Wessén.

Both stones are well executed and extraordinarily interesting artistically. The crosses are familiar typologically (B-4) but have a double outline (not hitherto attested). The C-type rune animal of U241 is attested thus far only in the now-lost U986; the one on U240, of Type B-3, can be compared to that of U356. Characteristic animal figures occur on both Lingsberg-stones.

Despite some irregularities on U241 (e.g., the short mainstaves of the **t** in **tan**, the **r** of **rita**, the **u** of **ulf**, and the **h** of **tuh**), the rune forms agree quite well with Asmund's; note for example the distinctive r-rune ᛘ in **hulmfriþr** on U240.

Typical of Asmund are the formulation *letu retta stæin þenna æftiR* and the prayer augmented with *ok Guðs moðiR*. The expression *faður þæiRa Dans* is similar to *sun þæiRa KætilmundaR* on U346 and U356.

Interesting is the spelling **tuh** *tu* 'two' on U241, which would tend to confirm the hypothesis advanced before that a superfluous final **h**-rune is the result of pronouncing the word in isolation, with aspiration accounting for the illusionary /h/. Such explanations as Brate's and Wessén's of this **h**-rune being a form of the **n**-rune—either "ornamental" or "miscarved"—cannot account for its presence in *tu*, which never concluded with /n/.

In view of this evidence, which makes the attribution to Asmund highly probable, it is interesting to note the somewhat rare (for Asmund) forms + and × as word dividers on U240.

In a runological report from 1904 (referred to by Wessén under U242), Erik Brate assumed that the fragmentary:

(28) U242 (Lingsberg, Vallentuna sn.):
—×**auk**×**st[u]** ... —×**raisa**×
... *ok St*–... *ræisa* ...

originally formed a part of the same complex of runic monuments as U240 and U241. In this case (and there is little evidence that Brate's assumption is valid), U242 would very likely be the work of Asmund.

Despite a few minor similarities in the rune forms, U242 has little in common with Asmund's stones, and the use of the word divider to mark off individual words (contrary to Asmund's practice of separating large word groups) makes the attribution fairly improbable.

(29) U322 (Stensta, Skånela sn.):
þiuþburh u lit rita stinꞏ**þina ibtiR[+nibiaR+ ... i+uibiast] ... ——a—bi an hos**
Þiuðborg let retta stæin þenna æftiR.ˉ.. hialpi and hans.

Wessén terms Brate's attribution to Asmund "extremely uncertain," and there are undeniably some minor features that make one hesitate to ascribe the stone to this master. The surface has not been worked (unlike most of Asmund's signed carvings), and the spellings **þina** and **hos** are not Asmund's usual ones. The former occurs only in **þinabtiR** on U824, and the latter only in **hosalu** on U956; otherwise they are spelled **þino** and **hons**.

These objections are not as telling as the many similarities that U322 has to Asmund's works. The design is very close to that of U301, from the same parish; note especially the way the animal's arched head, with its "Westlund bulb," is fitted flush against its body in both carvings, so that part of the text band and the head are depicted with a common line.

The rune forms correspond very closely with Asmund's; in the first word alone are found the typical forms Þ (twice), ʜ, and ʀ. The spellings þiuþburh with ✲ and ibtiR with ß are in accordance with Asmund's orthographic habits, and it is possible that the unorthodox form of the final rune in *þenna* indicates that an o-rune was originally intended.

Finally, the puzzling and superfluous u-rune that follows immediately on the word þiuþburh (Wessén's word divider is a natural feature of the stone's rough surface) finds its exact counterpart in the series kuþsumu-þiR on U956. U322 is, for these reasons, probably the work of Asmund.

(30) U343 (Yttergärde, Orkesta sn.). Now lost:

·karsi· uk...–rn þaiR litu raisa stai–þino' aftiR· ulf· faþur sin' kuþ hialbi hons...aukuþs muþi

Karsi ok ... þæiR letu ræisa stæin þenna æftiR Ulf, faður sinn. Guð hialpi hans ... ok Guðs moðiR.

(31) U344 (Yttergärde, Orkesta sn.):

in ulfr hafiR onklati' þru kialtakat þit uas fursta þis tusti ka–t' þa ————þurktil' þa kalt knutr

En UlfR hafiR a Ænglandi þry giald takit. Þet vas fyrsta þe(t)'s Tosti galt. Þa (galt) Þork(æ)till. Þa galt Knutr.

As in U240–U241, a connected inscription is contained on two rune stones, both undoubtedly the work of a single runographer. Von Friesen, Brate, and Wessén all agree that Asmund is the one in question. There is little doubt that these scholars are correct; all of them have pointed out well-known correspondences to Asmund's signed carvings. Among the less obvious similarities, mention should be made of (1) the reversed runes of U344 (cf. U884b), (2) the omission of the t-rune in þis *þet's* (cf. þas *þat's* on L1053, perhaps lans *lands* on L1049), (3) the spelling ulfr *UlfR* with ʀ instead of ↑, and (4) the rune forms ↑, ↾, ⅄, +, and ⼘.

The double monument to Ulf, a veteran of three campaigns in England, is comparable in many ways to U194/203 and U240/241, both multiple memorials that speak of similar events, and all attributable to Asmund.

(32) U357 (Skepptuna kyrka):

–arhas ˙ ukarn–il ˙ uk ontuitr ˙ uk hruþailfr ˙ muþur þiRa ˙ þaR þriR
bruþr ˙ litu ˙ rita ˙ staino þisa aftiR hulma faþur sin
*Vargas (?) ok Arn(k)ell ok Andvettr ok Hroðælfʀ, moðiʀ þæiʀa, þæiʀ
þriʀ brøðr letu retta stæina þessa æftiʀ Holma, faður sinn.*

Wessén writes: "As was already assumed by Brate, the stone is presumably carved by Åsmund Kåreson, though it is not signed." The evidence suggests that the attribution to Asmund is probably right. In
terms of design, U357 resembles U932 and U301, not only in type structure but in many details. Note, for example, the text band running up
the middle of the stone.

Orthographically there is much agreement with Asmundic practice:
the o-rune as /aⁿ/ (ontuitr, staino) and the consequent use of the u-rune
as both /o/ and /u/, the spelling þaR *þæiR* (cf. L1053), and the a-rune in
aftiR. Initial /h/ is preserved in the name *Hroðælfʀ*, as in U824. Note
also the use of the r-rune after /f/.

The rune forms ᚱ (in bruþr), ᚠ, ᚨ, ᛏ, and ᛚ are indicative of Asmund,
but somewhat disturbing are the several r-runes with the less typical
form ᛉ.

(33) U367 (Helgaby, Skepptuna sn.). Now in Skepptuna kyrka:

... ita ˙ istin þino ˙ aftiR ...
On the reverse: ... –noR–– ...
... retta stæin þenna æftiR ...

Brate considered this fragment part of the same rune stone as the fragmentary U368, which is probably signed by Asmund. Wessén terms this
notion "extremely uncertain" (under U368); he does not believe that Asmund could have carved U367.

It is most unfortunate that Wessén disposes of Brate's idea without
presenting a counterargument. Is it perhaps the cross form that Wessén
objects to? It is true that we have not yet met the pointed rays on Asmund's crosses of Type B-4, but an exact copy of this cross occurs on
U860, which Wessén does not hesitate to attribute to Asmund. (It is a
companion stone to the signed U859.) The cross on the reverse side of
U367 is identical with that of U356.

The spelling istin for *stæin* is not characteristic of Asmund, but the
first i-rune may have been brought about by pronouncing the word in
isolation, in the same way as the h-rune of þauh and tuh. The phrase

retta stæin þenna æftiR should bring Asmund to mind immediately, and, when one notes that *þenna* is spelled **þino** and *æftiR* **aftiR**, the connection with Asmund is indisputable. The spelling **þino** occurs on only thirty-nine other stones in all of Uppland. Of these thirty-nine stones, eight are connected to carvers active in western Uppland (Lifstæin, Tiðkumi, Arbiorn) and bear no resemblance to Asmund's work. The remaining thirty-one are either signed by Asmund (nine) or associated in another way with his work (twenty-two).[21] The form **aftiR** occurs on only fifty-one Upplandic stones (about 6%) but is common with Asmund (cf. U346, U356, U884, U932, U1144).

The rune forms of U367 strengthen these impressions. There is nothing about them that would preclude Asmund's having carved them, and the agreement is striking when one holds a photograph of U367 against the words *retta stæin þenna æftiR* in signed Asmund-stones, U871 and L1053, for example, or the unsigned U860 mentioned above. Note the mixture of short- and long-branched runes, found also on the nearby U356, and the form of the word divider.

It is unfortunate that the r-rune of **rita** has not been preserved. Had it been Asmund's characteristic form, and were there no initial i-rune in *stæin*, U367 could be viewed as "very likely" a work of Asmund. As it is now, the fragmentary work can only be tentatively attributed to Asmund.

If U367 could have been carved by Asmund, Wessén's principal objection to uniting U367 and U368 falls away. One is nevertheless reluctant to take such a stand because of the notorious unreliability of early drawings and because there is no evidence that U368 was, like U367, carved on the reverse side.

(34) U372 (Ånsta, Skepptuna sn.):

þurstain · uk þihn · uk sialfi · þaim hit kila muþiR · þaiR litu rita stain þinobtiR sihat · faþur sin · kuþ hialbi honsal

Þorstæinn ok Þægn ok Sialfi, þæim het Gilla moðiR, þæiR letu retta stæin þenna æftiR Sig(v)at, faður sinn. Guð hialpi hans sal.

Wessén cites Brate's attribution to Asmund without comment.

---

[21]The data are: **þino** not associated with Asmund: U646, U679, U688, U817, U864 (all Arbiorn or his school), U719 (Lifstæin), U771, U828 (Tiðkumi). Other occurrences, all associated with Asmund, are U194, U203, U240, U343, U346, U356, U367, U372, U374, U375, U409, U419, U431, U438, U629, U645, U847, U860, U866, U871, U875, U903, U932, U956, U986, U987, U998, U1009, U1031, U1043, U1145, U1149.

A comparison with Asmund's signed U956 reveals correspondences not only in the cross (as Brate pointed out), but also in the detail of the rune-animal's head. (The structure of the rune animal is otherwise unlike anything Asmund has signed, but it is reminiscent of that on U194, which we attributed to him.) The spelling þinobtiʀ is unique in the Upplandic inscriptions, but there are three other cases of a concluding o-rune used as the initial rune of *æftiʀ* (i.e., þinoftiʀ), all clearly associated in some way with Asmund (U194, U419, U1149). Asmund himself has written þinabtiʀ on his signed U824.

An ornamental line is used as the mainstaff of the final rune (l), and the h-rune serves to symbolize fricative /g/ (þihn, sihat).

Sporadic occurrences of the rune forms Þ and ⋏ remind one of Svæin, who indeed carved the þinoftiʀ on U1149, and but for the presence of typical Asmund-forms (and atypical of Svæin) ⌐, ⌐, ↑, ⋔, and Þ, it would be tempting to introduce him in connection with U372. Since this is not possible, one must judge U372 as probably the work of Asmund, and as one of his less impressive creations.

(35) U375 (Vidbo kyrka):

sikfastr · aukinla–h þauh litu rita stain þino aftiʀ uinoman sun si– in hon uarþ tauþr i buhi

Sigfastr ok Ginnlaug þau letu retta stæin þenna æftiʀ Vinaman, sun sinn. En hann varð dauðr i buhi.

Brate ascribed the Vidbo-stone to Asmund. Von Friesen and Wessén remark that its author was, if not Asmund, someone very close to him.

None of the stones that Asmund has signed affords an exact ornamental parallel to U375. The designs of U356 and L1049 are perhaps closest; in both one finds the same elongated tails, while the latter reveals a head of great similarity (nasal lobe, pointed ears, almond eyes). The figures in the center of U375 do not bear much resemblance to those on Asmund's U969 and U1144 or to those on inscriptions we have attributed to him (U240, U241), but the very presence of these figures is of some consequence.

An orthographic feature atypical of Asmund is the spelling sikfastr *Sigfastr*. Only in the uncertain reading si[k]riþr on U884 does Asmund break his habit of representing fricative /g/ with the h-rune. On the other hand, the name kinlauh *Ginnlaug* on U375 illustrates Asmund's practice, and the employment of the o-rune as /a^n/, the use of a single rune to end one word and begin the next, and the **h** in **þauh***þau* are features well known from this master's work.

Asmund's distinctive **r**-rune occurs twice (in **uarþ tauþr**), but the two **r**'s on the right side of the stone are, though attested, less characteristic. There are otherwise not enough divergences to warrant assuming a different runographer for each side of the stone, as in U1149, and the chief candidate for the right side (Þorfast) has a distinctively different **þ**-rune. It is therefore probable that Asmund carved U375.

(36) U409 (Lövstaholm, S:t Olovs sn.):

furkuþr×auk komal+litu rasa·stain þino abtiR+una+faþur sin+kuþ hialbi anta×una

Forkuðr ok Gamall letu ræisa stæin þenna æftiR Una, faður sinn. Guð hialpi anda Una.

Brate attributed this stone to Asmund, and Wessén agrees that there is "a good deal that suggests that this attribution is correct."

There is nothing in the technical execution or the formulation that would contradict Brate, and such unusual orthographic-linguistic features as **rasa** *ræisa* and **anta** *anda* could be accommodated without a great deal of difficulty. The design agrees in general structure with Asmund's signed U356, and the cross form with that of his unsigned U194, but there are ornamental details, such as the long, pointed ears and the mannered, arching tails, that are not familiar features of Asmund's art.

These divergences are augmented considerably when one takes a closer look at the rune forms on U409. While there are a few similarities, such as the **s**'s of **stain** and **sin**, there are some rune forms completely foreign to Asmund, for example, the first **b**-rune, which has the shape ᛒ, and the **s**-rune ᛋ in **rasa**. More significantly, there is a consistent occurrence of a **þ**-rune with a distinctively small, and sometimes angular, loop in the center of the mainstaff; this form ᚦ contrasts markedly with Asmund's typical ᚦ. Furthermore, none of the **r**-runes has the expected form ᚱ, but rather the form ᚱ. Nor is the word divider characteristic of Asmund. It is not necessary, however, to leave the authorship of U409 a matter of conjecture, for we are fortunately in a position to attribute this stone to a runographer whose works share with U409 both those features that are in agreement with Asmund's style and those that are not.

The Runographer Þorfast

The runographer Þorfast has affixed his name to two known Upplandic inscriptions. Despite the distance that separates them, there is no doubt that we are dealing with the same Þorfast:

(37) U599 (Hanunda, Hökhuvuds sn.):
orniutrˣakˣuihniutrˣakˣsi̱ihniutrˣ þiR li̱tu rasa stan þinsa aft–Ṛ...
mˣfaþur sinˣþurfostrˣhriti runoR
*Arnniutr ok Vigniutr ok Signiutr þæiR letu ræisa stæin þennsa æftiR
..., faður sinn. Þorfastr risti runaR.*

(38) U629 (Grynsta backe, Svarsta, Håbo-Tibble sn.):
+iluhi · nuk · fuluhi · þiR litu · rasa · s[tain ׃]þino+aftiR foþur sin +arn-
kisl · k[uþ · h]ia[l]bi · onta honsˣþurfastr hristi runoR
*Illugi ok Fullugi þæiR letu ræisa stæin þenna æftiR faður sinn Arn-
gisl. Guð hialpi anda hans. Þorfastr risti runaR.*

Þorfast has in common with Asmund some general features of formulation, some basic artistic structures (Type B), a few sporadic rune forms (ᚺ, ᚨ, ᛏ, ᚠ), and orthographic use of the o-rune as /aⁿ/ and the h-rune as fricative /g/. At the same time, however, Þorfast frequently uses the o-rune to symbolize non-nasal /a/, as in **orniutr** *Arniutr*, **þurfostr** *Þorfastr* U599, and **foþur** *faður* U629. The a-rune stands for a diphthong in **rasa stan** *ræisa stæin* U599 and **rasa** *ræisa* U629. An unetymological /h/ is restored in **hriti** U599 and **hristi** U629 *risti*.

An interesting feature of Þorfast's style is the position of the runes in the text band. In U629 those on the right side are placed on the outer line of the text band, while the runes on the left side stand in their usual position on the inner line. Both lines can thus be read in the same way.

Þorfast's most distinctive rune forms are ᚦ þ, ᚱ r, ᛋ s, and ᛒ b. His rune animals do not exhibit the graceful rhythm of Asmund's but are distorted by curves that seem unnaturally violent. The ears of his animals, which extend perpendicularly from the head, are pointed.

These characteristics serve to clarify many of the features of U409 that make one reluctant to attribute it to Asmund. Thus, the forms **rasa** *ræisa* and **anta** *anda*, the pointed ears and arched tails, the use of the word divider + and ×, the position of the runes in the right-hand text band,

and above all the rune forms ᚴ, ᚦ, and ᚱ make it very likely indeed that U409 is the work of Þorfast.[22]

In addition to U409, it is possible to attribute to Þorfast with great certainty the rune stone at Funbo Church:

(39) U987 (Funbo kyrka):

katil· aukuriþr· litu rosa stin þino×oftiR þurstin sun sin uiþi auk rikuiþr· þiR ristu ston aftiR bruþur sin×kuþ hialbi on þurstins·

Kætill ok Gyriðr letu ræisa stæin þenna æftiR Þorstæin, sun sinn. Viði ok Rikviðr þæiR ræistu stæin æftiR broður sinn. Guð hialpi and Þorstæins.

as well as the following fragment:

(40) U525 (Österlisa, Länna sn.):

...–ftiR suin×foþur sin...–––––n–usuns×auk––ṣ––þ––×

...æftiR Svæin, faður sinn...

The attribution of U987 to Þorfast is agreed upon by von Friesen, Brate, and Wessén. The fragmentary U525 has not been hitherto attributed to a specific runographer, but the evidence (the spelling **foþur**, the rune forms ᚽ, ᚦ, and ᚴ, the word divider ×, the length and curvature of the tail and neck band) makes the attribution conclusive.

Unsigned Runic Monuments with Asmundic Features (part 2)

(41) U418 (Brista, Norrsunda sn.):

þu̱[rfas]tr· aukitilui· þau· litu· stain[·]rito[·]ifti[R]· þurstain· faþur sin· kuþ hialbi hont· hons

Þorfastr ok Kætilvi þau letu stæin retta æftiR Þorstæin, faður sinn. Guð hialpi and hans.

Both Wessén and Brate attribute U418 to Asmund, but Wessén seems to have changed his opinion subsequently (see fn. 22). The stone bears an unmistakable resemblance to the works of Asmund. The design is closely paralleled by that of his signed U356. A rare feature that occurs on the heads of U346, U356, L1050, and the stone in question here is the elongated flap that hangs from the rune-animal's snout. The vertical text band in the middle of the stone is also typical of Asmund's ornamentation.

At the same time there are features in U418 that make the attribution to Asmund somewhat doubtful. Not the least of these is the poor quality

---

[22]Under U987, Wessén cites von Friesen as attributing "quite justifiably" U410, U418, and U419 to Þorfast. It is likely that "U410" is a misnumbering for U409.

of the stone, whose surface has not been smoothed, and the consequent awkward appearance of the lines and runes. Asmund characteristically selects granite or sandstone of high quality, whereas U418 is a schistose piece of material that suffers from weathering.

Moreover, an examination of the runes of U418 confirms what these technical observations suggest. The forms ᚺ, ᛒ, and ᛉ do not indicate Asmund but Þorfast, as does the use of the word divider to separate individual words rather than larger semantic groups. The relatively small cross is squeezed into a limited space between the two tails, as on Þorfast's U629.

One is nevertheless somewhat reluctant to give full credence to the attribution to Þorfast. It would be comforting, first of all, to find on U418 his typical þ-rune with the form ᚦ, instead of the consistent occurrence of the form with fully rounded loop. Nor do the heads of the rune animals correspond to those on U599 and U629; they are, as has been observed, characteristic of Asmund's.

There is, it seems, no way to escape the fact that U418 reveals evidence of both Þorfast and Asmund. It is of course possible that the author is a third runographer whose style illustrates this combination of features, but since we do not know of such a runographer it is reasonable to suppose that both Þorfast and Asmund had a hand in the creation of U418. The greater part of the labor would no doubt have been carried out by Þorfast.

(42) U419 (Norslunda, Norrsunda sn.). Now at Skansen:

þaun kulfinkr· auk stinfriþr· auk s[ikfast]r litu r[a]isạ ṣtin þinoftiR austnin· kun[a]rsu[n]s at iuria kuþ [h]ialbi hons–lu

Þaun KylfingR ok Stæinfriðr ok Sigfastr letu ræisa stæin þenna æftiR Øystæin, Gunnars sun... Guð hialpi hans salu.

The attribution to Asmund is Brate's. Wessén considers this doubtful but admits that the carver of U419 "stood quite close to Asmund and learned from him."[23] Jansson declares it "completely unlikely" that the stone is a work of Asmund.[24]

It is no doubt the þinoftiR that focused Brate's attention on this stone, and the rarity of such a spelling, found elsewhere only on U194 and U1149, justifies such attention. There are in fact other features reminiscent of Asmund, including the cross (cf. U356, U956), the structure

---

[23]But under U431 Wessén states that "Åsmund executed three carvings in Norrsunda parish: U418, U419, U431; none of them is signed." See also fn. 22.

[24]Sven B. F. Jansson, *Skansens runstenar*, p. 46.

of the rune animals (cf. U998, U956), and some sporadic rune forms
(ᚱ, ᚱ). The head of the rune animal bears comparison with that on
U375, attributed to Asmund.

Although it is undeniable that U419 is related in some way to Asmund's work, it is, however, very unlikely that he is its author. The unsure execution and the presence of atypical rune forms, such as ᚱ , ᚱ ,
ᚱ , and ᛁ\ , necessitate the assumption that U419 is the work of another,
less experienced carver, whose name is unrecorded. This carver is definitely not Þorfast, as von Friesen is said (see fn. 22) to have thought.
Whether he was an assistant of Asmund, working from a sketch by the
master, or an independent runographer whose style was influenced by
Asmund is impossible to determine, although the former seems more
likely.

(43) U431 (Åshusby, Norrsunda sn.). Now in Norrsunda Church:
tufa auk hominkr litu rita stin þino ꞏ abtiR kunor sun sin ꞏ in –– hon
uaR tau–r miR krikium ut ꞏ kuþ hialbi honsalukuþs m––iR
Tofa ok HæmingR letu retta stæin þenna æftiR Gunnar, sun sinn. En
hann vaR dauðr meðr Grikkium ut. Guð hialpi hans salu ok Guðs
moðiR.

Both Brate and Wessén attribute the stone to Asmund, citing, above
all, orthographic correspondences to other works (use of the o-rune,
double reading of a single rune, the word **abtiR**, infrequency of the word
divider). Wessén also notes the rune forms ᛁ , ᚦ , ᚠ , and ᛕ . The design
of Type A-1 is close to that of U956 (and the attributed U203); an earless
head of great similarity can be found on Asmund's Järsta-stone (L1053).
The vertical text band occupying the center of the stone is a trademark
found also on U932 and U998.

The spelling **miR** *meðr*, with loss of medial /þ/ and subsequent palatalization of /r/, occurs on the Söderby-stone (L1049). The expression
let retta stæin þenna æftiR is Asmund's standard formulation. The only
feature that might give one pause is the slight unsteadiness of the lines
that make up the text band and cross. In the absence of other atypical
evidence, however, the attribution to Asmund is probably correct.

(44) U438 (Ekilla, Husby-Arlinghundra sn.). Now in the park at Sten-
inge manor in the same parish:
rontr auk riki ꞏ aukuþrun ꞏ þaiR bruþr ꞏ litu r–isa stain þino ꞏ abtiR ꞏ
bruno ꞏ faþur sin ꞏ kuþ hialbi honsalu

(Þ)*randr ok Riki (?) ok Guðrun, þæiR brøðr letu ræisa stæin þenna æftir Bruna, faður sinn. Guð hialpi hans salu.*

Brate includes this among his attributions to Asmund; Wessén is in substantial agreement, if somewhat more reserved.

The similarities in orthography (the o-rune as /aⁿ/, the spellings **auk-uþrun, honsalu, abtiR**) are undeniable. The cross is a basic Type A, attested in Asmund's works (cf. U356) and otherwise very common in Uppland. Wessén claims to find additional "decidedly Asmundian traits" in the design, although he admits that it does not completely agree with anything encountered elsewhere. Perhaps he is thinking of basic structures, such as the Type A-3 rune animal, found also on U301.

The rune-animal's snout is unusually ornamented and has no parallels in Asmund's work. Nor can we accept Wessén's statement that the rune forms on U438 are Asmund's. The r-runes, above all, do not correspond to those in Asmund's work. In six of the nine occurrences of this rune on U438, the upper branch makes contact with the text band rather than the mainstaff, and in none of them do we find the characteristic form ᛉ. The f-rune of **faþur** is not Asmund's familiar ᚡ, and there is a frequent lack of parallelism in the position of the mainstaves.

For these reasons, the attribution to Asmund is not fully justified. The similarities to the master's work may be explained in much the same way as those on U419. There are in fact common features in U419 and U438, for example, the rune forms ᛉ (rune 5 on U438) and ᛒ (rune 12 on U419), the cross, and some irregularity in the fit of the mainstaves, but the evidence is probably not enough to permit the assumption of a common author.

(45) U540 (Husby-Lyhundra kyrka):
airikr·auk hokun·auk inkuar auk k rahn[ilt]r þouh——...—R·—na hon uarþ[tau]þr [a] kriklati·kuþ hialbi honsalukuþs muþiR
ÆirikR ok Hakon ok Ingvarr ok Ragnhildr þau...Hann varð dauðr a Grikklandi. Guð hialpi hans salu ok Guðs moðiR.

Otto von Friesen attributed the stone to Asmund after a lengthy discussion in an article from 1910.[25] He seems to have been unaware that Celsius made the same attribution two centuries earlier.[26]

---

[25]Von Friesen, "Hvem var Yngvarr enn viðforli?" pp. 199–209.

[26]A hastily written note in Celsius' *Svenska runstenar* (Fm60), I, 635: "Vid Osmundi pictura. Res. 34," makes this assumption evident. The reference is to Rhezelius' manuscript from 1636, signum R550 in the Uppsala Universitets Bibliotek. Number 34 in this col-

The correspondences in design that von Friesen points out are few, but the comparison of the intertwined lobe on U540 with a similar one on U346 is undeniably telling. One might add that a similar lobe occurs also on U418, in which Asmund's hand was evident. Such a detail can carry considerable weight when the basic structure of a design is, as here, largely unparalleled.

Von Friesen further cites rune forms, orthography, and formulation as grounds for attribution, pointing out the form of the word divider and the u- and s-runes, the use of the o-rune as /aⁿ/ and the h-rune as fricative /g/, and the wording of the prayer. To these arguments one might add a few supporting observations. Characteristic r-runes occur in **airikr** (the first **r**) and **kriklati**. Ornamental lines are used as the mainstaves of the a-, l-, m-, and u-runes in **honsalukuþsmuþiR**. The spelling **þouh** can be compared with **þah** on U884 and **þ--h** on U932.

U540 is very probably the work of Asmund, and from an ornamental point of view one of his most remarkable.

(46) U645 (Lundby, Yttergrans sn.):

usnikin · lit rita stin þino · ata bruþr sino · osua– . . . hiilbi ont þiRa
Osnikinn let retta stæin þenna at brøðr sina Asva(r). . . Guð hialpi and þæiRa.

Previous runographic discussion has not treated this stone, a somewhat surprising fact in view of the striking resemblances it betrays to Asmund's work.

The o-rune represents nasalized /aⁿ/ in **þino**, **sino**, **osua–**, and **ont**, and the u-rune is consequently used to write /o/ in *Osnikinn*.

The formulation includes *let retta stæin þenna*, but not *æftiR*. The prayer is conventional and not particularly distinctive.

The cross is Asmund's well-known Type B-1 with rounded blades between the arms. The rune animal (Type C) is not identical with anything in Asmund's work, but could be likened to a "compressed" version of U986. The snout is outfitted with a Westlund bulb. The triquetra-like knot behind the rune-animal's head is without parallel, but bears comparison with the knotted tail of U932.

There are rune forms undeniably characteristic of Asmund: the frequent s-runes with forms ꜱ and ꜱ, the a-, n-, and o-runes with short branches (ᛆ, ᚿ, ᚮ), the r and u of **bruþr** with forms ᚱ and ᚢ, and the word divider

---

lection is U540. Celsius no doubt attributed it to Asmund on the basis of orthography, since Rhezelius' drawing does not accurately reproduce the rune forms.

The stone is a masterpiece of execution; its surface is smooth and the incisions in it are the work of a sure and practiced hand.

In addition to these arguments, an interesting correspondence can be found between the form **ata** on U645, considered a mistake for *at*, and the form **oto** on Asmund's signed U847, which is there interpreted hesitantly as *at tva* 'in memory of two'. This suggests that the interpretation of one of these forms is incorrect; either U645 is raised "in memory of two brothers" or U847 contains a miscarving (repetition of the o-rune) in the word *at* 'in memory of'. For these reasons it is likely that Asmund carved U645.

(47) U846 (Västeråkers kyrka):

> iafurfast' . . . –nfast' uiku**þ**. . . **þ**aR litu r. . .––isaR –ftiR fa**þ**ur sin'
> asi' kitilbiurn' kair' iftiR' suir' s–. . . fti. . . bua. . .
> *Iofurfast, –fast, Viguð(r). . .þaR letu r. . .(þ)essaR (æ)ftiR faður*
> *sinn, Asi, Kætilbiorn, GæiRR æftiR svær s(inn) . . . (æ)fti(R)*
> *boa(nda) . . .*

Wessén makes no mention of Brate's attribution to Asmund.

Although U846 displays a slight similarity to works of Asmund, notably in the crosses (Brate's only observation), there can be no question of attributing this stone to the master. As a result of the unskillful execution of the stone, in fact, it is difficult to make any sense out of the apparently B-3 designs, and the reading is also in many respects uncertain.

Those features which can be interpreted do not point toward but rather away from Asmund. The rune forms ᛋᚼ s, ᛒ ᚴ b, ᚱ ᛁᚱ ᛁᚱ r, and ᛁᚿ ᛁᚿ u, the presumable formulation *letu rista runaR þessaR*, and the spelling **kair** *GæiRR* are not in accordance with Asmundic practice. U846 is, therefore, very likely the work of another runographer, who may have observed some of the nearby Asmund-stones.

(48) U860 (Måsta, Balingsta sn.). Now in the village of Balingsta:

> fa[s]tbiurn' uk þuru**þ**r' litu rita stin **þ**ino' [abtiR inkifast buanta sin]
> [k]u[i]**þ** hia[l]bi hons ant uku**þ**s [m]u**þ**iR
> *Fastbiorn ok Þoruðr letu retta stæin þenna æftiR Ingifast, boanda*
> *sinn. Guð hialpi hans and ok Guðs moðiR.*

As early as 1726 Olof Celsius attributed this stone to Asmund. Subsequent scholars are in agreement with Celsius. The reason for such a consensus is that U860 represents a companion stone to U859, which is signed by Asmund. Celsius in fact thought Asmund carved U859 as a replacement for U860 after discovering that he had made errors in the latter. The attribution is strengthened not only by the formulation of U859 but also by a comparison of the manner of execution. As Wessén points out,[27] on both U859 and U860 the bottoms of the incisions have not been smoothed but have been left "*skrovliga och ojämna*" (rough and uneven).

Correspondences in rune form are also enlightening. On U860 one finds again the typical forms ᚢ, ᚦ, ᚱ, and ᛋ. The animal figures can be compared with those on Asmund's signed stones U969 and U1144.

Since Asmund's authorship is almost beyond doubt, it is interesting to note that the design of the text band is zoomorphically unorthodox, consisting of two heads and one body, rather than of a head and tail or two heads and two tails. The design is thus a hybrid of Types A and B. A similar phenomenon can be observed on L1050, which appears to have three heads and one tail.

(49) U866 (Björnome, Gryta sn.):

krukr · lit[ri]t[a] stin þino · aftiR · kara fạ. . . [hi]albi honsalukuþs muþiR

KrokR let retta stæin þenna æftiR Kara, fa(ður sinn. Guð) hialpi hans salu ok Guðs moðiR.

The stone has been ascribed to Asmund by Nils Gustav Stahre (cited by Wessén under U866), with whom Wessén is in complete agreement. Brate does not treat U866.

The evidence shows that Stahre's attribution is correct. The memorial formula with *letu retta stæin þenna æftiR* and the prayer augmented with *ok Guðs moðiR* are typical. The design bears comparison with Asmund's signed (and nearby) U824, U847, U871, and U884, all of Type A-3. The smoothly worked surface and the details of carving (sketching, for example) are additional evidence; the rune forms (note the narrow **b**- and **þ**-runes) and such familiar spellings as **þino** and **honsalukuþs** make it very likely that Asmund carved U866.

(50) U875 (Focksta, Hagby sn.):

· þurui · auk · inkikirþ · auk · þialfi · þauh litu rita stin þino · aftiR kalf · buanta þuruiaR · kuþ hialbi honsalukuþs muþiR

Þyrvi ok Ingigærð ok Þialfi þau letu retta stæin þenna æftiR Kalf, boanda ÞyrviaR. Guð hialpi hans salu ok Guðs moðiR.[28]

[27]Through an error of numbering, Wessén writes U852 instead of U859.

[28]In disagreement with Wessén, I read **þauh** and **salu**.

Celsius was the first to connect this stone to Asmund; he was subsequently joined by von Friesen and Wessén. Brate makes no mention of U875.

Although the design of the rune animal is most unusual, there are ornamental details that are characteristic of Asmund. The cross (B-4 with rounded blades) and the head of the rune animal (including the bulb) are familiar. The formulation *(letu retta stæin þenna æftiR, Guð hialpi hans salu ok Guðs moðiR)* and the orthography (þauh, þino, aftiR) add supporting evidence to the attribution.

The surface of the stone has not been smoothed, a circumstance perhaps due in some way to its former use as an offering stone, but the chisel has been deftly wielded. Above all, the rune forms are Asmund's. One may note, in addition to the obvious s-, a-, n-, and o-runes, the forms ᚱ (in **inkikirþ**), ᚱ (in **rita**), ᚠ (in **kalf**), and ᚼ (in **þuruiaR**). Ornamental lines serve as the mainstaves of runes 7 (**u**) and 63 (**r**).

It is highly probable that Asmund carved U875.

(51) U901 (Hamö, Läby sn.). Now in the Statens historiska museum, Stockholm:

...arl·uk ihulbiurn·litu rita stono þisa·ukirua bru þisa·at iafur faþur si...hialbi ont hos

...*Karl ok Igulbiorn letu retta stæina þessa ok gærva bro þessa at Iofur, faður sinn. (Guð) hialpi and hans.*

(52) U904 (Västerby, Läby vad, Läby sn.):

+iarl+ukarl+uk ihulbiurn litu rita stino þisa+ukirua bru þisa+abtiR+ iufur+faþur sin

Iarl ok Karl ok Igulbiorn letu retta stæina þessa ok gærva bro þessa æftiR Iofur, faður sinn.

The runologists Brate, von Friesen, and Wessén are agreed in attributing both stones of the double monument to Asmund. Under U901 Wessén has put forth detailed arguments to support his conviction and has made it very clear that he has no doubts about the authorship of the stone.

A closer look at both stones, however, reveals not only features distinctive for Asmund, but also some characteristic traits associated with Þorfast, as well as features common to both of them. Both Þorfast and Asmund use the h-rune as fricative /g/ and let a single rune do service as the concluding sound of one word and the initial one of the next. The two carvers also share the rune forms ⟨, ⟨ , ⟨ , ⟨ , and ⟨ . Reversed runes (U901), the spelling **abtiR**, and pictorial representation can also be found in the works of both. Thus, these features cannot, strictly speaking, be used to distinguish them.

There are, however, runographic elements on both U901 and U904 that are characteristic of Þorfast and not of Asmund. The spelling **stono stæina** may well be one of these. Wessén assumes that Asmund carved the first o-rune under the influence of the second, but it seems more reasonable to compare the representation of the diphthong /æi/ by means of the o-rune in the word "stone" with its only other attested occurrence in the Upplandic inscriptions (**ston**) and with a similar representation of the same diphthong in the form **rosa** *ræisa* 'raise' on U987, an unsigned work of Þorfast. Þorfast is also well known for his curious use of the o-rune as oral /a/ and for his monophthongal spellings **rasa** *ræisa* (U599, U629) and **stan** (U599). A further feature of U901 that brings Þorfast to mind is the form of the first b-rune, ⟨ .

U904 appears to bear more evidence of Þorfast. Here one finds the word divider with the form +, the rune forms ⟨, ⟨ (wide, in contrast to Asmund's), and especially ⟨ **b** (in **abtiR**). The cross, too, with its angular rays, is more characteristic of Þorfast than of Asmund, as are the rune-animal's pointed ears.

What gives one pause, however, is the discovery of features on both stones that are associated with Asmund and not with Þorfast. These include, on U901, a consistent use of the word divider ', the r-rune ⟨ or ⟨ and the þ-rune ⟨ , the cross with rounded blades, the shape and detail of the rune-animal's head, and the occurrence in two out of three cases of the rune form ⟨ **b**. Similarly, on U904 one should note the basic design of the rune animal and the occurrence of two b-runes with the form ⟨ and one r-rune with the form ⟨ . It could also be argued that the smaller decorative serpents are features of Asmund's style rather than Þorfast's.

Such observations as the above tend more to cloud the picture than to clarify it. The conflicting features are intermingled to a degree that makes it impossible to discover a division of labor. If the two runographers shared in the creation of these monuments, as the evidence seems to suggest, our tools are not adequate to describe their relationship. The only safe conclusion is that Asmund probably did U901 and U904 with some collaboration on the part of Þorfast.

(53) U903 (Västerby, Läby sn.):

    sibiurn' auk sihtarf' ritu stin þino' abtiR' aisti[n] auk abtiR sitiarf'
    bruþr sina suniR hukals ritu sti þino'

Sigbiorn ok SigdiarfR rettu stæin þenna æftiR Øystæin ok æftiR Sig-diarf, brøðr sina. SyniR Hugals rettu stæin þenna.

Both Brate and Wessén attribute the stone to Asmund.

In contrast to the nearby U901 and U904, in which elements foreign to Asmund were discovered, U903 seems to be safely attributable to Asmund alone. The arch of the text band forms a point at the top that occurs also on U860 (according to older drawings). The cross is Asmund's familiar one. The rune forms are recognizable from the works that Asmund has signed. Especially characteristic are the forms in **þino** (first occurrence) and the narrow **b**-runes. An ornamental line is employed in the **a**-rune of **hukals** and the **þ**-rune of the second occurrence of **þino**.

Most orthographic traits of U903 are typical of Asmund, as is evident in the spellings **sihtarf, abtiR, þino**. The name that is written **hukals** is not altogether certain, since the **k**-rune in this name could stand for /gg/, as in the form *Huggalz*, attested from 1399 (cited by Wessén). The omission of the /g/ in *Sigbiorn* and *Sigdiarf* on U903 can be compared to Asmund's omission of the /þ/ in *faður*, *broður*, or with the spelling **sybiarn** on (Fot's?) U297, which indicates the extent to which the /g/ was weakly articulated.[29] The lack of a nominative ending in **sihtarf** is possibly matched by the **inkialt** on U932.

(54) U1003 (Frötuna, Rasbo sn.). Two fragments:

A: . . . þrihu̦i . . .

B: . . . btiRr . . .

(55) U1004 (Frötuna, Rasbo sn.). A picture stone, without inscription.

Bengt Bergman[30] attributed the fragments and the picture stone to Asmund, and Wessén, with some reservation, concurs. As grounds for attribution the pictorial representations are cited above all. The rider on U1003B is compared with the figures on U901, and the animal on U1004 is likened to that on the B-side of U884. Wessén further points to the use of reversed runes and the spelling . . . **btiR**, which he interprets as *æftiR*.

As Wessén acknowledges, there is considerable risk in attributing such fragmentary material to a known carver. In this case the runographer Þorfast—who also writes **abtiR**, uses reversed runes, and has depicted a horse and rider on his U599—must be reckoned with. Were

---

[29]See also the report of a newly found fragment with the same spelling, in Sven B. F. Jansson, "Uppländska runstensfynd," *Fornvännen* 48 (1953): 270–272.

[30]Bengt Bergman, *Uppländsk run- och bildstensristning*, p. 77.

the þ-rune of U1003A Þorfast's typical ↑, there would be little doubt that
he carved the fragments here in question. Since this is not the case and
since the horse and rider resemble not so much Þorfast's as Asmund's on
the attributed U375, the attribution to Asmund is more likely. In particular, it is characteristic of Asmund's animal representations to depict
the juncture of limb and body by means of a spiral. More telling resemblances than those that Wessén and Bergman point out are found in the
figures on U1144 (to U1004) and U375 (to U1003A). As a final piece of
evidence, the strange dotted r-rune of U1003B may be compared to the
dotted b-rune on L1049.

(56) U1009 (Yrsta, Rasbo sn.):

uaiþr...————·litu rita stin þino abtiR·fastbiurn·faþur siṇ
uaiþr... *letu retta stæin þenna æftiR Fastbiorn, faður sinn.*

Both Brate and Wessén view this stone as the work of Asmund.

The similarities to Asmund's stones are clear: the formulation; the
spellings **þino**, **abtiR**; the rune-animal's head and tail (cf. similarly
"split" tails on U301, U824, U871, U969, U986); the rune forms ⊣, ↑, ↑,
ʅ (in **stin**), and ʀ (in **fastbiurn**); the form and function of the word divider; and the cutting and carving technique. Atypical of Asmund are
the rune forms ʮ (in **fastbiurn**), ∿ (in **sin**), and ß (in **fastbiurn**), but
these divergences from his usual forms are not sufficient in themselves
to warrant assuming another carver.

The interpretation of **uaiþr** as the name *Veðr*, mentioned as a possibility by Wessén, gains probability in light of the spelling **hruþailfr** *Hroð-
ælfR* on U357, which was attributed to Asmund.

The design of U1009 is a puzzle for Wessén, who likens it somewhat
unconvincingly to that of U875. It seems more apt to compare it to U540,
which was also of unorthodox design. The most likely reconstructions of
the two rune animals have the forms shown in fig. 8.17. In view of such
similarities, the attribution of U1009 to Asmund seems very likely correct.

U540   U1009

Figure 8.17. Reconstruction of two rune animals

(57) U1012 (Rasbokils kyrka):

sbraki·uk þur·biurn·uk uþuhin·ukinlauh·uk aˌfriþr·þaun litu rita·
aftiR biurn faþụ–sin

*Spraki ok Þorbiorn ok Oþv(a)ginn ok Ginnlaug ok Afriðr (?) þaun letu
retta æftiR Biorn, faðu(r) sinn.*

The attribution to Asmund is made by both Brate and Wessén.

The design of U1012 is a variant of A-3, with the forepart of the rune
animal making a complete loop, as is also the case in U346. The split tail
can also be observed in Asmund's signed carvings (see above under
U1009), and the head, with its rounded ear and Westlund bulb, is almost
identical to those on Asmund's Ängeby-stone (U356), which also bears a
cross of exactly the same form.

The abbreviated memorial formula *letu retta æftiR* is not attested in
Asmund's signed works, and a prayer—usually distinctive—does not
occur.

Orthographically, U1012 is typical of Asmund; thus, **ukinlauh** *ok
Ginnlaug*, **aftiR, biurn**. The omission of the a-rune in **uþuhin** *Oþvaginn*
can be compared to the omission of the i-rune in **urlati** *Virlandi* on U346.
The word divider between **þur** and **biurn** in the name *Þorbiorn* is paralleled by the form **mar·kaþi** *markaði* on U346.

Above all, the rune forms of U1012 are Asmund's. There are none of
the atypical allographs found in some other works (e.g., U901, U904),
which make Asmund's authorship doubtful. Note especially the narrow
b-, þ-, and f-runes.

U1012 is without a doubt one of Asmund's most successful works.

(58) U1031 (Hånsta, Lena sn.):

[sihtia]rf· auk humbiurn· [auk þur]ḅiurn· þiR lit[uˌ r[i]ṭa stin þino
auk b[ru·kira at iu]n faþur·[sin]

*Sigdiarf(R) ok Ho(l)mbiorn ok Þorbiorn þæiR letu retta stæin þenna
ok bro gæra at Ion, faður sinn.*

Brate and Wessén both assign this work to Asmund. Prior to them,
Anders Grape termed U1031 "a stone in Asmund's manner."[31]

The key comparison here, as scholars have recognized, is with U1142,
signed by Asmund and Vigmar. As Wessén remarks, "with the help of
the Åbyggeby-stone one can reconstruct the original appearance of the
Hånsta-stone quite well." The artistic similarities are particularly strik-

---

[31]Anders Grape, *Studier över de i fornsvenskan inlånade personnamnen*, I, 80. Grape
seems to have derived his runologic judgments from von Friesen.

ing in such details as the form and position of the winged dragon and the cross, the latter with its extended lower arm.

The formulation agrees quite well with Asmund's practices except for the use of *at* instead of *æftiR*. The reading here is uncertain, however; one would have expected something like **bru kiruabtiR**, as on U859.

The shapes of the runes are not in conflict with Asmund's style, but one cannot avoid taking notice of an atypical unsteadiness in the positions of the runes, as in the mainstaves of **þino auk**, which are not all parallel or straight. The same unsteady lines are also found occasionally in the carving. Whether this unsteadiness indicates that an assistant executed part of the inscription is uncertain. What is clear is that Asmund is the only known carver to whom U1031 can be attributed.

(59) U1035 (Tensta kyrka):

> ... **kiat auk...u rita stin þinaftiR kuih faþur sin si[kr]iþr at buanta si...**
>
> ...*ok... (let)u retta stæin þenna æftiR Kvig, faður sinn, Sigriðr at boanda si(nn).*

This stone has not been associated with Asmund previously. Brate attributed it to "Tälve" by comparison with U948 (signed by Þialfi and Orøkia). Wessén quite rightly rejects this attribution, but he does not offer another. His suggestion that U1035 might be later than U460, U463, and U948 would, however, probably rule out Asmund.

It is true that a first look at U1035 does not bring Asmund to mind, probably because none of his signed rune animals possesses the same form, a design generally associated with carvers several decades younger than Asmund. Yet precisely the same design can be found on a stone signed by Asmund, not in the rune animal but rather in the decorative serpent on the right side of U1144. Note especially the manner in which the forepart of the animal is gracefully arched backward, its snout making contact with its body. Both have haunches ornamented by means of a spiral and similar feet or claws. The rune animals of U130 and U901 also exhibit these features.

Another ornamental likeness to Asmund's work can be seen in the form of the smaller serpents. Like those on U859 and U1142, their heads appear to be wedged firmly into corners formed by the cross or other intersecting ornamental lines. The cross itself has Asmund's characteristically rounded blades; it differs from his other crosses of Type B-4 only in that the ring is composed of one line rather than two. Precisely the same cross occurs, however, on U1043, a stone that will be attributed to Asmund.

The main memorial formula is Asmund's typical one, with *letu retta stæin þenna æftiR*. The additional commemoration, *Sigriðr at boanda sinn*, is not attested in Asmund's signed inscriptions, but occurs in the attributed U240.

Orthographically the inscription on U1035 corresponds to Asmund's practices, and, were there an example of the o-rune with sound value /aⁿ/, the stone would have probably been associated with Asmund long ago. The only occasion for this spelling feature would have been in the word *þenna*, and here the carver has made use of a different Asmundic practice by allowing an a-rune to serve simultaneously as the final rune of *þenna* and the initial one of *æftiR*; thus, **þinaftiR**. Compare the spelling **þinabtiR** on Asmund's signed U824, as well as **þinoftiR** on U194, U419, and U1149 and **þinobtiR** on U372. The fricative /g/ of *Kvig* is spelled with the h-rune, Asmund's usual practice, but that of *Sigriðr* with the k-rune, as in the same name on U884. The u-rune functions as /o/ in **buanta** *boanda*. No dotted runes occur.

The forms of the runes are for the most part like Asmund's: the a-, o-, and n-runes with branches on one side of the mainstaff; the s-rune ᚼ of **sin** with short, slightly falling middle bar; the ᚼ of **kuih**; and the ᛏ of **stin**. The r-rune with distinctive form ᚱ does not occur, but the other forms (ᚱ ᚱ) are well attested in Asmund's work. The þ-rune of **faþur** with form ᚦ can be seen in U859 (**kuþ**) and U871 (**auþulfr**); the same rune with form ᚦ (in **þinaftiR** on U1035), which is an inversion of the previous form, can be found in the **þino** of U871. The s-rune of **stin** with the atypical form ᚼ is attested twice in U1142 (**stin** and **risti**). Two unusual forms without exact correspondences remain: the a-rune (?) of ... **kiat** with the form ᚨ, and the "Swedish-Norwegian" t-rune ᛁ in **buanta**. The first may be compared to the forms ᚨ **n** (?) on U956, ᚼ **n** (= a) on U871, and (somewhat less appropriately) to the ᚦ **o** on U824; the short-branched t-rune is paralleled by a t-rune with the form ᚠ on U356. All these inscriptions are signed by Asmund. Among the works attributed to him, U904 and possibly U860 have short-branched t-runes with the form ᛁ .

U1035 is from a technical point of view in keeping with Asmund's high standards. It was originally an attractive piece of stone, of reddish granite, like many of Asmund's works. The lines are deeply and surely carved. "It was no doubt a very lovely stone," writes Wessén. It can be attributed to Asmund with a moderate degree of certainty.

(60) U1043 (Onslunda, Tensta sn.):

u[lfr·]auk·kuþfastr·aukuþ[muntr· þ-...it]u rita stin þino·aftiR
ufih·fa[þ]ur sịn·kuþ hinlbi ont h̲–ns

UlfR ok Guðfastr ok Guðmundr þ(æiR l)etu retta stæin þenna æftiR
Ofæig, faður sinn. Guð hialpi and hans.

The attribution to Asmund is by both Brate and Wessén.

Most of the correspondences with works by Asmund are obvious and have been pointed out by Brate and Wessén: the o-rune in þino and ont, the u-rune and h-rune in ufih *Ofæig,* the infrequency of a word divider and its form, the spelling aukuþmuntr with a single rune read twice, the form of the cross, and, especially, the winged dragon. The only element that Wessén finds difficult to explain is the "design, which is foreign to Åsmund," and "apparently determined by the shape of the stone." The notion that this design, a variant of Type C, is foreign to Asmund (and a result of the shape of the stone) can be dismissed by pointing out the same basic design on his signed U986 and his unsigned U240.

Many of Asmund's familiar rune forms occur (ᚽ, ᛏ, ᚦ, ᚼ), but at the same time there are atypical forms like ᚱ, ᚱ, ᚦ, and ᛁᛁ. These divergences do not carry enough weight by themselves to alter the traditional attribution to Asmund.

(61) U1138 (Hållen, Runhällsbacken [Storgransbotten], Hållnäs sn.):

...n...rais...t̲...insa×abtiR×ui--...n sin...n̲...--l×a...ai...u
--...-r-×u----n...-almuntar̄-×bryþR×   ---þ-×-u------×
marak...

...ræisa (stæin) þennsa æftiR...(su)n sinn...brøðr...markaði (?).

Brate read the signature [osmunt]r marka[þi] from a photograph by von Friesen and pointed to abtiR as further evidence of Asmund's authorship. Jansson dismisses the attribution on technical and ornamental grounds and agrees with von Friesen that U1138 shows greater correspondences with U1163 and U1175 (misnumbered in *Runverket* as U1164 and U1177).

The stone is perhaps too damaged to analyze fully, but many features that diverge from Asmund's style can be pointed out. Thus, bryþR with a dotted rune and palatal /R/ and the consistent use of the rune form ᚼ and word divider × are in conflict with Asmund's habits. It is very unlikely that Asmund carved U1138.

(62) U1145 (Yttrö, Tierps sn.):

꞉rikr ꞏ lit raisa stain þino ꞏ abtiR fasta faþur sin auk þauh kunþruþr ꞏ
k[uþ hial]bi honsalukuþs muþiR

RikR let ræisa stæin þenna æftiR Fasta, faður sinn ok þau Gunnþruðr.
Guð hialpi hans salu ok Guðs moðiR.

The first to link this stone with Asmund Karasun was Celsius. Both Brate and Jansson have subsequently voiced the same attribution.

In terms of design, the work by Asmund with which U1145 should be compared is U998; in both monuments two rune animals are juxtaposed head-to-tail and in identical positions. On U998 a third text band occupies the center of the stone, while on U1145 this space is reserved for the cross. There are no exact parallels to this cross, a Type A-3, in Asmund's signed works, that on U1149 being perhaps closest (Type A-5, an A-3 with rays). In fact, only seven other examples exist in Uppland of the cross that appears on U1145 (U18, U194, U258, U409, U924, U936, and U940); one of these (U194) is attributed to Asmund, another (U409) to Þorfast.

Of the rune-animal heads on U1145, only one can now be made out; it closely resembles the heads on U1149, L1049, and L1053. The formulation with *ræisa* is not Asmund's usual one, but it is attested twice (U356, U998) in his signed inscriptions. The prayer is Asmund's distinctive one.

Orthographically U1145 is in perfect accordance with Asmund's habits; thus, **þino**, **abtiR**, **honsalukuþs**, and above all **þauh**. The nominative ending after a velar consonant is written with normal /r/ in **rikr** *RikR*, as in the attributed U431, U540, and U866.

From a technical point of view, U1145 could well have been executed by Asmund, who typically selects granite of an attractive red hue and smoothes the surface before carving. The lines have been deftly hewn.

Thus far, everything about U1145 has pointed to Asmund. For the most part the same can be said of the rune forms, for example, ᛆ, ᚠ, ᚴ, ᚼ, ᛏ, ᚱ (in **rikr**, **raisa**, **faþur**), and ᛋ (in **fasta**, **hons**). Somewhat disturbing, however, are the two s-runes with form ᛐ in *ræisa stæin*. This shape is found rarely in Asmund's work, but occurs in Svæin's part of U1149 and L1049, as well as in the nearby U1142 and U1144, stones that Asmund executed with Vigmar and **hiriaR**, respectively. Unfortunately, it is impossible to attribute U1145 to Vigmar or to **hiriaR**, since we are in doubt about their share in the stones bearing their names. With Svæin we are in a better position, and were there additional evidence, such as **t**- and **l**-runes with branches consistently from the text band (↑ ↑) or a predominance of **þ**-runes with the overround form **Þ**, we would be justified in linking U1145 to Svæin. Since this is not the case, it is more reasonable to assign the stone to Asmund, with the suggestion that a second carver may have played a subordinate role, as in U1142 and U1144.

The following fragment was discovered in 1956 and was published by Jansson in *Fornvännen* 54 (1959): 259–260, where it is attributed to Asmund:

(63) Österlisa, Länna sn.:
     ...———u rita stin...
     ... *(let)u retta stæin* ...

Jansson cites carving technique, formulation (**litu rita**), and ornamentation as grounds for attribution.

There can be little doubt that Jansson is correct, in spite of the fact that Þorfast was active in the area from which the stone comes. The arch-necked animal figure on the Österlisa fragment bears comparison with those on Asmund's U240, U375, U901, and U1003.

OTHER MONUMENTS PERHAPS CONNECTED TO ASMUND

There remains a number of runic monuments bearing some apparent connection with Asmund (or Þorfast), but for which the evidence is insufficient to permit trustworthy runographic speculation, often because the monument is lost or damaged.

(64) U364 (Gådersta, Skepptuna sn.):
     karsi·auk·kar–...sin·han uaR tauþr i·huitauaþum
     Karsi ok... sinn. Hann vaR dauðr i hvitavaðum.

This fragment is known only through older sources. From these drawings the stone appears to resemble U343 (attributed to Asmund), and the inscription indicates that both stones were raised by the same people. Unfortunately the core of the memorial formula is missing, so that typically Asmundic features, such as **rita**, **stin**, **þino**, and **abtiR**, cannot be verified. What remains of the inscription bears no Asmundic traits, and the spelling **han** is, in fact, atypical. The heads of the rune animals are closer to Þorfast's style than to Asmund's, and a comparison with U629 is quite enlightening. Note also the bird depicted on U629 and what appears to be a similar creature on U365, from the same location as

U364. If we can trust the older drawing, the s-runes of U364 are not like Asmund's but rather like Þorfast's. It would be extremely risky, however, to base an attribution on such information. The most we can say is that U364 is clearly related to Asmund's style and could have been carved by Þorfast.

(65) U374 (Örby, Skepptuna sn.):

> ...litu' rita: stain þino·iftiR·o–hu...an hon fil o kriklontr kuþ hi–lbi sal...
>
> ...*letu retta stæin þenna æftiR...Hann fell a Grikkland(i). Guð hi(a)lpi sal(u).*

This stone is also lost and has not previously been discussed in relation to Asmund, but the formulation *letu retta stæin þenna æftiR* and the orthographic use of the o-rune (**þino, hon, o, kriklontr**) do bring Asmund to mind. The rune forms, insofar as they are trustworthy in Peringskiöld's drawing, are not contrary to Asmund's. Wessén's statement that "the inscription has a-, n-, o-, and t-runes with branches on one side" is ambiguous. Some of these runes are short branched, while others have normal forms, a mixture noted in stones signed by Asmund (e.g., U356). The design of U374 does not bear any striking resemblance to any of Asmund's works, but it does not stand in opposition to his style.

The third person singular preterite of the verb "to fall" occurs seven times in the Upplandic inscriptions, twice as *fioll* and five times as *fell*. Four of the latter are spelled **fil**, one of them on the famous Ekilla-bro-stone (U644), an Ingvar-stone not associated with Asmund. The remaining three cases of **fil** *fell* are the one in question here (U374) and Asmund's signed inscriptions U346 and U356.[32]

It is not easy to weigh the evidence regarding this inscription, largely because it is no longer accessible to examination. A cautious conclusion would be in order: Asmund could have carved U374.

(66) U442 (Prästgården, Odensala sn.):

> bṛusi' u–þ–...alụ...–t...rit... faþu...
> *Brusi...*

Unlike the preceding stone, this one is preserved. Unfortunately, almost all the surface of the stone has flaked off, so that the ornamentation and the inscription have for all practical purposes been lost. Since it was

---

[32]The data are **fal** U158; **fil** U346, U356, U374, U644; **fial** U611; **–ial** U616.

not discovered until 1895, there are no older drawings of U442 that might show the stone in better condition.

The rune animal of U442 appears to have been something like the Type C design of U1035 and the right serpent of U1144. The few runes that are preserved are reversed runes and have forms not unlike Asmund's: ᛁ, ᚨ, ᛋ,ᚱ. The word divider is a short vertical stroke. The word **rita** *retta* may be present.

It is therefore not impossible that Asmund·carved U442.

(67) U548 (Husby-Lyhundra kyrka).

In contrast to the previous stones, this one bears no inscription, but a depiction of an animal with horns. As early as 1876 the animal figure was likened to that on U1004, which has been tentatively attributed to Asmund.[33] In the case of U1004, supporting evidence was taken from U1003, but U548 does not appear to be related to any other stones in its vicinity. One can only suggest, therefore, that Asmund could have carved U548.

(68) U570 (Hållsta, Lohärads sn.):

ˣ**aki**ˣ**a̱uk**ˣ**su[ai]n[**ˣ**þiR**ˣ**litu raisa**ˣ**stain**ˣ**if]t̠iR utrika̱**ˣ**f̠[aþu]r**ˣ**sin**ˣ
Aki ok Svæinn þæiR letu ræisa stæin æftiR Otrygga, faður sinn.

This severely damaged rune stone is probably to be attributed to Þorfast. The design is very close to Asmund's U356, but an even more appropriate comparison is U418, which bears evidence of both Asmund and Þorfast. Unfortunately, the inscription, reconstructed with the help of older readings, does not reveal any of Þorfast's unusual spellings. On the other hand, it is possible that the reading of Bureus in Fa10:2, which has **rasa** for *ræisa*, is more accurate than other readings, which have **raisa**. (Wessén assumed that the i-rune of Fa10:2 was "skipped.") The spelling **rasa** is typical of Þorfast. There are no þ-runes preserved that would establish Þorfast's authorship beyond a doubt, but the s-runes are characteristic, as is the word divider.

(69) U856 (Frövi, Balingsta sn.):

hukal̠–r̠ˡ **–––r–**...**[in þin–at]**...**u–[a]uk br̠u k–rua**
...*(stæ)in þenna at* ... *ok bro gærva.*

This stone is in a condition similar to U570. The spellings **bru** *bro* (with the u-rune for /o/) and **k–rua** *gærva* (with semi-vowel preserved)

---

[33]*Upplands fornminnesförenings tidskrift* 5 (1876): 113.

are reminiscent of Asmund (cf. the nearby U859 with **bru kirua**), as is the probable formulation with *let retta stæin þenna*. Ornamentally the stone bears comparison with Asmund's works of A-3 design (e. g., U824, U847, U871). It also resembles U969, not only in terms of design but also from a technical point of view. On both there are lines that have only been shallowly sketched, giving the carvings an unfinished appearance.

Since the rune forms of U856 do not afford any convincing evidence, one cannot attribute the stone to Asmund, but merely admit that his authorship is not impossible.

(70) U885 (Ingla, Skogstibble sn.):
**uikR ' auk sihstain ' aukarl ' þaiR l[itu ']stain ' rita ' at sihat ' faþur sin '
iu**
*VigR ok Sigstæinn ok Karl þæiR letu stæin retta at Sigvat, faður
sinn...*

There is something undeniably reminiscent of Asmund in this stone. Although the surface of the stone has suffered somewhat from weathering, it is clear that the design of U885 agrees well with Asmund's nearby stones of Type A-3, especially U871 and U884. The abrupt dip that one line of the rune-animal's "neck" makes (just opposite the point at which the snout makes contact) is also a stylistic detail of the rune animal of U871. The pattern of figure eights on the right side of the stone is not unlike those on U859 and U986. The cross is a simple Type A, found also on U871. Unusual, however, is the placement of the cross within a looped band, a feature more frequent later in the century, in the work of Öpir and his followers. Yet, if we accept Wessén's identification of the two men named Vig on U884 and U885, then the latter is an earlier work than a (signed) Asmund-stone.

The formulation is not Asmund's usual one, but the inverted formula *let stæin retta* occurs also on U418, a stone associated in some way with Asmund.

Orthographic features with correspondences in Asmund's work can be seen in **aukarl** *ok Karl* (cf. L1053) and **sihstain** *Sigstæinn*. The spelling **sihat** *Sigvat* occurs on the attributed U372. On the other hand, the word divider is used with more frequency than is the case in Asmund's inscriptions; nor does the palatal /R/ after velar consonants (**uikR** *VigR*) correspond to Asmund's habits (cf. **krukr** *KrokR* on U866). This latter objection may be dismissed if one accepts the alternative reading **uikiR** *VigæiRR*; the identification with Vig on U884 then collapses.

In a similar fashion, the rune forms on U885 give conflicting evidence. Along with typical forms, such as ᚱ (in **karl, faþur**), ᛏ (in **stain**), ᚿ (in **auk**), and ᚦ (**þaiR, stain**), one notes the atypical form ᚦ (**þaiR, faþur**) and a consistently greater breadth than we are accustomed to finding in Asmund's work.

Thus, with some hesitation we may say that Asmund could have carved U885.

The final example of a rune stone that offers inconclusive runographical evidence is the following:

(71) U890 (Österby, Ålands sn.):

— — —i ꞏ auk fasṭaþr ꞏ auk þuruḷ … ṭaþur sin : aukuþui aṭ lu — — — su — —
an — — furu i ukrikis
… *ok Fastaðr ok Þorul(fR)…faður sinn, ok Guðvi (?) at (?)…*

The design is familiar from Asmund's U356, although the rune-animals' heads agree perhaps more with Þorfast's. An ornamental detail that definitely brings Asmund to mind is the round knob in which one of the decorative serpents terminates. This relatively rare feature is present on U824 (signed by Asmund) and U1043 (attributed to Asmund). Furthermore, what appears to be an animal with an extended neck is found on the lower left part of the stone.

Orthographically there is not much to go on, but the spelling **aukuþui** *ok Guðvi* would suggest Asmund. Some of the rune forms (short-branched **a-** and **n**-runes, the ᚱ in **sin**, the ᚱ in **ukrikis**) correspond to Asmund's while others (the **s**-runes of **fastaþr** and **-su-**) do not. The runes are in general poorly executed.

For these reasons it is not possible to attribute U890 to Asmund, but a connection with his work seems undeniable.

The Runographer Auðmund

A runographer who, like Þorfast, appears to represent a follower of Asmund is Auðmund. There are two inscriptions signed with this name, and although they differ in a number of points, it is probable that both are by the same carver. As Jansson points out, the name *Auðmundr* is relatively uncommon.

(72) U598 (Borggärde, Hökhuvuds sn.):

**raskuiþr×lit ꞏ akua staiṇ — — kum[i] litu×risa ꞏ stain ꞏ aftiR ꞏ broþur ꞏ sin
×inkibiarn [o]þmunt ꞏ risti ꞏ runaR**

Raskviðr let haggva stæin... Gummi letu ræisa stæin æftiR broður sinn Ingibiorn. Auðmundr risti runaR.

(73) U1132 (Gimo, Skäfthammars sn.):

:liutr·uk·þroti·uk·oþuiþr·uk·þaiR·litu·rita·ifitR×[faþur×sin: baorn·fasti]þi:moþur·sin:oþmontr· risti·r...naR·

Liutr ok Þrotti ok Auðviðr þæiR letu retta æftiR faður sinn Biorn (ok) Fasthæiði moður sin(a). Auðmundr risti runaR.

As Brate writes, the basic structures of the rune animals are the same: "the double ring by which the serpent's neck and tail are intertwined." Nevertheless, in ornamental detail, particularly the heads, the two carvings differ considerably.

The cross on U598 is a basic Type A, while that on U1132 is an A-5 resembling Asmund's on L1053. Both of Auðmund's crosses are placed at the end of a vertically extended arm.

A clear connection with Asmund can be seen in the two animal figures that decorate Auðmund's U598 (cf. U1144).

Auðmund's rune forms vary considerably. In both inscriptions ᛅ alternates with ᛆ, the latter dominating at the end of the inscription. The **n**-rune is consistently short branched (ᚿ). The **s**-rune has forms ᛋ, ᛋ, ᛍ, ᛋ, and ᛌ. The **o**-rune is written ᚬ on U598, but ᚬ, ᚭ, and ᚭ on U1132. Unusual forms ᚦ **þ** and ᛐ **t** occur on U598 but not on U1132. Various word dividers occur: × ı :

Auðmund shares with Asmund the practice of using an ornamental line as the mainstaff of a rune.

The formulations of U598 and U1132 are both characterized by awkwardness; they have little in common otherwise.

Like Þorfast, Auðmund is inconsistent in his use of the **o**-rune, writing /o/, /u/, and /au/ with it, but not /aⁿ/. In **oþmunt**ı **risti** *Auðmundr risti* on U598 a single rune serves to conclude one word and begin the next (unless one assumes that the nominative ending *-r* has been omitted).

A stone not previously attributed can now be assigned to Auðmund:

(74) U1123 (Tuna kyrka):

...[ụ]h[i]·lituı **risa stain**ı **if[t]iR [o]ṭ k[a]iR**ı **faþur sin**

... *letu ræisa stæin æftiR OddgæiR, faður sinn.*

The design is not of the same structure as that of Auðmund's signed works, but the animal figure (originally perhaps two of them) can be likened to those on U598, and the cross is placed on a long arm. A "Swedish-Norwegian" t-rune (↑), attested in U598, occurs in **litu**. The o-rune is used as /o/ and has the form ↯ . The n-rune is short branched throughout; the a-rune varies. The spelling **risa stain** occurs in both U598 and U1123. Both inscriptions are also distinguished by unusual placement of the runes, which stand on the outer line of the text band and run from the lower right side upwards and around toward the left.

Brate speculates that "since Ödmund perpetuated some of Åsmund's carving characteristics and was active in a district not far from Åsmund's carving area, but through his use of o as an o-rune reveals that he is younger than Åsmund, it is possible that he is an apprentice of the latter, or perhaps son, as Torgöt to Fot."

It seems likely that both Þorfast and Auðmund were directly influenced by Asmund. In contrast, a number of runic monuments with superficial resemblances to Asmund's work indicate that he also exerted an indirect influence on Upplandic runography. Thus, U352 and U494 seem to imitate U301 with regard to design, and U484 is artistically reminiscent of U372 (attributed to Asmund). The design of Asmund's U346 may have influenced U361, a work by Uppland's arch-imitator Viseti. The nonsense inscription U483 boasts rune forms and a cross similar to Asmund's. The A-3 rune animals of Asmund's signed U824, U847, U871, and U884 may have inspired a host of similar stones, for example, U821 and U826 (the latter with **rita** and a cross like Asmund's). If the attribution of U1035 to Asmund is correct, we may reckon with additional artistic influence, for a number of other stones, no doubt later than Asmund's, have this design.

Summary of Signed and Attributed Stones

In the preceding investigation, thirteen runic monuments were found that clearly bear Asmund's signature and no other; such was considered highly probable for two further monuments. In addition, six inscriptions were discovered with multiple signatures containing Asmund's name. To these twenty-one signed monuments an additional fifteen were attributed to Asmund with considerable confidence, and sixteen more were deemed to be works probably by this master. In five of these sixteen, however, evidence of a co-runographer was suspected. Finally, six inscriptions were found that could have been executed by Asmund but that lacked sufficient evidence to permit a serious attribution.

To the runographer Þorfast, whose signature was found on two stones, three unsigned inscriptions were attributed with a fair degree of certainty. In another his authorship was considered likely. Another runographer revealing associations with Asmund was found in Auðmund, who signed two inscriptions. A third was attributed to him. These findings can be illustrated in tables 8.2 and 8.3.[34]

Table 8.2. Signed Inscriptions

Asmund alone	Probably Asmund alone	Asmund with others	Þorfast	Auðmund
U301	U368	U884	U599	U598
U346	L1050	U932	U629	U1132
U356		U1142		
U824		U1144		
U847		U1149		
U859		L1049		
U871				
U956				
U969				
U981				
U986				
U998				
L1053				

Table 8.3. Attributed Stones

Very likely Asmund	Probably Asmund	Could be Asmund	Very likely Þorfast	Probably Þorfast	Auðmund
U130	U193*	U367	U409	U570	U1123
U194	U322	U374	U525		
U203	U357	U442	U987		
U240	U372	U548			
U241	U375	U856			
U343	U418*	U885			
U344	U431				
U540	U645				
U860	U901*				
U866	U904*				
U875	U1003				
U903	U1004				
U1009	U1031				
U1012	U1035				
Österlisa	U1043				
Fragment	U1145*				

*Refers to those monuments that may have been executed in collaboration with another runographer.

[34]These figures may be compared with those of previous scholars: von Friesen (*Upplands runstenar*, p. 35) said that there are "not fewer than forty preserved stones carved

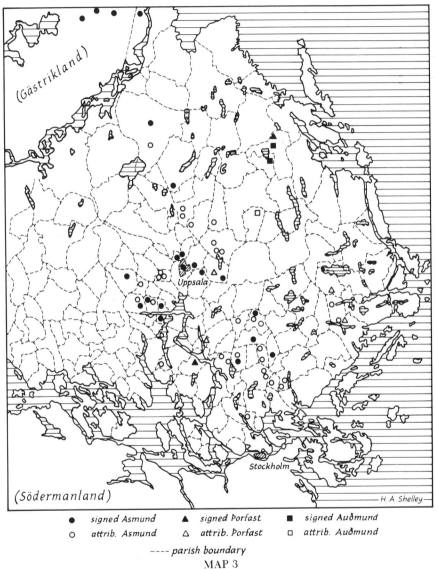

●	signed Asmund	▲	signed Þorfast	■	signed Auðmund
○	attrib. Asmund	△	attrib. Þorfast	□	attrib. Auðmund

---- *parish boundary*

MAP 3

by Asmund's hand. Half of them are signed." Brate found twenty-two stones signed by Asmund and attributed twenty-four more. Þorfast, according to von Friesen (ibid., p. 46), carved "six or seven stones in central and eastern Uppland." Brate assigned three stones to Þorfast: U599, U629, and U987. He also attributed (through a misreading) U1158 to a Þorfast, but he considered him a different carver with the same name.

As is evident from the map on page 150, these runic monuments are distributed over a relatively large area. They are conspicuously absent only in the far west, where Lifstæin, Tiðkumi, and Balli are the dominant runographers. On the other hand, Asmund's activity in Gästrikland is remarkable. He has executed three (four with the nearby Fleräng-stone, just over the border) monuments in an area that is relatively poor in runic antiquities. With the attribution of U645 to Asmund, it can no longer be maintained that Håbo härad lay "completely outside Asmund's field of activity" (Wessén under U438).

Interesting is the activity of Asmund's close followers, Þorfast and Auðmund. While the latter appears limited to a narrow geographic locality, Þorfast is active in various parts of Uppland, and his works can be found near Asmund's. This proximity is especially striking in the case of U525 (attributed to Þorfast) and the Österlisa fragment (attributed to Asmund), both from the same place. Similarly, U987, U409, and U570, attributed to Þorfast, appear in the vicinity of Asmund's U998, U431, and U540, respectively. Such evidence suggests that Þorfast was more than just a "follower" of Asmund; he was perhaps an assistant who worked very closely with the master. A similar conclusion was drawn from the analyses of U418, U901, and U904, in which traits characteristic of Þorfast seemed to appear side by side with those indicative of Asmund.

A remarkable feature of the signatures on both U956 and L1053 is the occurrence of the patronymic; the runographer describes himself as the son of a certain Kari: *Asmundr Karasun*. Both Asmund's name and that of his father are relatively common throughout the north and are well attested in the runic inscriptions. However, over half of the occurrences of the name *Asmundr* in Swedish runic inscriptions refer to Asmund Karasun himself. In Uppland the name is attested, excluding references to the runographer, only twice: on U233 and U479. (Neither inscription appears to be associated in any way with Asmund's work.) *Kari* is more frequent in Uppland, occurring in some eight or nine inscriptions in addition to U956, where it refers to Asmund's father.[35] The occurrence of *Kari* on U866, a stone attributed to Asmund, is no doubt a coincidence.

'One might well wonder what prompted Asmund to include the patronymic *Karasun* in two of his signatures. The use of the father's name

---

[35]These are U16, U37, U172 (?), U259, U532, U683, U797, U866, and U1146. The information given in *Runverket* under U797, that the name *Kari* is "attested ten times in Swedish runic inscriptions," is incorrect. Perhaps the word "Upplandic" was intended.

to identify the son is not common in the runic inscriptions, and most of the occurrences employ the word *arfi* 'heir, son', reflecting perhaps the importance of inheritance rights. Thus, *(æftiR) Vafra arfa* U354, *Kari Munulfs arfi* U259. Asmund's signatures are clearly not intended as legal documents. Nor is there another known runographer with the name *Asmundr*, from whom Asmund Karasun might wish to distinguish himself.

On the other hand, there is one Upplandic inscription that parallels U956 and L1053 in its use of the patronymic in a signature. U308 is signed with the words *Þorgautr risti runaR þessaR, Fots arfi*. Unlike Asmund's father, Þorgaut's can be more precisely identified; he is the master runographer Fot, who has himself signed six or eight runic monuments.

In the absence of further evidence it is rather bold to suggest that Kari was also a runographer, who transmitted his art to his son Asmund. Nevertheless, the suggestion has been made that runography was an inherited profession.[36] But until such time as an inscription is discovered bearing the signature of a *Kari*, this hypothesis must remain purely speculative.[37]

CHRONOLOGICAL QUESTIONS

Dating the Upplandic inscriptions constitutes one of the most difficult runological problems, for, although the general outlines are clear, the evidence provided in the inscriptions is so slight that a fine chronology involves great risks. None of the rules that have traditionally been employed is without exception, and most of them are based on assumptions that are tenuous indeed. The use of the o-rune, first advocated by Hildebrand in 1878, is a case in point. This rule states that, since stones commemorating those who died "with Ingvar" employ the o-rune as

[36]Jacobsen and Moltke, eds., *Danmarks runeindskrifter, Text*, Sp. 930: "In the case of professional carvers the trade was no doubt passed on from father to son."

[37]Speculation of a different sort may be found in Bengt Bergman's highly derivative article, "Asmund Kareson," in *Gästrikland*, ed. Märta Lindeberg, pp. 339–351. Bergman took over the notion that Asmund was a priest from von Friesen and considered the raising of runic monuments to be an organized effort on the part of the missionary church. As a kind of supporting evidence he offered the following (p. 349): "Why would the carvers themselves exhibit their names if not possibly because a good deal of them were missionaries and their names in connection with those of the members of the parish could be of a certain significance."

both /aⁿ/ and /o/,[38] the transition of sound values must have been occurring at the time they were erected, and since Ingvar is said to have died in 1041 (and his men with him), all inscriptions can be dated before or after this time according to whether the o-rune represents /aⁿ/ or /o/, respectively. This argument assumes that (1) the occurrence of the o-rune with multiple sound values indicates a transitionary period, (2) the Ingvar mentioned in the inscriptions is identical with the hero of *Yngvars saga viðførli*, (3) the traditional dating of Ingvar/Yngvar's death is trustworthy, (4) the news of Ingvar's death reached Uppland within a few years, and (5) the stones that commemorate men on this expedition were raised at the same time, and shortly after the news reached Uppland. If any of these assumptions were proven false, the entire argument would collapse, and the use of the o-rune would be of no value as a chronological criterion. In view of the considerable doubt concerning the date of Ingvar's death,[39] it is extremely risky to base a chronology on this orthographic rule, which indeed is sometimes directly contradicted in individual cases.[40]

To arrive at an absolute chronology it is necessary to relate the information found in the inscriptions to real historical events, which in the works of Asmund can be done to a limited extent.

Since the interpretation of **þasataimunt** on L1053 as "Æimund was king at that time" was rejected, the only information of historical character on a stone signed by Asmund is the reference, on L1049, to FrøygæiR's expedition. Unfortunately it is impossible to pinpoint the date of this expedition, and all attempts to do so thus far must be considered unsuccessful. The most influential has been that of Bugge, who does not date the expedition but the rune stones that speak of it:

The Swedish inscriptions carved in memory of Fröygeir and his men are carved by Christians. The oft-mentioned rune carver Aasmund Kaaresön was involved

[38]In reality the evidence of the Ingvar-stones is far from convincing. There are only two unambiguous uses of the o-rune as /aⁿ/—in the expression **o sirklanti** *a Særklandi* on Sö131 and Sö281. The spellings **ont**, **onunt**, and the like on U644, U654, U661, and U778 probably indicate the umlaut vowel /ǫ/, regardless of the nasal-oral contrast (cf. **foþur** on U654, U661). The o-rune is used as /o/ only in **for bort** on U1143, no longer readable. The carver of Vm19 uses the o-rune as non-nasal /a/ (or /æ/?) in **hiolbi.**

[39]1041, "eleven years after the fall of King Olaf Haraldsson the Holy," according to one version of the saga. The same year is given in various annals, which may have derived their information from the saga. See Elias Wessén, *Historiska runinskrifter*, pp. 35–36 (with additional references).

[40]For example, U844 and U845, or U513 and U540.

in the carving of the Gefle-stone's inscription [L1049]. These four Swedish rune stones seem to be approximately contemporaneous, even if L.324 [U611] and L.702 [U698] present a somewhat younger type of inscription than D.II, 251 [U518] and L1049. I should like to date them to ca. 1030.[41]

This method of dating assumes that we already possess sufficient knowledge of runic chronology to date the stones, when in fact we are seeking to establish just such a chronology by reference to the events related by the stones.

Erik Brate suspected that FrøygæiR's expedition took place as early as 1016.[42] He arrived at this dating by identifying the Svæin who commemorates FrøygæiR on U518 with the Svæin in whose memory U539 was erected, a stone that von Friesen dated ca. 1016. In view of the great frequency of the name *Svæinn* in the Upplandic inscriptions, the identification must be rejected. Von Friesen's dating of U539, moreover, is not without its weaknesses.[43]

Von Friesen himself dated Asmund's Söderby-stone, with its reference to FrøygæiR, by means of the following argument: "On the Söderby-stone at Gävle mention is made of a man who fell in Tavastland on Fröger's expedition. This undertaking is mentioned on the Danish Tirsted-stone, which exhibits the use of the ås-rune as a sign for *o* and unnasalized *a* (*æ*), a characteristic of the Ingvar-stones. From this it might be concluded that Asmund was active during the 1040s."[44] As has been noted, the use of the o-rune is an extremely unreliable criterion for dating. More importantly, the Tirsted-stone (DR216) cannot be used as a reference to FrøygæiR because of the highly uncertain character of the inscription, which has not yet been interpreted in a satisfactory way.

Of inscriptions attributed to Asmund there are two that refer to "Knut's payment," U194 and U344. There is little doubt that this expression refers to the tribute that Knut took from the English and used to repay his army of mercenaries after his successful invasion of England in 1015–1016. His troops were released to return home in 1018, a year

[41]Brate and Bugge, *Runverser*, pp. 55–56. Bugge includes the Danish Tirsted-stone (DR216) as evidence, viewing its inscription and design as an attempt at archaization.

[42]Brate, *Svenska runristare*, pp. 17, 20, 41.

[43]Von Friesen assumes Svæin died in Jutland while waiting to attack England with Knut. Such an assumption is not imperative, since there were several raids on England, and the inscription does not specify which.

[44]Von Friesen, *Runorna*, p. 208.

that therefore constitutes a *terminus post quem* for the execution of U194 and U344.[45]

It may also be possible to achieve a *terminus ante quem* for an inscription attributed to Asmund if we can identify the Ingvar on U540 as the Ingvar of the saga. Both von Friesen and Wessén admit that such an identification is possible.[46] If the year 1041 is accepted as the date of Ingvar's death, U540 must have been erected before this time.

Two remaining references in the works of Asmund may involve historical figures. In the opinion of Celsius, Brate, and von Friesen, the Vinaman in honor of whom U375 was erected was named for the kinsman of Saint Sigfrid who was martyred around the beginning of the eleventh century.[47] The chronological results achieved by this argument are not, however, very enlightening.

Similarly, the Knut who co-sponsored U1149 is thought to have been named for Knut the Great, who died in 1035. Since it is believed that naming children after living persons was contrary to Viking Age practice,[48] U1149 would have been erected sometime after the year 1035.

If all the above arguments are accepted, we may conclude that Asmund carved U375 sometime after the beginning of the eleventh century, U194 and U343–U344 sometime after 1018, U1149 after 1035, and U540 before 1041. Although these results seem to agree with the traditional dating of Asmund's activity,[49] they do not indicate whether this activity began before 1018 or continued beyond 1041. Also, we do not possess both a *terminus post quem* and a *terminus ante quem* for any of Asmund's rune stones.

Scholars have naturally been reluctant to remain content with such a vague chronology. To determine the end points with greater exacti-

[45]See von Friesen, *Runorna*, p. 208, and Wessén, *Historiska runinskrifter*, pp. 13–15. Note that U241 mentions "payments" but does not indicate whether one of them was Knut's.

[46]See U540 for details. The discussion was initiated by F. Braun in "Hvem var Yngvarr enn viðfǫrli?" *Fornvännen* 5 (1910): 99–118, who identified the names on U513 and U540 not only with the family of the saga hero but also with members of the Swedish royal family. Von Friesen rejected the latter identification but remarked that "it might be maintained with a certain degree of probability that the rune stones L605 [U540] and 601 [U513] pertain to Yngvar and his siblings."

[47]Wessén does not commit himself regarding this question. Anders Grape (*Studier över de i fornsvenskan inlånade personnamnen*, p. 42) believed that the name was borrowed from England independently.

[48]See Elias Wessén, *Nordiska namnstudier*, pp. 18–23 (with additional references).

[49]Brate: ca. 1025–1040; von Friesen: ca. 1025–1050's.

tude and to establish a chronological ordering of the inscriptions between these two points, they have employed a number of arguments,
all involving risky assumptions. Thus, it is argued that the monument
to Ulf (U343–U344) was raised shortly after his return from Knut's conquest, since Ulf is said to have taken two previous payments, the first
possibly falling in the 990's.[50] One is obviously worried about Ulf's age
at the time of his death; unfortunately there is no way of knowing his
age at the time of his first voyage to England. Were he twenty-five years
old in 995, he could have died in 1045 at the age of seventy-five. (Egil
Skallagrimsson, whom Ulf resembles in more ways than one, lived
eighty years.) In general, arguments based on the life span of the eleventh-century Swede and on the succession of generations are quite
shaky.[51] The dating of U343–U344 as "about" 1025–1030 is, strictly
speaking, without solid foundation.[52]

Another method employed to achieve a finer chronology involves the
internal relationships of the Upplandic rune stones. Necessarily, the
occurrence of the same name in two or more inscriptions must indicate
one and the same person. The degree of certainty in this matter varies
greatly from case to case. The relative chronology established in this
way is used to achieve an ordering of the entire corpus of runic monuments on stylistic (usually artistic) grounds. It is assumed that the art
of the rune stones went through the stages of rise, culmination, and
degeneration. All historical events mentioned in the inscriptions may
then contribute to the absolute dating of all the monuments.

The validity of such typological dating has been widely debated. On
the one extreme there are such statements as Wessén's: "If one disre-
gards the many fragments that are unsuitable for a characterization and

---

[50] "If the first tribute mentioned on the Yttergärde-stone, the one that Toste paid, dates
back to the tenth century, then this is a strong reason for not going too far from the boundary year 1018, at least as far as this inscription is concerned" (Wessén, *Historiska runinskrifter*, p. 15).

[51] Note that Alli erected U203 over his son, who was already a father. A woman named
Gyrið lived long enough to sponsor memorials over her father (U328), her husband (U225–
U226), and one of her sons (U100).

[52] Wessén, *Historiska runinskrifter*, p. 15. It seems more justified to date U194 shortly
after 1018, since Alli raised the stone in his own honor while still alive, and U194 can be
viewed in conjunction with U203 as a clarification of inheritance rights. The assumption
would then be that Alli returned home wealthy, found his son had died, and erected U194
to declare his wealth and (at the same time) U203 to establish Frøygærð as heir to it.

a dating based on this, as well as a few carvings of deficient quality, there are very few of Uppland's rune stones that cannot be fitted into this development and thus dated at least approximately."[53] At the other extreme are the art historians, such as Hans Christiansson (see chapter 3) and Sune Lindqvist, who maintain that the typological method cannot provide a trustworthy ordering of the rune stones within a period of time as brief as the eleventh century.[54]

To discuss the validity of the typological method in general and to evaluate the system that von Friesen and Wessén have achieved through an application of this method would require an entire volume. We may instead summarize their reasoning concerning Asmund.

Both von Friesen and Wessén consider the "unornamented" stones the earliest stage in Upplandic runography, but they differ slightly in absolute dating. Von Friesen believed that Upplandic runography owed its beginnings to insular impulses transmitted by Swedes like Ulf returning from Viking expeditions, such as Knut's, and that the unornamented stones were to be dated before and around 1025.[55] The works of Gunnar (U225–U226) and Ulf (U160–U161) are not differentiated chronologically from strictly unornamented monuments, such as U323. Asmund's works are considered to follow immediately upon the unornamented stones.

Wessén, on the other hand, wishes to separate the unornamented stones from Asmund's by at least a decade. He argues that the impulses of which von Friesen speaks could well have been transmitted by Vikings who were Ulf's predecessors and who returned from England earlier in the century (or by Ulf himself at an earlier stage of his life). Unornamented stones would then stem from the first two decades of the eleventh century, and the works of Ulf and Gunnar would provide a transition from them to Asmund, whose activity begins around 1025.[56]

In his assumption that the stones that mention "gelds" (U194, U240–U241, U343–U344) mark the beginning of Asmund's activity, Wessén

---

[53]Ibid., p. 7.

[54]Sune Lindqvist, "Jarlabanke-släktens minnesmärken," in *Nordiska arkeologmötet i Stockholm 1922*, pp. 123–141. Lindqvist does not indict the typological method as a whole but shows its limitations for a certain group of stones. Another great skeptic in matters of chronology was the Danish runologist Lis Jacobsen.

[55]Von Friesen, *Upplands runstenar*, p. 33; *Runorna*, pp. 205–206.

[56]Wessén, *Historiska runinskrifter*, pp. 19–20.

again makes use of the typological method, for he considers these stones
to be "early works":

> None of these stones, however, is among Åsmund's best works. They are strik-
> ingly simple, even though they are obviously raised in honor of important men.
> This is especially true of the two Knut-stones U344 and U194. A possible ex-
> planation is that they belong to an early stage in Åsmund's activity, before he
> had developed his technique and found his style. Curiously enough, U344,
> which moreover is extraordinarily awkward in its ornamentation for an Åsmund
> work, is carved with so-called reversed runes; it is therefore read most easily
> in its mirror image.[57]

Not everyone will accept this esthetic evaluation or the consequences
it entails. To my mind the Yttergärde-stones, and certainly the two at
Lingsberg, are not "strikingly simple." These words apply much more
appropriately to stones like U203, U372, U431, and U956. Nor is it certain that simplicity should be equated with poor quality, as Wessén's
reasoning assumes, and one might well take exception to Wessén's notion that U344 is "unusually awkward" artistically. Finally, to say that
Asmund had not yet found his style in U194, U240–U241, and U343–
U344 is to eliminate the very basis for attributing the stones to Asmund
in the first place. What is clear is that Wessén and von Friesen want
U344 to be an early work of Asmund, so that his career can find its niche
in the typological scheme that has been worked out.

Wessén does not discuss Asmund's activity outside of these "early
works,"[58] but von Friesen was committed to a further chronology, having accepted Sander's interpretation of the Järsta-stone (L1053) as referring to the reign of King Emund the Old. But, although the Järsta-stone
would then be dated in the 1050's, the nearby (and typologically similar) Söderby-stone (L1049) was dated in the 1040's because of the reference to FrøygæiR. The Fleräng-stone (U1149), because of the occurrence of the name *Knutr*, and the Vidbo-stone (U375), erected in memory of Vinaman, are dated in the 1040's or 1050's.[59] Von Friesen also

---

[57]Ibid., p. 12.

[58]Under U518, however, Wessén expressed the opinion that L1049 (Asmund and
Svæin's Söderby-stone) was contemporaneous with U518, a strictly unornamented stone.
This opinion was written a number of years before *Historiska runinskrifter,* in which Wes-
sén seeks to establish a clear boundary between the two stylistic groups.

[59]In *Upplands runstenar,* p. 34, von Friesen argues that the Knut on U1149 was named
after King Knut's fame reached Sweden and that he would have grown up before the rune
stone was erected. "The Knut of this carving ought to have reached maturity when he with

remarks that "younger inscriptions are frequently signed not only by Asmund but also by a further carver,"[60] indicating that he would view U884, U932, U1142, U1144, U1149, and L1049 as late works. U981 is also deemed a late work.[61] On the other hand it is unclear what von Friesen had in mind when he says that Þorfast carved stones "using Asmund's late ornamentation as a model."[62] Þorfast's works show greatest similarity to Asmund's U356, which von Friesen likens to the "early" U343.[63] In von Friesen's later discussion of Þorfast, the word "late" is omitted; Þorfast is "a carver who took Asmund as a model."[64]

Asmund's carvings can, of course, be grouped in a number of ways. They can be classified artistically according to each of several features: shape of the rune animal, structure of the cross, style of the rune-animal's head, complexity of the design as a whole. Asmund's work could also be ordered in accordance with the degree of excellence in the technical execution, on the assumption that poorly executed works represent early attempts. The same type of analysis might be applied to orthography, formulation, and rune forms. Again, one might simply group the stones geographically and assume that stones in the same area were done at the same time.

Very few of these groupings will coincide, and all of them will be difficult to reconcile with what few historical touchstones we possess or with our suppositions about Upplandic chronology as a whole. The clearest instances of coinciding groups would be (1) U824, U847, U859, U866, U871, U884: all in Södra Hagunda, all of Type A-3, all with elongated heads and tear-drop eyes, and all featuring a complex and dynamic interplay of decorative serpents; (2) U1145, U1149, L1049, L1050,

---

his brother raised a monument over the father. If he was born about 1020, the stone ought then to have been raised ca. 1040 at the earliest." In *Runorna*, however, von Friesen believes that the Knut on U1149 must have been born after King Knut's death (1035), but he does not demand that he reach maturity (p. 208).

[60]Von Friesen, *Runorna*, p. 210.

[61]Because the Vifast on U981 (by Asmund) also occurs on U980, which von Friesen attributes to Fot, and "Fot's activity begins ca. 1050, see below page 217" (*Runorna*, p. 209). The argument is circular, however, since on page 217 von Friesen announces that "we saw above, page 209, that one of Uppland's most productive rune masters, Fot, begins his activity at the time Asmund Kareson concludes his, viz. during the 1050's."

[62]Von Friesen, *Upplands runstenar*, p. 46.

[63]Otto von Friesen, "Historiska runinskrifter," *Fornvännen* 4 (1909): 57–85. The comparison occurs on pp. 57–58.

[64]Von Friesen, *Runorna*, p. 210.

L1053: all in Gästrikland or northern Uppland, all with designs of Type B and heads with almond eyes and pointed ears (or no ears), and all but one executed in sandstone; (3) U1031, U1043, U1142: in north-central Uppland and bearing similar crosses and winged dragons.

Using the typological method, one might speculate that the first group, which is artistically the most developed, is from a late stage in Asmund's career; the co-signers of U884 would then be assistants. On the other hand, the hypothesis could be advanced that group (2) above marks Asmund's beginnings, as an assistant of Svæin. It is Svæin who has executed the most substantial part of the inscriptions on U1149 and L1049, and, contrary to the practice on other stones that Asmund has signed jointly, Asmund's name occurs in secondary position in the signatures *(Svæinn ok Asmundr)*. [65]

Using the methods of von Friesen and Wessén, one can achieve results that are directly opposed to the conclusions they have drawn. [66] One must be satisfied with the vague chronological results (which indicate that Asmund was active during the 1030's) until an air-tight runo-

[65]The most puzzling view of Asmund's relative chronology is surely to be found in Friedrich Plutzar's *Die Ornamentik der Runensteine*, published in 1924. At the end of this study appears a table that attempts to order the monuments belonging to the "Asmundkreis." Plutzar groups as late works of Asmund some of the stones in Södra Hagunda found under group (1) (see page 159), and considers Asmund's collaboration with Svæin to fall into a middle period (presumably the time scale is to be read down the chart). He also attributes U885 to Asmund, and groups U1142 and U1031 (both with winged dragons) and U598 and U1123. At the same time, however, he mistakenly groups the latter two (U598 and U1123) under "Hiriar," when U598 is signed by Auðmund and U1123 is attributable to him. Similarly, U1132 is signed by Auðmund but grouped under Asmund. Plutzar does not indicate that U969, U986, U884, and U847 are signed by Asmund, or that U629 is signed by Þorfast. L1049, signed by Svæin and Asmund, is listed as unsigned, and U1149 (also signed by these two) is represented as signed only by Svæin. Like Brate, Plutzar misread U1158 as signed by Þorfast (but Brate did not believe it to be the same Þorfast as on U599 and U629; see fn. 34) and attributed U846 mistakenly to Asmund. Svæin is somehow associated with U901, U903, U904, and U875. It is easier to understand how Plutzar associated him with L1053 and L1050. The connection of U448, a stone in Fot's style, with "Vihmar" remains a complete mystery.

[66]One can "prove," for example, that the unornamented stones date from after 1035 by the following argument: U518 is an unornamented stone and was carved at the same time as L1049 because both commemorate men of FrøygæiR's expedition. But L1049 is contemporaneous with U1149, since both were done by Asmund and Svæin and are stylistically similar. U1149, in turn, was raised after 1035 because of the occurrence of the name *Knutr*. Therefore, U518 (unornamented) was erected after 1035. It is also interesting to note that Andreas Lindblom (*Sveriges konsthistoria*, p. 33) sees influence of Balli in Asmund's U871. But, according to von Friesen and Brate, Asmund preceded Balli.

graphic ordering is achieved or until new finds reveal additional historical information.

THE ASMUND-OSMUNDUS QUESTION[67]

In the article on Asmund written for the Swedish biographical lexicon, Otto von Friesen contradicts his own view that Asmund was runographically active during the 1040's. He was instead "presumably gone
from Sweden at the beginning of the 1040's, for he carved none of the
Ingvar-stones, which are common in the regions where he was active."[68]
The motivation behind this somewhat dubious reasoning is that Asmund
must have undertaken extensive travels sometime before 1050 if he is
to be identified, as von Friesen desires, with a certain English pseudo-
bishop of the name Osmundus.

The chief source of our knowledge of Osmundus is the church history
of Adam of Bremen.[69] According to Adam (III, 14–15), the Swedish
King Emund the Old had at his court a certain "irregular" *(acephalum)*
bishop by the name of Osmundus. This Osmundus had been a companion of Bishop Sigfrid in Sweden, who had sent him to Bremen for
schooling. Osmundus then went to Rome in an attempt to have himself
ordained, but he was turned away and forced to wander about until a
Polish (?) bishop consented to ordain him.[70] Returning to Sweden, Osmundus professed to be a bishop especially chosen by the Pope to represent him in those parts. Legates to Sweden from the Church of Hamburg-Bremen were turned away, and Osmundus continued to "corrupt
the barbarians" with Emund's consent. Adam goes on to describe the
calamities that befell the Swedes until upon Emund's death the pious
Stenkil ascended the throne. Adam's description is clearly colored by
political bias, so that it is difficult to determine the accuracy of his report.

According to the history of Ely monastery in England, a certain Osmundus, who had previously been in Sweden, arrived at the court of

[67]Much of the material in this section appears in slightly altered form in C. W. Thompson, "A Swedish Runographer and a Headless Bishop," *Mediaeval Scandinavia* 3 (1970):
50–62.

[68]Otto von Friesen, "Asmund Kareson," in *Svenskt biografiskt lexikon*, II, 379. This
statement contradicts von Friesen's dating of the Söderby-stone as contemporary with the
Ingvar-stones.

[69]Adam von Bremen, *Hamburgische Kirchengeschichte*, ed. B. Schmeidler; Francis J.
Tschan, ed. and trans., *Adam of Bremen: History of the Archbishops of Hamburg-Bremen*.

[70]In "Biskop Osmund," *Fornvännen* 42 (1947): 54–56, T. J. Arne demonstrated that
Osmund was probably ordained in Kiev at about 1050.

King Edward the Confessor (1042–1066), remained with the king for a while, enjoying his favor, and subsequently retired to Ely, where he died sometime around 1070.[71]

Von Friesen championed the identification of Asmund the runographer and Osmundus the "bishop" in several publications, throughout which one can trace his increasing enthusiasm for the idea. In 1907, he states, it is "not impossible that he is identical with the Osmundus who after extended travels is said to have been ordained in Poland," and concludes on a cautious note: "it will probably never be proven."[72] By 1913, however, he is less cautious and declares that the identification is "more than possible,"[73] and, when the biographical article on Asmund was written in 1920, the idea is considered "probable to a high degree," something about which one "scarcely need hesitate."[74] In 1928, and finally in 1933, von Friesen found much to support the identification.[75] Despite his early caution, von Friesen sought, if not to prove the validity of the identification, at least to offer as much supporting evidence as possible. This evidence can be summarized as follows:[76]

1. Asmund's carvings betray an unusual education.

2. Asmund's Christian enthusiasm suggests that he was a clergyman.

3. The reference to Emund the Old on the Järsta-stone (L1053) proves that Asmund was active during Emund's reign.

4. Asmund's activity centers around Uppsala, the seat of royalty, and his influence can be seen in the vicinity of royal domains throughout central and northern Sweden.

5. Asmund's familiarity with Knut's payment indicates a close connection with England.

6. Asmund's zoomorphic ornamentation and cross forms have their origins in the British Isles.

7. The orthographic use of the h-rune as fricative /g/ in Asmund's inscriptions reveals influence from English runography.

---

[71]*Historia Eliensis,* ed. David James Stewart, I, 220–221.

[72]Von Friesen, "Upplands runstenar," p. 471. Von Friesen assumes that Asmund is a Scandinavian settler in England.

[73]Von Friesen, *Upplands runstenar,* p. 38.

[74]Von Friesen, "Asmund Kareson," pp. 378–379.

[75]Otto von Friesen, *Runorna i Sverige,* pp. 64–65; *Runorna,* p. 210.

[76]These arguments can be found in the following works by von Friesen: "Upplands runstenar," pp. 470–471; *Upplands runstenar,* pp. 37–38; "Asmund Kareson," pp. 376–377; *Runorna i Sverige,* pp. 64–67; *Runorna,* pp. 206–210.

8. The language of Asmund's inscriptions shows influence from Anglo-Saxon.

Some of von Friesen's arguments are completely transparent, and one has already been refuted. None of them is binding. The first argument may be dismissed at once, for Asmund's carvings do not, any more than the carvings of other runographers, reveal an "unusual education," whatever von Friesen may have meant with this expression. His inscriptions follow the usual patterns of Upplandic runography. Similarly, Asmund's inscriptions treating Viking expeditions to England do not presuppose a background in English history. Surely Knut's conquest of England and the attacks that preceded it were common knowledge in eleventh-century Scandinavia. (We undoubtedly know less today of these matters than the eleventh-century farmer.) It is, moreover, unlikely that Alli of Väsby would have sought to glorify himself as a taker of Knut's geld (U194) had it required special knowledge on the part of his neighbors to understand the reference.

The evidence of the Järsta-stone is inadmissible, since it is unlikely that þasataimunt indicates the reign of Emund the Old (see pages 85–86). The origin of Swedish rune-stone ornamentation is the subject of widespread disagreement. Models have been sought not only in the west (Britain, Ireland), but also in the east (the Orient) and even the south (Germany).

It is not surprising that Uppsala constitutes the nucleus in the distribution of Asmund's works, a fact more or less true of Upplandic runic inscriptions as a whole. Like Fot's and Öpir's, and unlike, say, Lifstæin's, Asmund's activity is not particularly limited geographically. The runographic influence that von Friesen finds in other parts of Sweden associated with royalty is of a very general nature indeed and would not be considered Asmundic at all did this influence not follow logically from von Friesen's view of Asmund as the first runographer to work in the ornamented style and thus ultimately responsible for all succeeding runography.

While it is true that Asmund was the first known runographer to employ the **h**-rune as a symbol for fricative /g/, it is very unlikely that this orthographic trait owes its origin to English runographic practice. In English runic inscriptions, the rune form ᛤ is a variant of the **j**-rune (ᛡ, ᚼ, ᚽ) and usually represents /j/, although this sound may be a reflex of /g/, as in the name *Gislheard* ᚷᛁᛋᛚᚻᛠᚱᛞ (Dover-stone). Old English /g/ is normally written ᚷ, whether palatal or velar. The

Ruthwell cross attempts to distinguish the velar spirant by employing the symbol ᚸ, no doubt derived from ᚷ. The Brunswick casket, a rare exception, writes /g/ with ᚵ.[77]

It is more reasonable to seek the origin of Asmund's use of the **h**-rune in the orthographic system of the younger Scandinavian runic alphabets. One of the major structural differences between these alphabets and the older futhark is the orthographic loss of the voice distinction; thus, each of the pairs /k/ and /g/, /þ/ and /ð/, /p/ and /b/, /t/ and /d/, and /f/ and /v/ is written with a single rune. It is logical to maintain this pattern, in which occlusion is distinctive, by removing the fricative /g/ from the **k**-rune (phonetically, a stop) and assigning it to the **h**-rune.

If Asmund were to have been influenced by the English futhorc, one would rather expect him to have adopted its most striking feature—the use of diacritics to encompass more phonetic distinctions. But, as we have seen, no dotted runes occur in Asmund's works.

The evidence of Anglo-Saxon linguistic influence in Asmund's inscriptions is also extremely dubious. According to von Friesen, the noun *sal(a)* 'soul' and the verb *marka* 'mark, carve' are borrowed from Old English. In the case of the former it should be noted that the word for 'soul' does not appear in Old English as *sāl*, as von Friesen states, but rather in the forms *sāwol*, *sāwul*, *sāwel*, *sāwl*, and *sāul*. In runic inscriptions it appears on the Thornhill cross as (accusative singular) **saule**, and on the Great Urswich cross as **saulæ**. Whatever its ultimate origin, the Scandinavian form *sāl(a)* is first and foremost West Norse, not English.[78] What von Friesen means no doubt is not that Asmund uses an Anglo-Saxon form, but that he uses the Scandinavian (West Norse) form of the word "soul," which may ultimately derive from Old English. Both *sial* and *sal(a)* are borrowed terms, but their derivation is a matter of some disagreement.[79]

Nor are there sufficient grounds to suppose that *marka* is a loan translation of Old English *mearcian*. The word is attested in Gothic *(gamarkōn)*, Old Frisian *(merkia)*, and Old High German *(marcōn)*, in addition to Scandinavian and Old English. There was no need for Asmund to borrow semantic content; the verb *marka* occurs in Old Norse in the sense 'cut, carve' (see Fritzner).

[77]See R. W. V. Elliott, *Runes: An Introduction*, pp. 33–44 and 76–109; Lucien Musset, *Introduction à la runologie*, pp. 181–212.

[78]Another West Norse form that Asmund employs in contrast to all other runographers in Uppland is the preterite singular *hio* 'carved' (instead of *hiogg*).

[79]See Carl-Eric Thors, *Den kristna terminologien i fornsvenskan*, pp. 450–457.

It is fair to say that, had not Adam's pseudo-bishop been associated with England, no one would have "discovered" Anglo-Saxon influence in Asmund's works.[80] On the other hand, this cannot be said for von Friesen's remaining argument, which is based on Asmund's alleged religiosity. The idea that Asmund's runic monuments reveal the piety of a cleric impresses one not by virtue of scientific or logical merit but rather because of its hoary ancestry. As will be shown, the identification of Asmund and Osmundus can be seen as part of a tradition extending as far back as the early eighteenth century.

Christian influence in the Upplandic runic monuments of the eleventh century consists of (1) the decorative crosses, (2) prayers, (3) Christian names, (4) references to good works performed for spiritual benefit, (5) references to pilgrimages, (6) mention of baptism, and (7) the occurrence of the word "church" and the like. Of these, only the first three are found in Asmund's work, and the third is not evidence of the Christianity of the runographer but of the person who bore the name. In Asmund's signed works, crosses occur on fifteen of the eighteen monuments that can be checked, or about 83%. It should be remembered that crosses occur on some 64% of the Upplandic monuments as a whole. A prayer occurs on some 58% of Asmund's signed works (versus 26% for Uppland). While these figures may indicate that Asmund was, in fact, a Christian (and it could be argued that the figures are of no more value as evidence of the runographer's religion than are Christian names), it is difficult to understand the logical processes by which they can be used to conclude that Asmund "fights for the Christian faith in pagan Sweden."[81]

Perhaps it is the form of Asmund's prayer, with its characteristic mention of "God's mother," that von Friesen considers especially pious. It is dangerous, however, to place excessive emphasis on a literal interpretation of what is, after all, a formulaic expression that can be found in the works of other carvers, even outside of Sweden.[82] If one wishes to find unusually pious prayers, one should turn to Lifstæin's U719 with its *Kristr lati koma and Tuma i lius ok paradis ok i þann hæim bæzta kristnum*, or to U942, by the runographer Æsbiorn: *Guð signi oss,*

---

[80]According to Otto Janse, Osmundus did not represent the English mission at all, but rather the Greek-Catholic one ("Har Emund den gamle sökt införa den grekisk-katolska läran i Sverige?" *Fornvännen* 53 [1958]: 118–124).

[81]Von Friesen, "Asmund Kareson," p. 377.

[82]For example, in the Danish inscription DR354, which is unrelated to Asmund's work. See also Thors, *Den kristna terminologien i fornsvenskan*, pp. 395–396.

gumna valdr, hæilagR drottinn. In short, it is uncertain to what extent prayers and crosses indicate a zealous Christian runographer; even if Asmund's piety were established beyond a doubt, the assumption that he was a priest is not justified.

Throughout his writings, von Friesen acknowledges his debt to Fredrik Sander, who in 1898 identified Asmund with Adam's Osmundus.[83] What is less well known is that Sander's adversary, Hjalmar Kempff, came upon the idea independently at about the same time.[84] Kempff's attitude was less than enthusiastic, however ("Let the rune-carver Asmund be the same as Bishop Osmund"), and he never championed the identification.

But the curious notion that Asmund was related in some way to the church goes back further than Kempff and Sander. In 1832 Johan Gustaf Liljegren gave Asmund the title "Prestmannen."[85] Liljegren in turn was probably indebted to Brocman, who in 1762 held that runography was transmitted from Uppland to Hälsingland by "Christianity and its preacher Osmund Kareson."[86] The ultimate source of this idea is no doubt to be found in Olof Celsius, who in 1726 wrote of Asmund: "He was nevertheless a Christian and a zealous papist, as is evident, for example, in the fact that he is almost the only one who never neglects to mention the Mother of God in his carvings, where there is sufficient space."[87]

The pedigree described does not, however, lend authority to the identification of the runographer and the bishop. It speaks not well of early runology but ill of modern, for the idea that Asmund was a priest is but one example of a long list of curious and mistaken notions that have gradually been abandoned as runology has progressed. To maintain that Asmund is Osmundus is in the tradition of Dijkman, who

---

[83]Fredrik Sander, *Runinskrifter ånyo granskade,* p. 11. Sander states that he had discussed the identification earlier with "H. H. Erkebiskopen" when presenting him with a copy of *Marmorlejonet från Piræeus* (1896).

[84]Kempff, *Söderby runsten vid Gefle,* "Senare efterskrift II," written in July, 1898, a couple of months before he had received Sander's *Runinskrifter ånyo granskade.*

[85]Johan Gustaf Liljegren, *Run-lära,* p. 59. For the entire quotation consult the Appendix.

[86]Brocman, *Sagan om Ingwar Widtfarne,* p. 257.

[87]Olof Celsius, "Monumenta quædam Sveo-Gothica suis temporibus reddita Auct. O. C.," *Acta Literaria Sveciæ* 2 (1725–1729): 196.

thought Öpir was the son of a priest and agreed with Verelius that Lif-stæin was the grandson of the Guðfast who is mentioned on U766 and U767.[88]

Although von Friesen's arguments were rejected as early as Brate's *Svenska runristare*, they have never been without a following. Sune Lindqvist accepted them in his work on the Eskilstuna sarcophagus.[89] Brate called the identification "daring to say the least" because "the activity of a rune-carver in such demand seems to agree little with that of a bishop, and the name Asmund is not unusual in either Sweden or England."[90] Sven B. F. Jansson has remarked that "the reasons given as support for this rather bold idea do not appear sufficiently strong."[91] Andreas Lindblom, who considered Brate to have "refuted" von Frie-sen, believed that the identification "has contributed to an overestima-tion of Åsmund's significance."[92] As late as 1946, however, von Friesen's argument was accepted as dogma.[93]

---

[88]On Öpir as a priest's son see the discussion in the Appendix. Verelius' comment, which is based on the occurrence of the word *fæðrga*, is found in *Manuductio compendiosa ad runographiam...*, p. 60. Dijkman agrees with him on page 96 of his *Historiske An-märckningar*.

[89]Sune Lindqvist, *Den helige Eskils biskopdöme*, p. 94.

[90]Brate, *Svenska runristare*, p. 28.

[91]Jansson, *Skansens runstenar*, p. 22.

[92]Lindblom, *Sveriges konsthistoria*, p. 33.

[93]Bergman, "Asmund Kareson," pp. 339–351.

9. Appendix: Previous Studies

The existence of known runographers has been recognized since the earliest days of Swedish runology, but, although a great deal of effort has been devoted to the collection of runic inscriptions, the study of these inscriptions, and of runography in particular, has often been the victim of sketchy or unscientific treatment. In the following pages some previous investigations touching upon Swedish runography will be reviewed.

THE SEVENTEENTH AND EIGHTEENTH CENTURIES

The work of Johan Bure, or Bureus (1568–1652), Sweden's first great antiquary, was quite understandably concerned primarily with the inventory of inscriptions. By his own efforts and with the assistance of men like Jon Håkansson Rhezelius, Johan Henriksson Axehielm, Mårten Aschaneus, and Caspar Cohl, a total of 663 runic inscriptions were collected, among these 543 from Uppland.[1]

Although Bureus and his associates did not investigate the problem of rune-carvers, it is clear that they were aware of it. Evidence of this can be found in Bureus' untitled manuscript Fa6 in the Royal Library in Stockholm, in which the signature of a carver is underlined in many of the inscriptions. In the same manuscript (pp. 14–16), one can note

[1] Elisabeth Svärdström, *Johannes Bureus' arbeten om svenska runinskrifter*, p. 39. The misleading information in *Svenskt biografiskt lexikon*, VI, 696 ("200 in number"), would seem to reflect the number of *published* inscriptions.

the beginnings of an investigation, basic to any runographical study, of the variant rune forms found in the inscriptions—not only obvious variants like ᚼ ᛁs and ᛏ1 t, but also the characteristic b-rune ᛒ of the runographer Balli.[2] Similarly, on page 38 some variant spellings of the word *æftiR* 'in memory of' are noted (aftiR, iftiR, yftiR, eftiR, oftiR, abtiR, aftir), although no attempt is made to connect these with individual carvers.

It is in a note by Bureus' assistant Aschaneus that we find the first explicit reference to a rune-carver. On page 101 of Fa6 the inscription U629 (Grynsta backe, Svarsta, Håbo-Tibble sn.) is found, a stone bearing the signature **þurfastr hristi runoR**. Aschaneus remarks that "this Durfaster seems also to have raised many runes," and goes on to speculate on the puzzling, unetymological *h* in the word *risti* 'carved'. "This ✳ h," he notes, "is his nickname and signifies 'hawk', since there is a hawk on the stone."

After the death of Bureus the task of collecting inscriptions fell to Johan Hadorph (1630–1693), on whose initiative the so-called *Ransakningar* was undertaken.[3] The materials gathered by Hadorph and his workers were to constitute a large work, *Monumenta Runica Sueo-Gothica*, which, however, lay unfinished at Hadorph's death in 1693. The task was turned over to Johan Peringer, or Peringskiöld (1654–1720), whose plan was to publish a comprehensive survey of Sweden's antiquities under the title *Monumenta Sueo-Gothorum*. Although only two parts of this work reached completion,[4] we possess Peringskiöld's preliminary manuscript in ten large volumes.[5]

With the advent of Peringskiöld the runic inscriptions of Sweden are made the subject of study and discussion, and the topic of runography is fully recognized. Toward the end of the first volume of Peringskiöld's large manuscript appears a list of "stenhuggare"—stone-carvers—which includes twenty-eight names,[6] and in the handwritten preface to

---

[2]In Denmark, Bureus' younger contemporary, Ole Worm, showed a similar interest in rune forms. See his "Tabella varietatum literarum Runicarum," in *Runer seu Danica Literatura Antiqvissima vulgo Gothica dicta*, p. 60.

[3]*Ransakningar om antikviteterna 1667–84*, MS in the Royal Library, Stockholm, signum Fl9.

[4]Johan Peringskiöld, *Monumenta Uplandica per Thiundam* and *Monumenta Ullerakerensia*.

[5]Signum Fh in the Royal Library, Stockholm.

[6]Fh1, p. 507b. Peringskiöld notes the following carvers (some of them based on misreadings): "Gunir, Uni, Thurbiurn Skalt, Lugi, Uraidr, Lifstein, Bali, Þurgutr, Foter, Ub-

this volume Peringskiöld refers to the "remarkable artists like Gunnar, Une, Thure, Gadir, Bali, Girmund Skalt, Thurbiorn Skalt, Thorder, Ubber, and Fot, together with innumerable others."[7]

That Peringskiöld was conscious of the manifold variation in rune forms is evident from his records concerning the acquisition of type fonts for his *Monumenta*. He makes some rather fine distinctions, acquiring, for example, symbols for ↑ and ↑, ↑ and ↑, and six types of word divider, as well as the more obvious variants, such as ↳↳, ▷▷, ▷▷, and ◁ ⧣ ⊦⧣.[8] Like Bureus, Peringskiöld nowhere links these rune forms to specific carvers, schools, or geographic areas, but it is likely that he had such categories in mind. These same type fonts were put to use, though not always accurately, in the two published parts of the *Monumenta*.

More significantly, Peringskiöld appears to have been the first to make an explicit attribution of an unsigned rune stone to a known carver. In *Monumenta Ullerakerensia* Peringskiöld draws a parallel between U916 (Ängeby, Börje sn.) and U912 (Börje kyrka) and links both stones with U946 (Danmarks kyrka) and U951 (Säby, Danmarks sn.):

> The rune stone in the foundation of the door of Börje Church [U912] / and this Engeby stone [U916] / are of the same age / being executed by one and the same Stone carver / as is only too evident from the nature and design of the runic band; which likeness also agrees well with the two memorials cited in Wakshalda Härad I. Fl. *pag.* 275. [U946] and 305. [U951] on which the Skald is called *Girmund Scald . . .*[9]

In making these attributions, which are probably correct (although we now read the runographer's name as *GrimR Skald*), Peringskiöld appears to use design as his principal criterion *("runoslingarnes art och ritning")*. The same reliance on similarity of ornamentation is evident elsewhere in Peringskiöld's writing, as in his comment on U907 (Bärby, Vänge sn.): "The interweaving of serpents here is arranged in the same way as the Blacksta-stone in Jomkil [U919]."[10] Similarly, the design of

---

bir v. Ybbr, Þurdr, Gadir, Irinfast, Viseti, Ismuntr, Orslugr, Giulin, Sighvastr, Oddvakin, Þurir Trani, Þordr, Ketil, Girimuntr Skalt, Hurmsr, Osmunt ok Vihmar, Osmunt ok Hiriar, Odmontr."

[7]Ibid., p. 17.
[8]Ibid., pp. 358, 361–374.
[9]Peringskiöld, *Monumenta Ullerakerensia*, p. 344.
[10]Ibid., p. 334.

a cross could be linked to an individual style, exemplified by Pering-skiöld's handwritten remark on U1086: "Högsta Södergärde in Bäling parish with a cross like Ubir's design."[11]

Peringskiöld's broad interests led him to speculate on the dating of Upplandic runographers, usually with considerable error. By assuming that the journeys to Greece mentioned in the inscriptions actually refer to the migration of the Goths, dated "about the years 261 and 266" in *Monumenta per Thiundam* (p. 300), Peringskiöld placed Öpir in the third or fourth centuries.[12] In a similar fashion, history, or pseudo-history, was employed to date the carvers with cognomen *Skald*:

Skalds were Poets and Historians among Kings and Earls / whom they accompanied to war / always positioned within the Shieldwall / nearest the Kings / in order to observe what of their manly deeds should be remembered and recorded as History. Such a Historian was this Girmund Skalt. There is also a Thorbiurn Skalt mentioned on the Hillershög rune rock [U29]. From the time of King Ragnar Lodbrok Anno Christi 750 until Birger Jarls' time / we find the catalogue of Skalds recorded in Sturluson's Edda... therein we find no Girmund Skald, nor Thorbiorn Skald; thus, the two Skalds probably lived before Ragnar Lodbrok's time.[13]

The presence of a cross, in fact, did not always indicate for Pering-skiöld that a rune stone was done in Christian times; rather, it could be interpreted as a symbol of the god Thor,[14] although it was conceded that inscribed prayers to God or the Virgin Mary were evidence of Christianity.[15] There is an interesting note to this effect on a scrap of paper in Fh1 (p. 249); Peringskiöld confesses: "I said that Thurbiurn Skald's rune rock [U29] was carved in the fourth century," and proceeds to correct this earlier misunderstanding: "That Thurbiörn skalt lived in the time when Christianity first began to take root in Sweden can be concluded from the rune stone in the porch of Bro Church, Bro Skepplag [U532], which reads: Sigrid had the stone raised in memory of Kari, her husband, God help his soul, Thurbiurn skalt carved the runes."

---

[11]Fh1, p. 501b.

[12]Ibid., p. 507b. Also in Peringskiöld, *Monumenta per Thiundam*, p. 244, and in *Monumenta Ullerakerensia*, pp. 41 and 325.

[13]Peringskiöld, *Monumenta per Thiundam*, p. 306.

[14]U936, for example, is described as showing "a lion under the mark of Thor" in *Monumenta Ullerakerensia*, p. 322.

[15]Christian runographers were generally placed in the eighth or ninth centuries. Thus Fh1, p. 507b: "Foter—guds moder!—Sec. 8 v. 9." and "Bali... i hvita vadum. Sec. 9."

Peringskiöld was also among the first to attempt a geographic localization of a particular runographer. In discussing U893 (Högby, Uppsala-Näs sn.), a stone signed by Öpir, Peringskiöld writes: "That the rune-carver Ubbir / had his residence in Näs parish here in Ulleråker Härad / is apparent from the fact that the two farms 'Ubby' seem to bear his name / and also two 'Ubby' with a mill in Jumkils parish; besides the fact that most of Ubbir's stone carvings are found around Uppsala in Uppland."[16]

Speculation of a similar nature can be found in the work of Peringskiöld's contemporary and fellow Rudbeckian, Petter Dijkman, whose *Historiske Anmärckningar* was written in 1708 but not published until 1723.[17] Runography is only of peripheral interest to Dijkman, whose typical concerns are biblical history, etymology, and the Christianization of Sweden; but from time to time he comments on rune-carvers, as when he notes that "those stones which have the names of the rune-carvers Ubir, Fatr, Ingulfur, Visti, Fair, and Lifsten / besides many others / are likewise carved in Christian times / which observation is supported by the fact that on some of the carved stones is found the Christian prayer / that they pray God to preserve their souls."[18]

Of more significance is a story Dijkman relates concerning the carver Öpir. It is typical of the fantastic speculation that can result from the total misunderstanding of a runic inscription and is quoted here in full:

> Since the principal aim of this work is to gain a more detailed knowledge concerning the introduction of the Evangelical Doctrine into Sweden / together with the history of the rune stones / and I find on a great many stones the name of the stone carver Ubr, or Ubir / I believe it would not be unpleasant for the curious reader / nor inappropriate to this work / to relate what knowledge I acquired in the year 1711 at the end of May and the beginning of June / during my travels past Härad Parish Church in Södermanland / concerning the parentage of this Ubir / from a red stone, hard as flint, two and a half ells in length / lying in the Church porch / just before the Church door itself / with a figure and an inscription in runic staves.
>
> The figure is of a man with shaven or sheared hair / beard / and on his head a clergyman's cap, worn as in former times down over the ears / and in accordance with the old custom a clergyman's robes with the inscription: *Ubr risti stan, iftir Svini Fadur san*, that is / Ubr the son carved the stone after his father, Sven, in

---

[16]Peringskiöld, *Monumenta Ullerakerensia*, p. 331.

[17]Petter Dijkman, *Historiske Anmärckningar, öfwer/och af en dehl Runstenar, i Swerige, Angående dhe Uhrgambla/Sviar- och Giöthers Kyrkie- och Werdzliga Wäsende/ Uthi åthskilliga Måhl, Åhr Christi 1708.*

[18]Ibid., p. 7.

his memory. Which circumstances shed light upon the darkness of antiquity / that Ubir was a Clergyman's son / and at the time the rune stones were erected / which he carved / heathendom was gone / and secondly / that Runic was maintained long into Christian times. The wife of the parish clerk told me / that Ubir's father is said to have been / as the story goes / a clergyman / and have lived in Näsby / Härad parish / at the judge's estate in that district.[19]

The stone Dijkman refers to is Sö325 (Härads kyrka, Åkers hd.), which according to Wessén reads:

:kaubi•resti⁝stin⁝eftiR⁝
•suini⁝faþur⁝sin⁝

That is, *Kaupi ræisti stæin æftiR Svæini, faður sinn.* Dijkman has apparently overlooked the first two runes and misconstrued the fifth rune (i) as r, possibly with the aid of an ornamental line (see photograph in *Runverket*). Considerably more imagination was required to interpret the zoomorphic design as illustrating a human figure (much less a priest).

It is with a great sense of relief that one turns to the sober reasoning and sound insight of Olof Celsius (1670–1756). Though Celsius was not primarily concerned with runology,[20] it can be said that his great runological talent—in both the study and the field—places him in a class with renowned runologists, such as L. F. A. Wimmer and Otto von Friesen. Above all, the two handwritten volumes of *Svenska runstenar*,[21] which constitute Celsius' notebooks during part of the 1720's, bear witness to this skill. *Svenska runstenar* is at once a collection and a study; Celsius' basic plan seems to have been to devote one page to each inscription, with the readings taken from earlier literature, but as further study and experience bore fruit the inscriptions were subjected to analysis from many points of view, and the pages of *Svenska runstenar* are filled with corrected readings and notes on the history, dating, distribution, and internal relationships of the primarily Upplandic rune stones. Above all Celsius took an interest in runographical matters and had a sharp eye for discerning characteristic features of individual carvers. He

[19]Ibid., pp. 23–24.
[20]Olof Celsius was the son of Magnus Celsius (1621–1679), who first deciphered the so-called *Hälsingerunor,* and was an uncle of Anders Celsius (1701–1744), whose name is linked to the centigrade thermometer. He was professor of Greek in 1703, of Oriental languages in 1715, and of theology in 1727, at Uppsala.
[21]Signum Fm60 in the Royal Library, Stockholm.

was probably the first to notice Viseti's characteristic f-rune with the abbreviated lower branch (ᚠ).[22]

In making attributions Celsius exhibits cautious reasoning, and although he was capable of mistakes his judgments are a great advance over his predecessors'. Typical is his comment on U74 (Husby, Spånga sn.):[23]

> Seems to be the same runographus as in
> Orkesta 1:116 [= U337]
> 1. same name Viseti
> 2. same 1
> 3. Helsing ᛏ

Similarly, it is noted that the same "Osmuntr" of U956 (Vedyxa, Danmarks sn.) carved the stone in Järsta, Valbo sn., Gästrikland (L1053), U986 (Kungsgården, Samnan, Gamla Uppsala sn.), and U998 (Skällerö, Marielund, Funbo sn.).[24]

Celsius also attributed unsigned stones, making use of a variety of criteria. Thus, under his transcription of U860 (Måsta, Balingsta sn.) Celsius remarks: "Seems to be Osmunder's writing,"[25] and under U1145 (Yttrö, Tierps sn.) he writes: "Appears to be Osmuntr Kara son's writing. Vid. Gersta and Wedyxa stones."[26] Concerning U875 (Focksta, Hagby sn.) Celsius comments: "Not unlike careless Osmuntr."[27]

What Celsius meant by "writing" (*Skrifft*) is somewhat uncertain, but it is likely that the attributions are based primarily on orthographic features. Elsewhere Celsius noted typical Asmundic spellings, such as þino þenna, osmunrt Asmundr, and ukuþs ok Guðs.[28] Indeed, Celsius remarks that "Osmund does not repeat the same consonants if they occur at the end of one word and the beginning of the other,"[29] and it is probably this characteristic orthographic trait above all that Celsius had in mind when attributing U860, U875, and U1145 to Asmund. (All three stones have the spelling ukuþs ok Guðs.)

---

[22]Ibid., I, 166 (U337).
[23]Ibid., II, 446.
[24]Ibid., I, 85.
[25]Ibid., I, 215.
[26]Ibid., I, 404.
[27]Ibid., II, 150.
[28]Ibid., I, 60, 95.
[29]Ibid., I, 313.

Yet we cannot rule out the possibility that rune forms played a role in Celsius' recognition of Asmund's style. The inscriptions in *Svenska runstenar* that are based on first-hand experience are remarkable for their faithfulness to details in the shapes of the runes; indeed, the runologist of today who is trained to recognize at a glance an Asmund-stone by virtue of rune forms alone can often do the same thing with an inscription in Celsius' book.[30]

That design was a factor in Celsius' attributions is clear from several comments in *Svenska runstenar*. On the basis of the cross U732 (Grillby, Sörskog, Villberga sn.) and U755 (Kälsta, Litslena sn.) are assigned to Balli,[31] while U1092 (Nyvla, Bälinge sn.) is attributed to Öpir, "as can be seen from the head of the serpent and from the simple cross."[32]

Finally, Celsius recognized formulation as a criterion in attributing rune stones. Writing in *Acta Literaria Sveciæ*, he notes that U860 (Mästa, Balingsta sn.) can be attributed to Asmund, among other reasons "because he is almost the only one who never omits 'Mother of God' in his carvings, if there is sufficient space on the stone."[33]

In dating runographers Celsius again showed his talent for objective reasoning. Since stones carved by both Öpir and Asmund were found in the foundation of the Uppsala cathedral, Celsius reasons, it is clear that the two runographers lived before 1260 (a traditional date for the construction of the cathedral).[34] Moreover, it is obvious to Celsius that most of the runographers are Christian, not only evident from his comments in *Svenska runstenar*,[35] but also the primary subject of Celsius' essay in *Acta Literaria Sveciæ*, an essay that attempted to do away once and for all with the fantastic chronological speculation of earlier runologists.[36]

Although Celsius did not convert all his contemporaries, his influence is quite apparent in N. R. Brocman's interesting book on Yngvar the Far-traveled, published in 1762.[37] With help from Celsius, Brocman is able

---

[30]Note for example the excellent reproduction (Fm60, II, 150) of the runes of U875, especially the k's of **inkikirþ**, the t of **aftiR**, and the s's of **honsalukuþs**.

[31]Fm60, I, 131, 134.

[32]Ibid., II, 629.

[33]Olof Celsius, "Monumenta quædam Sveo-Gothica suis temporibus reddita Auct. O. C.," *Acta Literaria Sveciæ* 2 (1725–1729): 196.

[34]Fm60, I, 27, 29–30, 571.

[35]Ibid., I, 24 (Öpir) and 451 (Balli).

[36]Celsius, "Monumenta quædam . . .," *Acta Literaria Sveciæ* 2–4 (1725–1736): *passim*.

[37]Nils Reinhold Brocman, *Sagan om Ingwar Widtfarne och hans Son Swen, från gamla Isländskan öfwersatt, och Undersökning om Wåre Runstenars Ålder, i Anledning af sam-*

to speculate on chronological and runological matters without falling into the absurdities of the Rudbeckian school. In fact, working under the assumption that most rune stones were raised during a relatively short period of time, Brocman brings up some interesting questions concerning relationships among runographers. Unfortunately, it must be said that Brocman's answers are unsatisfactory in almost every case. Typical of the way Brocman poses important problems, only to offer untenable solutions, is his discussion of Asmund's so-called Söderby-stone (L1049), which mentions an expedition to Tavastaland (Finland). Brocman writes:

From the lifetime of Osmund, who carved this stone, and from the war on Tavastaland after the conquest and subjugation of southern Finland, one can conclude concerning the age of this stone that it was prepared and hewn after Ubbe, who seems to have survived his contemporary Bale and become Osmun's master. It therefore cannot be older than 1160, but presumably somewhat younger.[38]

The sources of Brocman's confusion are several. From Peringskiöld he got the idea that the rune-carver Þorð was Öpir's predecessor.[39] He then identified this Þorð with the Þóroddr rúnameistari mentioned in a prologue to the grammatical treatises of Codex Wormianus[40] and assumed that this Þorð brought runography to Sweden.[41] Finally, Brocman borrowed from Celsius the notion that Öpir and Balli were contemporaries[42] and appointed them the teachers of the remaining runographers. Thus, Brocman notes during a discussion of U141 (Fittja, Täby sn.): "But otherwise, considering the more distinct serpent foot and the beast's mouth over its own body, the design resembles the advances Ubbe and Bale introduced into rune-carving, and their apprentices subsequently improved upon."[43] It is unfortunate that Brocman is unable to control the material and to separate the good from the bad, since his approach is basically sound and his eye for runographical detail unusual-

---

ma Saga, samt Företal om Sagans Trowärdighet; Hwaruti de förr hos oss utgivna Sagors Wärde tillika stadfästes.

[38]Ibid., p. 176.

[39]Peringskiöld, *Monumenta Ullerakerensia*, p. 334. Þorð's connection with Öpir is based on a misreading of several stones.

[40]*Codex Wormianus (The Younger Edda)*, folio 36.

[41]Brocman, *Sagan om Ingwar Widtfarne*, pp. 277–280.

[42]Celsius, "Monumenta quædam...," *Acta Literaria Sveciæ* 3 (1730): 93–94.

[43]Brocman, *Sagan om Ingwar Widtfarne*, p. 177.

ly sharp, permitting, for example, the observation of a distinctive feature of Asmund's rune forms.[44]

THE NINETEENTH CENTURY

For most of the nineteenth century runological work in Sweden is surprisingly disappointing, scarcely representing any advance over the state of affairs manifested in Brocman's work. It is true that editions and collections of the inscriptions continued to be expanded and improved,[45] but an understanding of the runological problems was not achieved until the end of the century, after the work of such runologists as Wimmer in Denmark had cleared the ground for a more scientific approach. Thus, scholars like Carl Säve (1812–1876), George Stephens (1813–1895), and Richard Dybeck (1811–1877) were characterized more by their unbounded enthusiasm for antiquity rather than any runological perspicacity.

That runographical ideas in 1832 had advanced little since the work of Celsius and Brocman can be shown by citing a passage in the *Run-lära* of Johan Gustaf Liljegren:

Several experienced masters seem also to have contributed much to the spread of these carvings. When Ubbe, *Ubir*, undertook carvings in the Uppsala district, which he then continued southward through Uppland and Södermanland, and Bolle, *Bali*, again in a southwest direction through Uppland to Västmanland and western Södermanland, together with (the clergyman) Osmund Kåre's son who betook himself throughout the upper part of Uppland north to Gästrikland and Hälsingland, and since in the places where these rune-carvers were present such commemorative monuments appear more frequently and generally than elsewhere, then such considerations can only be evidence of the prevalent custom of erecting this type of monument, which they furthered by their labor and talent; but it also had its influence on runology, since in the aforementioned places there were also monuments containing only the rune row, or a depiction of runes for their own sake. Again, when soon many other rune-carvers are mentioned in addition to these, and finally the rune stones do not record any carver, then runology was no longer anything particularly distinctive, but reveals its greater and more general distribution.[46]

The view presented here is derived largely from the eighteenth century. Like Celsius, Liljegren sees Öpir and Balli as contemporary, and

[44]Ibid., p. 257 ("the long necks he often gives the u-rune").

[45]Johan Gustaf Liljegren's *Run-urkunder* is still used today for inscriptions as yet unpublished in the Swedish *Runverket*.

[46]Johan Gustaf Liljegren, *Run-lära*, p. 59.

like Brocman he makes them the standard bearers of Upplandic runography. To these two is added Asmund, whom Brocman had already held responsible for the diffusion of runes into Hälsingland.[47] The fallacious idea that signed rune stones must be earlier than unsigned ones follows naturally from the assumption that Öpir, Balli, and Asmund are originators, for these three runographers alone account for almost half of the signed stones of Uppland (83 of 182).

Nor did the survey of Upplandic inscriptions that Upplands fornminnesförening began publishing in the early 1870's contribute anything of value to the understanding of Upplandic runography. Only an occasional comment, of no originality, dealt with the subject, such as Carl Säve's remark concerning U532 (Roslags-Bro kyrka): "This is perhaps the same Thorbjörn skald who carved the splendid runic inscription on the Runerock in Hillersjö in the Färentuna district,"[48] or P. J. Lindal's note that "there are nearly forty inscriptions from the hand of the rune-carver Upper..."[49]

One of the first steps toward a modern scientific treatment of the inscriptions was taken by Hans Hildebrand in 1878 and 1879.[50] Hildebrand attempted to arrive at both a relative and an absolute chronology by means of orthographic, stylistic, and historical arguments. The orthographic transition by which the old a-rune received the sound value /o/ is recognized, and this transition is seen to be at work on the so-called Ingvar-stones (stones commemorating those who fell on the expedition of Yngvarr in viðfǫrli). Since we are told in Icelandic sources that Yngvar died in 1041, argues Hildebrand, we can date these stones (and the change of ᛆ ᚠ ᚦ ᚴ from /a/ to /o/) around the middle of the eleventh century.

Hildebrand also presents a somewhat crude grouping of the rune stones on the basis of ornamental features—the form of the runic band, the shape of the head, the number of serpents. As a general principle, Hildebrand dates the simpler designs earlier, so that Öpir's work is no longer viewed as coming at the beginning of Upplandic tradition. The arguments that Hildebrand presents are often confused, and his knowledge of the runic material is somewhat sketchy, but many of his conclu-

---

[47]Brocman, *Sagan om Ingwar Widtfarne*, p. 257.

[48]*Upplands fornminnesförenings tidskrift* 2 (1872): 12.

[49]Ibid., 10 (1882): 218.

[50]Hans Hildebrand, "Kronologiska anteckningar om våra runstenar," *VHAA månadsblad*, 1878, pp. 710–713; 1879, pp. 8–18.

sions have gained acceptance and are current today in a more refined form.

The Twentieth Century

Not until the present century has the Upplandic material been subjected to an analysis that recognizes the basic importance of runography. The tentative beginnings of Hildebrand have been elaborated by modern Swedish runologists, of which the names Otto von Friesen, Erik Brate, Elias Wessén, and Sven B. F. Jansson stand out as most prominent.

Of these it is perhaps Otto von Friesen, "the founder of modern Swedish runology,"[51] whose views have been most dominant. Von Friesen contributed to *Upplands fornminnesförenings tidskrift* in 1908,[52] and in 1907 he had written a brief survey of runic inscriptions for use in a large descriptive work on Uppland.[53] This essay, revised, enlarged, and published separately as *Upplands runstenar* in 1913, remains in many respects von Friesen's best work and is still the most useful introduction to the stones of Uppland.

Upplands runstenar does not deal exclusively with rune-carvers but treats other runological matters as well. Inscriptions in the older futhark are touched upon briefly, and the importation of the "Danish" futhark into Sweden is discussed. Von Friesen also surveys the number, distribution, and locations of the Upplandic monuments and provides a map to elucidate his findings. After brief discussions of the ornamentation of the stones and the problem of dating the inscriptions, von Friesen surveys Upplandic runography, establishing a chronology that to a great extent remains standard today. First, the "unornamented" stones (those without elaborate zoomorphic design) are treated, then the stones associated with carvers like Asmund, Lifstæin, Tiðkumi, Æirik, Fot, Balli, Viseti, and finally Öpir. Lesser-known carvers are related to the main ones.

Von Friesen's chronology is based on arguments reminiscent of Hildebrand's articles of 1878–1879. Historical criteria, such as Knut's conquest of England or Ingvar's expedition to "Särkland," are used to arrive at an absolute dating. Generational relationships of the families found

---

[51]Dedication to von Friesen in part 1 of *Upplands runinskrifter.*

[52]*Upplands fornminnesförenings tidskrift* 24 (1908): 147 (attributed U904 to "Asmund Karasun or his school").

[53]"Upplands runstenar," in *Uppland: Skildring af land och folk*, II, 449–490.

in the inscriptions are employed to establish relative chronology. Underlying these criteria is the notion that Upplandic rune-stone art proceeds from simple ornamentation to a "classical" phase and concludes with a period of degeneration.

Throughout *Upplands runstenar* there is a tendency to treat an assertion as a fact and to dispense with detailed proof.[54] It is above all evident that von Friesen has attributed a great many stones to the carvers without demonstrating his arguments. We are told, for example, that Fot executed the so-called Jarlabanki-stones, but this attribution is nowhere argued in detail. Often merely a hint of a carver's activity is given, as in the case of Þorfast, "who, using Asmund's later ornamentation as a model, carved six or seven stones in central and eastern Uppland."[55] Lack of explicit proof also typifies von Friesen's other major survey of the Upplandic stones, which appeared in the sixth volume of *Nordisk kultur*.[56] Attributions are made, without evidence, as when U455 (Näsby, Odensala sn.) is called "an unsigned but characteristic Fot stone."[57]

To find a detailed analysis of an attributed stone in Otto von Friesen's work one may turn to an article from 1910.[58] The stone in question is U540 (Husby-Lyhundra kyrka), which von Friesen attributes to Asmund on the basis of ornamentation, rune forms, orthography, and formulation. This attribution is a masterpiece of analysis and exposition; one only wishes that von Friesen had gone to similar lengths elsewhere, for example in the attribution of the Jarlabanki-stones to Fot.[59]

The work of the Swedish runologist Erik Brate offers a contrast in many ways to that of von Friesen. Where von Friesen was intuitive and bold, Brate was laborious and cautious. There is no doubt that von Friesen was the better runologist and that his audacity and intuition gave him an understanding of Upplandic runography that has perhaps never been equaled. Nonetheless, Brate often serves as a useful check on von Friesen's speculative tendencies, and one is forced more than once to take Brate's side of the argument.

[54]In his "Historiska runinskrifter," *Fornvännen* 4 (1909): 57–85, von Friesen attempted to supply some of the proofs that are lacking in *Upplands runstenar*.

[55]*Upplands runstenar*, p. 46.

[56]Otto von Friesen (ed.), *Runorna*.

[57]Ibid., p. 218.

[58]Otto von Friesen, "Hvem var Yngvarr enn viðfǫrli?" *Fornvännen* 5 (1910): 199–209.

[59]Von Friesen's important article on Asmund for the Swedish Biographical Lexicon is discussed in chapter 8.

Svenska runristare, Brate's main contribution to Upplandic runology, was originally put together in 1904 as a lecture for his entrance into the Vitterhets, Historie och Antikvitets Akademien on March 7, 1905, although it was not published until 1925. It is the only work that deals exclusively with rune-carvers, unfortunately, one must conclude, in a most unsatisfactory way.

The book begins with a brief introduction that sketches clearly the nature of the task—"to investigate the distribution of carvers of our runic inscriptions and to try to establish the chronology of the groups thus established"[60]—and acknowledges the work of Hildebrand and von Friesen. Brate's method is, "first, to go through the carvers' signed carvings and investigate which features are characteristic of [each carver] and, then, point out these features in anonymous carvings."[61] The sound value of the o-rune will assist in dating the carvers.

In Uppland and environs, *Svenska runristare* treats 406 inscriptions (including one on a copper box and one on a grave slab). Brate finds 195 bearing the signatures of runographers and attributes 211 unsigned stones to 71 carvers, of which two are anonymous and six are assistants.

Although Brate nowhere discusses the criteria he uses to distinguish carvers, one can conclude from his attributions that there are three major ones. The first is design. The shapes of the rune animal, the animal's head, and the cross are frequently mentioned as being distinctive. The second includes orthographic features: the use of the o-rune, the contrast between monophthongal and diphthongal spellings, the use of a single rune to conclude one word and begin the next, the employment of the h-rune to represent post-vocalic /g/, and the various spellings of the word *æftiR* 'in memory of'. Third, Brate recognized characteristics of formulation, such as the wording of the prayer, the use of place names and verse, and the choice of vocabulary, such as *ræisa:retta* 'raise, erect', *risti:markaði* 'carved', and *þenna:þennsa* 'this'.

On the other hand, Brate seems to have made very little use of rune forms as a basis for distinguishing runographers. Only the most obvious variants are noted, such as long-branch versus short-branch runes, Viseti's f-, s-, and t-runes, and Balli's b-rune. No fine allographic distinctions are made.

It seems likely that the great number of errors in *Svenska runristare* can be explained partially by assuming that Brate's first-hand experi-

[60]Erik Brate, *Svenska runristare*, pp. 5–6.
[61]Ibid., p. 7.

ence with the rune stones was insufficient, for, while the design, orthography, and formulation can be studied fairly adequately from older drawings (Bautil, Dybeck) or collections (Liljegren), only fieldwork can provide the necessary familiarity with rune forms and other details of the stone-carver's technique. If, however, Brate did devote an adequate amount of his time to fieldwork, one is forced to conclude that he was not a first-rate runologist. It is otherwise difficult to understand how Brate could attribute twenty-eight stones (practically all of von Friesen's "unornamented stones") to the runographer Gunnar, when even the most inexperienced eye can perceive subgroupings.[62]

Besides errors of judgment, Brate is also plagued by unreliable information, usually in the actual text of the inscriptions. Whether this misinformation stems from sources like Liljegren or from Brate's own readings, the results are often catastrophic. The situation is further aggravated by occasional misinterpretations of the readings. By misunderstanding U203 (Angarns kyrka), U828 (Bodarne, Fittja by, Fittja sn.), and U1067 (Åkerby kyrka), Brate creates three carvers who never existed at all, among them a woman.[63]

In short, *Svenska runristare* is of little value today, despite Lucien Musset's comment to the contrary.[64] It is riddled with errors of judgment and with faulty information. It is not systematic and does not take into consideration sufficiently detailed runographic distinctions to provide trustworthy attributions.

A great many of Brate's mistaken attributions are countered by recent volumes of *Runverket*. The four volumes of *Upplands runinskrifter*, to which a fifth (containing inscriptions on loose objects, newly found inscriptions, and presumably a survey of the material) will eventually be added, are the work of Elias Wessén and, to a lesser extent, Sven B. F. Jansson; they provide us with the third major contribution to Upplandic runographic research in the twentieth century.

Upplands runinskrifter is a monumental piece of scholarship and offers the best readings, the most reasonable interpretations, and the finest pictorial representations of the runic inscriptions that have thus far been provided. In addition it contains much useful information con-

---

[62]Ibid., p. 15. Brate insists that it is "impossible to determine whether they should be attributed to Ulv i Borresta or Gunnar or possibly other carvers of the same school," and opts for Gunnar.

[63]Ibid., "Frögärd i Osby" (p. 13), "Ödkume" (p. 63), "Sigröd" (p. 120).

[64]"...*toujours fondamental.*" Lucien Musset, *Introduction à la runologie*, p. 256.

cerning previous study of the Upplandic monuments, including early drawings. Small wonder, then, that it should assume the status of a definitive work.

Yet features inherent in the nature of this work make it less than definitive from the point of view of runography. In the first place, *Upplands runinskrifter* is a collection primarily and a study only incidentally; its format precludes a systematic analysis of runographic problems. Moreover, the first four volumes of *Upplands runinskrifter* were published over a period of time extending from 1940 to 1958. It would not be surprising, therefore, to find a certain uneven quality in a work with such a long genesis, and indeed it is possible to observe how Wessén develops new views, changes his mind, and falls into certain inconsistencies as the work progresses.[65] It can be shown, furthermore, that *Upplands runinskrifter* is not without factual error, so that to follow it uncritically is to invite disaster.[66]

Nevertheless, out of the 1181 articles in these four large volumes emerge a great many attributions, evaluations of rune-carvers, descriptions of runic styles, and discussions of runographic principles. Of great significance is the addition of *"huggningsteknik"* (carving technique) to the traditional criteria of design, formulation, orthography, and rune forms.

Other scholars have published works during the past fifty years that relate in one way or another to Upplandic runography, yet they are usually limited to one aspect of the subject and have therefore been discussed where appropriate. Thus, the ornamentation of the rune stones has been studied by Plutzar, Bergman, and Christiansson, among oth-

[65]For example, in volume 2 (1945), p. 267, Wessén rejects Brate's connection of U460 and U463 to U948 ("There is undeniably a certain superficial resemblance, but, the more closely one looks at the details, the more striking are the differences") and refuses to attribute the stones to a single carver ("It is certainly not the same carver"). Later, in volume 4 (1953), p. 65, during the discussion of U948, Wessén revises his opinion ("Brate's comparison with the two carvings U460 and U463 remains, however, very plausible") and attributes all three stones to the same carver.

[66]Aside from a number of typographical or printer's errors, and a handful of unfortunate misnumberings of inscriptions, one can note errors in (a) the localization of a stone (U372 is north, not south, of the Ånsta-Skoby road); (b) the reading of the inscription (**ulfr**, not **ulfR** in U510); (c) Wessén's comments "till läsning" (it is not true that on U203 "all the s-runes have the form ᚾ"; the first two have the form ᚱ, the third is ᚿ, and the final one ᚻ); and (d) the photographs (the small **n**-rune of **ant** *and* 'spirit' is not visible in the photograph of U945). An error of even greater magnitude is the treatment of a single stone as two separate stones (U199 and U235).

ers.[67] Individual stones or groups of related stones have been treated by Lindqvist, Wessén, Wideen, and Jansson.[68] There are surveys of inscriptions[69] and articles in encyclopedias.[70]

The attribution of an unsigned rune stone to a known carver, practiced as we have seen for over 250 years, continues to fascinate anyone who comes into contact with the material. Attributions crop up today where one least expects them, as is demonstrated in a recent book on Scandinavian art by the Danish author R. Broby-Johansen.[71] On page 156 of this book the inscriptions U251 (Sursta, Vallentuna sn.) and U80 (Sundby, Spånga sn.) are said to be "both by the stonemaster Fot." The attribution of U251 to Fot, which is clearly incorrect, seems to be the product of Broby-Johansen's highly independent imagination.

[67]Friedrich Plutzar, *Die Ornamentik der Runensteine*; Bengt Bergman, *Uppländsk run- och bildstensristning*; Hans Christiansson, *Sydskandinavisk stil: Studier i ornamentiken på de senvikingatida runstenarna*.

[68]Sune Lindqvist, "Jarlabanke-släktens minnesmärken," in *Nordiska arkeologmötet i Stockholm 1922*, pp. 123–141; Elias Wessén, "Runstenarna i Bromma," *Bromma hembygdsförenings årsskrift* 3 (1932): 21–35; idem, *Historiska runinskrifter*; Harald Wideen, *Västsvenska vikingatids-studier*; Sven B. F. Jansson, articles on newly found inscriptions in *Fornvännen*, 1946 ff.

[69]Sven B. F. Jansson, *The Runes of Sweden*; idem, *Runinskrifter i Sverige*; Musset, *Introduction à la runologie*; Klaus Düwel, *Runenkunde*; Wolfgang Krause, *Runen*.

[70]For example, the articles on "Asmund," "Fot," and "Balle" in *Svensk uppslagsbok* and *Svenskt biografiskt lexikon*.

[71]R. Broby-Johansen, *Oldnordiske stenbilleder*.

BIBLIOGRAPHY

Adam of Bremen. *Hamburgische Kirchengeschichte*. Edited by Bernhard Schmeidler. Scriptores rerum Germanicarum in usum scholarum ex Monumentis Germaniae historicis separatim editi. 3d ed. Hannover and Leipzig: Hahnsche Buchhandlung, 1917.

—————. *History of the Archbishops of Hamburg-Bremen*. Translated with an introduction and notes by Francis J. Tschan. Records of Civilization, vol. 53. New York: Columbia University Press, 1959.

Andersen, Harry. "Det yngre runealfabets oprindelse." *Arkiv för nordisk filologi* 62–63 (1947–1948): 203–227.

—————. "Til u-omlyden i dansk." *Acta Philologica Scandinavica* 16 (1943): 258–286.

Antonsen, Elmer H. "The Proto-Norse Vowel System and the Younger Futhark." *Scandinavian Studies* 35 (1963): 195–207.

Arne, T. J. "Biskop Osmund." *Fornvännen* 42 (1947): 54–56.

Bautil. SEE Göransson, J.

Bellander, Erik. "Gästriklands järnåldersbebyggelse: 1. Fornlämningar och fynd." In *Från Gästrikland, 1938*. Gävle: Gästriklands kulturhistoriska förening, 1939.

Bergman, Bengt. "Asmund Kareson." In *Gästrikland*, edited by Märta Lindeberg. Uppsala: Lindblad, 1946.

—————. *Uppländsk run- och bildstensristning*. Stockholm: Privately printed, 1948.

Bergman, Gösta. *Utvecklingen av samnordiskt ē i svenska språket: En dialektgeografisk undersökning*. Uppsala: Almqvist & Wiksell, 1921.

Bliss, Harry A., ed. *Memorial Art, Ancient and Modern*. Buffalo: H. A. Bliss, 1912.

Brate, Erik. *Svenska runristare*. Kungl. Vitterhets historie och antikvitets akademiens handlingar, 33:3. Stockholm, 1925.

—————, and Sophus Bugge. *Runverser*. Antiqvarisk tidskrift för Sverige, 10. Stockholm, 1887–1891.

Braun, F. "Hvem var Yngvarr enn viðforli?" *Fornvännen* 5 (1910): 99–118.

Broby-Johansen, R. *Oldnordiske stenbilleder*. Copenhagen: Gyldendal, 1967.

186 *Bibliography*

Brocman, Nils Reinhold. *Sagan om Ingwar Widtfarne och hans Son Swen, från gamla Isländskan öfwersatt, och Undersökning om Wåre Runstenars Ålder, i Anledning af samma Saga, samt Företal om Sagans Trowärdighet; Hwaruti de förr hos oss utgivna Sagors Wärde tillika stadfästes.* Stockholm, 1762.

Bureus, Johannes. MS without title. Signum Fa6 in the Royal Library, Stockholm.

Celsius, Olof. "Monumenta quædam Sveo-Gothica suis temporibus reddita Auct. O. C." *Acta Literaria Sveciæ* 2–4 (1725–1736): *passim*.

———. *Svenska runstenar.* 2 vols. Signum Fm60 in the Royal Library, Stockholm.

Christiansson, Hans. *Sydskandinavisk stil: Studier i ornamentiken på de senvikingatida runstenarna.* Uppsala: Almqvist & Wiksell, 1959.

Codex Wormianus (The Younger Edda). Introduction by Sigurður Nordal. Corpus codicum islandicorum medii aevi, 2. Copenhagen: Levin & Munksgaard, 1931.

Cutts, Edward L. *A Manual for the Study of the Sepulchral Slabs and Crosses of the Middle Ages.* London, 1849.

Day, E. H. *Monuments and Memorials.* London and Oxford: Mowbray, 1915.

Dijkman, Petter (den äldre). *Historiske Anmärckningar, öfwer / och af en dehl Runstenar, i Swerige, Angående dhe Uhrgambla / Sviar- och Giöthers Kyrkie- och Werdzliga Wäsende / Uthi åthskilliga Måhl, Åhr Christi 1708.* Stockholm, 1723.

Düwel, Klaus. *Runenkunde.* Stuttgart: Metzler, 1968.

Ebel, Else. "Die Terminologie der Runentechnik." Ph.D. dissertation (Göttingen), 1963.

Elliott, R. W. V. *Runes: An Introduction.* Manchester: University Press; New York: Philosophical Library, 1959.

Erdman, Axel, and Karl Hildebrand, eds. *Uppland: Skildring af land och folk.* 2 vols. Stockholm: Kungl. Humanistiska Vetenskapssamfundet i Uppsala, 1901–1908.

Foote, Peter, and David M. Wilson. *The Viking Achievement.* London: Sidgwick and Jackson, 1970.

von Friesen, Otto. "Asmund Kareson." In *Svenskt biografiskt lexikon*, II, 375–379. Stockholm, 1920.

———. "Historiska runinskrifter." *Fornvännen* 4 (1909): 57–85.

———. "Hvem var Yngvarr enn viðforli?" *Fornvännen* 5 (1910): 199–209.

———. "Om de uppländska runstenarnas och upplandslagens språk." In *Uppland: Skildring af land och folk*, II, 491–504.

———. "Run- och offerstenen vid Focksta i Hagby socken." *Uppsala Nya Tidnings Julnummer*, 1913.

———, ed. *Runorna.* Nordisk kultur, 6. Stockholm: Albert Bonnier, 1933.

———. *Runorna i Sverige.* 3d ed. Uppsala: Lindblad, 1928.

————. "Upplands runstenar." In *Uppland: Skildring af land och folk*, II, 449–490.

————. *Upplands runstenar: En allmänfattlig öfversikt*. Uppsala: A.-B. Akademiska Bokhandeln, 1913.

Fritzner, Johan. *Ordbog over det gamle norske sprog*. 3 vols. Kristiania, 1886–1896.

Gardell, Sölve. *Gravmonument från Sveriges medeltid*. 2 vols. Stockholm: Kungl. Vitterhets historie och antikvitets akademien, 1945–1946.

Göransson, Johan. *Bautil, det är: Alle Svea ok Götha Rikens Runstenar, upreste ifrån verldenes år 2000 til Christi år 1000*. Stockholm, 1750.

Grape, Anders. *Studier över de i fornsvenskan inlånade personnamnen*. Vol. 1. Uppsala: Almqvist & Wiksell, 1911.

Haugen, Einar. "On the Parsimony of the Younger Futhark." In *Festschrift für Konstantin Reichardt*, edited by C. Gellinek. Bern and Munich: Francke, 1969. Reprinted in E. S. Firchow et al., *Studies for Einar Haugen*, pp. 591–597. The Hague: Mouton, 1972.

Henning, Sam, ed. *Upplandslagen enligt Cod. Holm. B199 och 1607 års utgåva*. Samlingar utgivna av svenska fornskrift-sällskapet, 240, 70:1. Uppsala, 1967.

Hesselman, Bengt. "Några nynordiska dialektformer och vikingatidens historia." In *Ordgeografi och språkhistoria*. Nordiska texter och undersökningar, 9. Stockholm: Hugo Gebers Förlag, 1936.

————. *Omljud och brytning i de nordiska språken*. Nordiska texter och undersökningar, 15. Stockholm: Hugo Gebers Förlag, 1945.

————. *Sveamålen och de svenska dialekternas indelning*. Uppsala: K. W. Appelbergs Boktryckeri, 1905.

Hildebrand, Hans. "Kronologiska anteckningar om våra runstenar." *Vitterhets historie och antikvitets akademiens månadsblad*, 1878, pp. 710–713; 1879, pp. 8–18.

Historia Eliensis. In *Liber Eliensis*, edited by David James Stewart. Vol. 1. London, 1848.

Högbom, A. G. "Land och vatten." In *Uppland: Skildring af land och folk*, I, 3–64.

Jacobsen, Lis, and Erik Moltke, eds. *Danmarks runeindskrifter*. 2 vols. Copenhagen: Ejnar Munksgaard, 1941–1942.

Janse, Otto. "Har Emund den gamle sökt införa den grekisk-katolska läran i Sverige?" *Fornvännen* 53 (1958): 118–124.

Jansson, Sven B. F. "Ännu några runfynd från senare år." *Fornvännen* 54 (1959): 241–267.

————. "Möjbrostenens ristning." *Fornvännen* 47 (1952): 124–127.

————. "Några okända uppländska runinskrifter." *Fornvännen* 41 (1946): 257–280.

————. "A Newly Discovered Runic Stone from Västerljung, Södermanland."

188   Bibliography

In *Nordica et Anglica: Studies in Honor of Stefán Einarsson*. The Hague: Mouton, 1968.

―――. *The Runes of Sweden*. London: Phoenix House, 1962.

―――. "Runinskrifter i Norrtäljetrakten." In *Norrtäljetrakten under forntiden*. Antikvariska studier, 2. Stockholm: Kungl. Vitterhets historie och antikvitets akademien, 1945.

―――. *Runinskrifter i Sverige*. Stockholm: Almqvist & Wiksell, 1963.

―――. "Runstenen i Ryssby kyrka (Sm39)." *Fornvännen* 59 (1964): 225–235.

―――. "Runstensfynd i kyrkmurar." *Fornvännen* 53 (1958): 241–257.

―――. *Skansens runstenar*. Skrifter från Skansen, 4. Stockholm: Stiftelsen Skansen, 1967.

―――. "Uppländska runstensfynd." *Fornvännen* 48 (1953): 262–280.

Johnsen, Ingrid Sanness. *Stuttruner i vikingtidens innskrifter*. Oslo: Universitetsforlaget, 1968.

Jones, Gwyn. *History of the Vikings*. London: Oxford University Press, 1968.

Jónsson, Guðni. *Annálar og nafnaskrá*. Reykjavík: Íslendingasagnaútgáfan, 1948.

Kempff, K. Hjalmar. *Söderby runsten vid Gefle*. Gävle, 1897–1898.

Knoop, Douglas, and G. P. Jones. *The Mediæval Mason*. 3d ed. Manchester and New York: Manchester University Press, 1967.

Kock, Axel. "Fornsvenskans behandling av diftongen *ia*." *Arkiv för nordisk filologi* 5 (1889): 371–384.

―――. *Svensk ljudhistoria*. 5 vols. Lund: C. W. K. Gleerup, 1906–1929.

―――. *Umlaut und Brechung im Altschwedischen*. Lund: C. W. K. Gleerup, 1911–1916.

Krause, Wolfgang. *Runen*. Berlin: Walter de Gruyter, 1970.

Kruuse, E. "De lefvande folkmålen." In *Uppland: Skildring af land och folk*, II, 537–552.

Liber Eliensis. SEE *Historia Eliensis*.

Liljegren, Johan Gustaf. *Run-lära*. Stockholm, 1832.

―――. *Run-urkunder*. Stockholm, 1833.

Lindblom, Andreas. *Sveriges konsthistoria*. Stockholm: Nordisk rotogravyr, 1944–1946.

Lindqvist, Sune. *Den helige Eskils biskopdöme*. Antikvarisk tidskrift för Sverige, 22, 1. Stockholm, 1915.

―――. "Jarlabanke-släktens minnesmärken." In *Nordiska arkeologmötet i Stockholm 1922*. Stockholm: Kungl. Vitterhets historie och antikvitets akademien, 1923.

―――. "Onaturliga runstenstransporter." *Fornvännen* 42 (1947): 50–51.

Loman, Bengt. "Rökrunorna som grafematiskt system." *Arkiv för nordisk filologi* 80 (1965): 1–60.

Lundgren, M. F., Erik Brate, and E. H. Lind. *Svenska personnamn från medeltiden*. Uppsala, 1892–1934.

Markström, Herbert. *Om utvecklingen av gammalt ǎ framför u i nordiska språk: Tilljämning och omljud.* Skrifter utgivna av institutionen för nordiska språk vid Uppsala Universitet, 2. Uppsala, 1954.

Moberg, Lennart. *Om de nordiska nasalassimilationerna mp > pp, nt > tt, nk > kk, med särskild hänsyn till svenskan.* Uppsala: Lundequistska bokhandeln, 1944.

Moltke, Erik. SEE Jacobsen, Lis.

Musset, Lucien. *Introduction à la runologie.* Bibliothèque de philologie germanique, 20. Paris: Aubier-Montaigne, 1965.

Noreen, Adolf. *Altisländische und altnorwegische Grammatik.* 4th ed. Halle: M. Niemeyer, 1923.

———. *Altschwedische Grammatik mit Einschluss des Altgutnischen.* Halle: M. Niemeyer, 1897–1904.

Nygaard, Marius. *Norrøn syntax.* Kristiania: Aschehoug, 1905.

Ólsen, Björn Magnússon. *Den tredje og fjærde grammatiske afhandling i Snorres Edda, tilligemed de grammatiske afhandlingers prolog og to andre tillæg.* Copenhagen, 1884.

Olsen, Magnus. "Ordblinde runristere." *Fornvännen* 48 (1953): 327–329.

Olson, Emil. *Yngvars saga víðfǫrla, jämte ett bihang om Ingvarsinskrifterna.* Samfund til udgivelse af gammel nordisk litteratur, 39. Copenhagen: S. L. Møllers Bogtrykkeri, 1912.

Palme, Sven Ulric. *Kristendomens genombrott i Sverige.* Stockholm: Albert Bonnier, 1959.

Peringskiöld, Johan. *Monumenta Sveo-Gothorum.* 10 vols. Signum Fh in the Royal Library, Stockholm.

———. *Monumenta Ullerakerensia.* Stockholm, 1719.

———. *Monumenta Uplandica per Thiundam.* Stockholm, 1710.

Petersen, Jan. *Vikingetidens redskaper.* Skrifter utgitt av videnskapsakademi i Oslo, Hist.-Filos. Klasse, 1951, no. 4. Oslo, 1951.

Pipping, Hugo. "Gömda bindrunor." Studier i nordisk filologi, 23:2. Helsingfors: Svenska litteratursällskapet i Finland, 1933.

Plutzar, Friedrich. *Die Ornamentik der Runensteine.* Kungl. Vitterhets historie och antikvitets akademiens handlingar, 34:6. Stockholm, 1924.

Ransakningar om antikviteterna 1667–84. Signum Fl9 in the Royal Library, Stockholm.

Rhezelius, Jon Håkonson. *Afrytningarr / och Afskriffter aff RuneStenar och Rymstafwar / Skråer och Privilegier / Crönikor / Inrykes och Uthrykes Mynt, Som fundne äre uti Rodanom eller Attundaland uthi Upplands. Anno 1636.* Signum R550 in the University Library, Uppsala.

———. *Monumenta Uplandica: Reseanteckningar från åren 1635, 1636, 1638.* Edited by C. M. Stenblock and Oscar Lundberg. Uppsala: Upplands fornminnesförening, 1915–1917.

Rischel, Jørgen. *Phoneme, Grapheme, and the "Importance" of Distinctions:*

Functional Aspects of the Scandinavian Runic Reform. KVAL Interim Report, 1. Stockholm, no date.

Sander, Fredrik. *Marmorlejonet från Piræeus med nordiska runinskrifter.* Stockholm, 1896.

——. *Runinskrifter ånyo granskade.* Stockholm, 1898.

Scheidig, Walther. *Die Holzschnitte des Petrarca-Meisters.* Berlin: Henschelverlag, 1955.

Schmeidler, Bernhard. *Hamburg-Bremen und Nordost-Europa vom 9. bis 11. Jahrhundert.* Leipzig: Dieterich, 1918.

Seip, Didrik Arup. *Norsk språkhistoria til omkring 1370.* 2d ed. Oslo: Aschehoug, 1955.

Sernander, Rutger. "Läby-Bron. En uppländsk brobyggnad från slutet af den yngre järnålder." *Upplands fornminnesförenings tidskrift* 5 (1905–1908): 142–149.

Söderwall, K. F. *Ordbok öfver svenska medeltidsspråket.* 2 vols. Lund, 1884–1935.

Stenberger, Mårten. *Det forntida Sverige.* Stockholm: Almqvist & Wiksell, 1964.

Storm, Gustav. *Islandske annaler indtil 1578.* Christiania, 1888.

Styffe, Carl Gustaf. *Skandinavien under unionstiden.* 2d ed. Stockholm, 1880.

Svärdström, Elisabeth. *Johannes Bureus' arbeten om svenska runinskrifter.* Kungl. Vitterhets historie och antikvitets akademiens handlingar, 42:3. Stockholm, 1936.

Svenskt biografiskt lexikon. Stockholm: Albert Bonnier, 1918–.

Svensk uppslagsbok. 2d ed. Malmö: Förlagshuset Norden AB, 1947–1955.

Svensson, John. *Diftongering med palatalt förslag i de nordiska språken.* Lundastudier i nordisk språkvetenskap, 2. Lund: Håkan Ohlssons Boktryckeri, 1944.

Sveriges runinskrifter. Stockholm: Kungl. Vitterhets historie och antikvitets akademien, 1900–.
   I. *Ölands runinskrifter.* Edited by Sven Söderberg and Erik Brate. 1900–1906.
   II. *Östergötlands runinskrifter.* Edited by Erik Brate. 1911–1918.
   III. *Södermanlands runinskrifter.* Edited by Erik Brate and Elias Wessén. 1924–1936.
   IV. *Smålands runinskrifter.* Edited by Ragnar Kinander. 1935–1961.
   V. *Västergötlands runinskrifter.* Edited by Hugo Jungner and Elisabeth Svärdström. 1940–1971.
   VI–IX. *Upplands runinskrifter.* Edited by Elias Wessén and Sven B. F. Jansson. 1940–1958.
   XI. *Gotlands runinskrifter.* Edited by Sven B. F. Jansson and Elias Wessén. 1962.
   XIII. *Västmanlands runinskrifter.* Edited by Sven B. F. Jansson. 1964.

Bibliography 191

Thompson, Claiborne W. "Nonsense Inscriptions in Swedish Uppland." In *Studies for Einar Haugen*, edited by E. S. Firchow et al., pp. 522–534. The Hague: Mouton, 1972.

———. "Öpir's Teacher." *Fornvännen* 67 (1972): 16–19.

———. "A Swedish Runographer and a Headless Bishop." *Mediaeval Scandinavia* 3 (1970): 50–62.

Thors, Carl-Eric. *Den kristna terminologien i fornsvenskan.* Studier i nordisk filologi, 45. Helsingfors: Svenska litteratursällskapet i Finland, 1957.

Tschan, Francis J. SEE Adam of Bremen.

Uppland: Skildring af land och folk. SEE Erdman, Axel.

Upplands runinskrifter. SEE *Sveriges runinskrifter.*

Verelius, Olaus. *Manuductio compendiosa ad runographiam Scandicam antiquam, recte intelligendam.* Uppsala, 1675.

Weiss, Eugen. *Steinmetzart und Steinmetzgeist.* Jena: Diederich, 1927.

Wessén, Elias. "Det svenska runverket: Ett 350-arsminne." *Fornvännen* 47 (1952): 193–210.

———. *Historiska runinskrifter.* Kungl. Vitterhets historie och antikvitets akademiens handlingar, filol.-filos. serien, 6. Stockholm, 1960.

———. *Nordiska namnstudier.* Uppsala Universitets årsskrift, filosofi, språkvetenskap och historiska vetenskaper, 3. Uppsala: Lundequistska Bokhandeln, 1927.

———. "Runstenarna i Bromma.' *Bromma hembygdsförenings årsskrift* 3 (1932): 21–35.

———. *Svensk språkhistoria. I. Ljudlära och ordböjningslära.* Stockholm: Filologiska förening vid Stockholms Högskola, 1941.

———. *Våra folkmål.* 2d ed. Stockholm: C. E. Fritze, 1945.

———, and Sven B. F. Jansson. SEE *Sveriges runinskrifter.*

Westlund, Börje. "Om runstensfragmenten vid Hagby i Täby socken." *Fornvännen* 59 (1964): 152–156.

Wideen, Harald. *Västsvenska vikingatids-studier.* Skrifter utgivna av Göteborgs arkeologiska museum, 2. Göteborg, 1955.

Worm, Ole. *Runer seu Danica Literatura Antiqvissima vulgo Gothica dicta.* Antiqvitates Danicæ, 1. Hafniæ, 1651.

INDEX

INDEX OF INSCRIPTIONS